cavendish
Q&A
series

Employment Law

4th Edition

DEBORAH J LOCKTON, LLB, MPHIL,

*PROFESSOR OF EMPLOYMENT LAW AND
DEPUTY HEAD, DEPARTMENT OF LAW,
DE MONTFORT UNIVERSITY, LEICESTER*

Cavendish
Publishing
Limited

London • Sydney • Portland, Oregon

Fourth edition first published in Great Britain 2006 by
Cavendish Publishing Limited, The Glass House,
Wharton Street, London WC1X 9PX, United Kingdom
Telephone: + 44 (0)20 7278 8000   Facsimile: + 44 (0)20 7278 8080
Email: info@cavendishpublishing.com
Website: www.cavendishpublishing.com

Published in the United States by Cavendish Publishing
c/o International Specialized Book Services,
5804 NE Hassalo Street, Portland,
Oregon 97213-3644, USA

Published in Australia by Cavendish Publishing (Australia) Pty Ltd
45 Beach Street, Coogee NSW 2034, Australia

© Lockton, DJ	2006
First edition	1996
Second edition	2000
Third edition	2002
Fourth edition	2006

British Library Cataloguing in Publication Data
Lockton, Deborah J
Employment law – 4th ed – (Q&A series)
1 Labour laws and legalisation – Great Britain
2 Labour laws and legalisation – Great Britain – Case Studies
I Title
344.4'101

Library of Congress Cataloguing in Publication Data
Data available

ISBN 1-85941-978-X
ISBN 978-1-859-41978-6

1 3 5 7 9 10 8 6 4 2

Printed and bound in Great Britain

Preface ──────────────

Since writing the last edition of this Questions and Answers book, a great deal has happened in the area of employment law. The implementation of a number of European Directives has impacted greatly on areas such as discrimination.

Major changes brought about by the Employment Act 2002 implemented by secondary legislation have affected areas such as institutions, employment protection, equal pay and unfair dismissal. All of these are in addition to changes in interpretation as a result of cases in the national courts and the European Court of Justice. As a result, a number of questions now have slightly different answers. I have also inserted a number of new questions and answers to take into account some of the recent additions to legislative protection.

This book has always been intended to help students when faced with assessments in employment law. It is meant to be used in conjunction with textbooks in this area and to this end I have followed the format I used in my book *Employment Law* (5th edn, 2006). The questions in each chapter, however, do not cover all the details in individual areas, nor are the answers intended to be the definitive answers. The aim is to give the student an example of the approach to answering questions in each area and to identify the key issues to be learned and understood.

As always I give my thanks to my colleagues who have kindly given their consent to my use of questions which are not my own. My thanks also to my colleagues and friends who, within the book, have faced some horrendous employment problems, including those friends who, upset at not being in previous editions, I have endeavoured to include in this one! My thanks again to Keith for unlimited support and caffeine and to my son James, old enough now to be thrilled that his name appears in a book but still unable to grasp the concept that computers are used for work and therefore cannot be used for games all of the time. Despite all of this help, any mistakes are my own.

The law is stated as I understand it to be on 1 October 2005.

DJ Lockton
Thrussington

November 2005

Contents

Table of Cases

Table of Statutes ───────────────

Statutory Instruments

EU Legislation

1 Institutions of Employment Law

Introduction

Invariably, the first topics studied in employment law are the sources and the institutions. This is because employment law has its own specific adjudicative forums and bodies which oversee the operation of the law. As such, it is necessary to learn the nature of these institutions to be able to study the subject. General questions may arise on the institutions, or more specific questions may be set, given that the Trade Union Reform and Employment Rights Act (TURERA) 1993 gave to the Secretary of State power to increase the jurisdiction of the employment tribunals and this was introduced by the Employment Tribunals (Extension of Jurisdiction) Order 1994 (now the Employment Tribunals Act 1996). Further changes have been introduced by the Employment Tribunals (Constitution and Rules of Procedure) Regulations 2004, Equal Pay Act (Rules of Procedure) Regulations 2004 and the Employment Act (Dispute Resolution) Regulations 2004.

In addition, the House of Lords decision in *R v Secretary of State for Employment ex p EOC* (1994) led to the Employment Protection (Part-time Employees) Regulations 1995, equating the rights of part-time employees with those of full-timers and establishing the basis on which the commissions may seek judicial review. Apart from this, European law has had a major impact in certain areas, particularly sex discrimination, equal pay and transfers of undertakings, in addition to the Human Rights Act (HRA) 1998, implementing the European Convention on Human Rights. As such, issues relating to jurisdiction can also arise in questions on other areas, as will be seen in later chapters.

The issues to be considered are:

- the role and nature of the institutions;
- the relationship between the institutions and the relevant areas of employment law in which they operate;
- the legalism in employment tribunals debate;
- the impact of European law in this area.

This will mean that the student must have an in-depth knowledge of a broad area. Remember as well that, unless jurisdiction comes up in other areas, any questions on this topic are likely to be essay questions rather than problems.

Checklist

Students should be familiar with the following areas:

- the jurisdiction of the tribunals and the Employment Appeal Tribunal (EAT);
- changes in jurisdiction, composition and procedure;
- the effect of European Treaty Articles and Directives;
- the functions of the different commissions and commissioners;
- the attack on legalism in employment tribunals;
- the impact of the HRA 1998

Question 1

While employment tribunals can provide a quick and efficient remedy for an aggrieved employee, the restrictions placed upon them created problems for employees who wished to sue their employer. Changes made by the Trade Union Reform and Employment Rights Act (TURERA) 1993 eradicated these problems and provided tribunals with a comprehensive power to protect employees against infringement of all of their rights.

Critically evaluate this statement.

Answer plan

This question falls neatly into two parts: the first part asks about the problems facing employees before the TURERA 1993. The second part asks for a discussion of the changes made by the Act and consideration of whether these changes eradicated the problems identified. In a question like this, it is important to answer the question: a list of the past problems and the changes in the jurisdiction is not an adequate answer. Some problems will not be extinguished by an extension in jurisdiction and it is important to note that the question is asking for all the problems and not merely those caused by jurisdictional limits.

The issues to be considered are:

- tribunal jurisdiction before the TURERA 1993;
- limits on the jurisdiction;
- the problems such limits caused;
- other problems caused by restrictions in making tribunal claims;
- how the jurisdiction was extended in 1994;
- whether the present jurisdiction has met the problems identified earlier.

Answer

Employment tribunals were established by the Industrial Training Act 1964 with limited jurisdiction. Over the years, however, the jurisdiction was extended until, prior to amendments by the TURERA 1993, tribunals had the jurisdiction to hear almost all individual disputes based on statutory claims. It is important to note, however, that, until the 1994 amendments, tribunals only had jurisdiction to hear statutory claims and, as such, would hear *inter alia* unfair dismissal disputes, redundancy disputes, sex and race discrimination claims and equal pay claims. Tribunals had no jurisdiction to hear common law claims, which had to be heard by the ordinary courts. In addition, other criticisms have been levelled against tribunals, which jurisdictional changes will not address. These further criticisms will be discussed below.

Perhaps the major problem facing an employee before the changes made by the 1993 Act was the fact that tribunals could not hear common law claims. While on the face of things this did not appear to be a major problem, in fact, an unfair dismissal claim would often also involve a common law claim for damages for breach of contract. While the employee could sue for the unfair dismissal in the tribunal, the damages claim could only be heard by the ordinary courts, thus necessitating the employee taking two actions in different forums in relation to the same act by the employer. For example, in *Treganowan v Robert Knee and Co Ltd* (1975), the applicant was instantly dismissed when the typing pool refused to work with her after she kept discussing details of an affair she was having with a work colleague. The tribunal found that she had been fairly dismissed. It further stated that her conduct did not justify instant dismissal and that she should have received the six weeks' notice she was entitled to by her contract. The tribunal, however, had no jurisdiction to hear the breach of contract claim or award damages for what the tribunal considered to be a breach of contract. To pursue an action for damages, Ms Treganowan had to take action in the county court. Furthermore, if the notice had been considerable and, therefore, the damages had been outside the county court jurisdiction, Ms Treganowan would have had to pursue her claim in the High Court. Breach of contractual notice provisions are obviously not the only breach of contract an employer can commit: many cases arise over breaches of express or implied terms in the contract. The tribunals, until 1994, had no jurisdiction over these claims, leaving the employee to use the ordinary courts.

While there had been much criticism of the jurisdictional limit placed upon the tribunals, the extent of the restrictions came to the fore with the introduction of the Wages Act 1986 (now the Employment Rights Act (ERA) 1996). This was brought in to remedy the deficiencies in the Truck Acts 1831–1940 and provides that there must be a statutory or contractual right to deduct from wages before any such deductions can be made. Section 13(1) of the 1996 Act states that an employer must not make a deduction from the wages of an employee unless the deduction is:

(a) required or authorised by statute; or

(b) required or authorised by a provision in the contract of employment which has been given to the employee or notified to the employee previously in writing; or

(c) agreed to by the employee in writing before the making of the deduction.

Section 14 then contains a list of exceptions to which s 13(1) does not apply. The Act has been widely criticised and, prior to the changes in tribunal jurisdiction, led to a series of cases on interpretation. The major problem was whether the Act applied to given situations. An illegal deduction gave an employment tribunal jurisdiction, normally within three months of the deduction being made. Any other deduction had to be recovered in the ordinary courts. This led to a series of cases defining the terms 'wages' and 'deduction' for the purposes of s 13(1) to see if the tribunals had jurisdiction in certain situations.

Section 27 of the ERA 1996 lists payments which can be regarded as wages. In particular, s 27(1)(a) refers to 'any fee, bonus, commission, holiday pay, or any other emolument referable to his employment, whether payable under his contract or otherwise'. This definition led to a number of cases discussing whether wages in lieu of notice are 'wages' for the purpose of s 13(1) and, therefore, whether employment tribunals had the jurisdiction to hear complaints about deductions from such payments. In the House of Lords decision of *Delaney v Staples (trading as De Montfort Recruitment)* (1992), their Lordships decided that a payment in lieu was damages for a breach of contract. Such a payment did not arise out of the employment but as a result of the termination of employment and as such was not within the definition in s 27, even if the employer had a contractual right to pay wages in lieu. This decision meant that the tribunals could not hear complaints about deductions from such payments. Such complaints could only be heard by the ordinary courts, a situation acknowledged by the House of Lords, who ended with a plea that the jurisdiction of the tribunals be extended to hear breach of contract claims. Further cases have decided that, while *ex gratia* payments are not wages, it depends on the construction of the contract. In *Kent Management Services Ltd v Butterfield* (1992), an ex-employee complained that on his dismissal his employer had refused to pay him commission which was outstanding. The employer argued that the commission was discretionary as a clause attached to the contract said it would not be paid in exceptional circumstances such as bankruptcy. Wood P in the EAT held that, on interpretation, the anticipation of both parties must have been that in normal circumstances, commission would be paid. As such, it was wages for the purposes of s 27(1)(a) and the tribunal had the jurisdiction to hear the complaint about the deduction.

The Kent case demonstrates another problem of interpretation which arises from the Act. How far is a total non-payment a deduction? The Court of Appeal in the *Delaney* case held that a non-payment was a 100% deduction and, as such, tribunals would have the jurisdiction to hear such complaints. The issue was never raised before the House of Lords so presumably this is still the law. If the jurisdiction of tribunals had been extended at this time, these problems would not have arisen.

While the limits on the tribunal jurisdiction have raised the major criticisms, other problems can also be identified. The first is the time limits that apply to different claims. These are different depending upon the claim brought. For example, an employee must present a claim for unfair dismissal within three months of the effective date of termination, whereas the time limit is six months on a redundancy claim. While different time limits can be confusing, there are further problems in that the tribunal has the discretion to allow a claim out of time if it was not reasonably practicable for a claim to be made within the three month period (s 111(2) of the ERA 1996). Given that tribunal decisions are not reported, this can lead to a variation in practice in different tribunals, although some guidelines have been laid down by the courts (see, for example, *London International College v Sen* (1993)). Reporting of tribunal decisions would ensure more consistency.

A further problem lies in the fact that an applicant cannot obtain legal aid for a tribunal claim. Given that a large number of applicants are unemployed at the time of pursuing a case in a tribunal, this can be a major set-back. In addition, until changes made in 2001 and 2002, a tribunal had limited powers to award costs where the claim was considered to be frivolous or vexatious and could only award costs of up to £500, a power exercised infrequently. In 1997–98 and 1998–99, they were awarded in less than 0.5% of cases. Changes made by the Employment Tribunals (Constitution and Rules of Procedure) Regulations 2001 now give a tribunal the power to award costs where a party or a party's representative has acted improperly. Furthermore, a tribunal must consider awarding costs where a party or its representative has acted 'vexatiously, abusively, disruptively or otherwise unreasonably, or the bringing of the proceedings by the party is misconceived' (reg 14). 'Misconceived' includes having no real prospect of success (reg 2). The amount of costs a tribunal can award has increased to £10,000. While this may benefit a claimant, costs may also be awarded against a claimant and thus the effect of these changes may be to deter potential applicants.

Given the amount of legislation in the past few years in the area of employment law, claims are getting much more complicated and often the applicant will need the skills of a lawyer or other experienced representative to present his or her case. The problem may be exacerbated since the proposals introduced by s 20 of the Employment Act 1989 have come into effect. This section gave the Secretary of State power to make regulations for a pre-hearing review procedure which would allow the tribunal, after such a review, to order one party to pay a deposit before continuing with the case. The initial amount of the deposit was £150, but this was increased to £500 in 2001. Pre-hearing reviews were introduced by the Employment Tribunals (Rules of Procedure) Regulations 1993. Section 38 of the TURERA 1993 gave the Secretary of State power to extend the jurisdiction of the tribunals to cover claims for damages for breach of contract subject to a financial limit. This extension of jurisdiction was introduced by the Employment Tribunals (Extension of Jurisdiction) Order 1994 (now the Employment Tribunals Act 1996). Personal injury claims are, however, still excluded as are claims for breach of a term requiring the employer to provide accommodation, breach of a term relating to intellectual property, breach of a term imposing an obligation of confidence and breach of a restraint of trade covenant.

In addition, the tribunal jurisdiction applies only where there is a termination of the contract (see *Capek v Lincolnshire County Council* (2000)) and is subject to a £25,000 limit. The extended jurisdiction means that the situation in *Treganowan* will not arise again, as the tribunal can now hear both claims as long as the damages claim is within the financial limits set. Furthermore, the problems raised in *Delaney* relating to wages in lieu of notice are also resolved as, even though such payments are damages for breach of contract, the tribunal has jurisdiction to hear complaints in relation to deductions from such payments. As such, the amendments allowed by the TURERA 1993 have met the problems arising from the restricted tribunal jurisdiction in these types of cases and prevented the duplicity of actions, one in the tribunal and one in the ordinary courts, which used to be necessary.

The other problems identified above were not answered by the 1994 Order. In an area of law that has become increasingly complex over the years, legal aid is still unavailable and, now that the proposals of 1989 in relation to pre-hearing reviews have been enacted, this can only further restrict the number of applicants who can claim. In addition, different time limits in respect of different rights and unreported tribunal decisions, particularly when allowing an applicant to present a claim outside of the statutory time limit, emphasise the need for legal aid to be available. Furthermore, the restriction as to the type of breach of contract claims that the tribunal can hear, plus the fact that the jurisdiction arises only on termination of the contract, lead one to question whether, in practice, the changes will make that much difference. While the changes engendered by the 1993 Act are to be welcomed, the lack of other changes will still mean that not all employees have the opportunity to have their cases heard by an industrial jury.

Notes

_____

_____

_____

_____

_____

_____

_____

_____

_____

_____

_____

_____

Question 2

Recent years have seen an attack on legalism in employment tribunals which has led to both procedural and substantive changes. It can be argued, however, that the changes have gone too far and that there is no longer a balance between flexibility on the one hand and certainty on the other.

Discuss.

Answer plan

This is a very specific question and calls for a detailed discussion of the literature and the case law. It is not the sort of question that can be answered with a vague knowledge of some of the issues. In this sort of question, if the student has not read the relevant articles and cases, it is best to leave well alone. On the other hand, if the student has done the required reading, this is a simple question to answer.

The issues to be considered are:

- rights of appeal from the tribunals to the EAT;
- procedural changes in the tribunals since 1985;
- the classification of issues as issues of fact;
- the disapproval of appellate courts laying down guidelines for tribunals to follow in recurring cases;
- the narrow approach to what is a 'perverse' decision.

Answer

Employment tribunals were first established as an adjudicative forum in 1964. Since then, their jurisdiction has expanded with the increase in employment rights introduced by statute. A tribunal consists of a legally qualified chairperson and two wing members who are not legally qualified, one appointed after consultation with representatives of employers and the other appointed after consultation with representatives of employees. Tribunals were established to provide a method of speedy resolution of industrial disputes and, as such, to a large extent govern their own procedure, which should be flexible. An appeal from an employment tribunal lies to the EAT on a point of law. To appeal, a party must show that the tribunal was wrong in law. The Court of Appeal in *British Telecommunications plc v Sheridan* (1990) has stated that this means either that there is an error of law or that the tribunal's decision was perverse.

While the aim of providing a forum for a speedy and flexible resolution of an industrial dispute is to be applauded, it must be recognised that employment law is not a simple area to administer and that, in recent years, the law in this area has become increasingly complex. As such, employment tribunals have needed to consider more and more legislation, new concepts introduced by European law, and interpretations from the EAT, the ordinary courts and the European Court of Justice. Such considerations have led some commentators to raise concerns that tribunals are getting increasingly legalistic. It is this debate to which the question relates.

To a large extent, tribunal hearings are like those of a court. Both parties present evidence, call witnesses and are often represented. The Rules of Procedure, however, specifically state that a tribunal should seek to avoid formality. This means that a tribunal may hear evidence which would not be admissible in an ordinary court. Wood P, in *Aberdeen Steak Houses Group plc v Ibrahim* (1988), however, has stated that too much informality may itself lead to perceived unfairness, so leading to the conclusion that the Appeal Tribunal wishes to see more formalised hearings. Such increase in legalism has to some extent been prevented by the Rules of Procedure themselves. While the EAT may be concerned about the conduct of the hearings, the rules allow a tribunal to give reasons for its decision in summary form only. To this rule, however, there are a number of exceptions: first, where the case concerns sex or race discrimination, equal pay, trade union victimisation, the closed shop or unreasonable exclusion or expulsion from a union; secondly, where it later appears to the tribunal that full reasons should be given; thirdly, where a party orally requests full reasons at the hearing; and, fourthly, where a party requests full reasons in writing within 21 days after receiving the summary reasons.

While this means that a party has a right to full reasons in any case, the Court of Appeal, in a series of cases, including *Varndell v Kearney and Trecker Marwin Ltd* (1983), has stated that the tribunals do not have to set out their reasons in full, although a later EAT has said (in *Levy v Marrable and Co Ltd* (1984)) that, where there is a conflict of fact, the tribunal should state that there is a conflict and which version it prefers. In *Yusuf v Aberplace Ltd* (1984), it further stated that a case may be remitted back to a tribunal if the EAT is unable to see why the tribunal reached the decision it did. Furthermore, in *Meek v City of Birmingham District Council* (1987), Bingham LJ emphasised that tribunals should outline their conclusions and reasoning so that an appeal court can see why the decision was made and whether a point of law is involved. This again suggests that later higher courts wish to see more legalism in the tribunals.

To some extent, however, it is how a tribunal's reasons, in whatever form, are used by the appeal courts which is the crux of the matter. Smith and Wood (Industrial Law, 8th edn, 2003, London: LexisNexis Butterworths), while discussing the cases above, argue that there has been an attack against legalism. They quote the procedural changes as an example, but argue that the main attack has been substantive and has occurred on three fronts: the classification of as many issues as possible as questions of fact; the disapproval of appellate courts laying down guidelines for tribunals to follow in recurring cases; and the narrowing of the definition of what constitutes a perverse decision.

In relation to the first point above, Smith and Wood cite many cases where it has been held that the issue is one of fact and, therefore, cannot be subject to appeal. For example, in *O'Kelly v Trusthouse Forte plc* (1983), the Court of Appeal held that whether a contract was one of service or for services was a question of fact. Such an interpretation is surely debatable at best and leaves the party with no right of appeal unless he can argue that the tribunal decision is perverse. This, however, ties in with the third point stated above, that is, the narrowing of what is defined as a perverse decision. In *RSPB v Croucher* (1984), Waite J said that perverse decisions would be exceptional and that the EAT could only call a tribunal decision perverse if the decision was not tenable by any reasonable tribunal properly directed in law. In *Neale v Hereford and Worcester County Council* (1986), May LJ gave his famous definition of perversity when he said that the EAT could only reverse a decision of the tribunal if it could be said 'My goodness, that must be wrong' and, although this has had its critics, Wood P, in *East Berkshire Health Authority v Matadeen* (1992), said that a decision can only be called perverse if it was not a permissible option; it offended reason; it was one which no reasonable tribunal could reach or it was so clearly wrong it could not stand. Such an interpretation is much wider than that of Donaldson MR in *Piggot Bros and Co Ltd v Jackson* (1992) and almost appears to be the Neale test in a more specified form.

Smith and Wood argue that such an approach demonstrates a policy to return to the tribunals. While commending the policy, they argue that there is a danger it has gone too far and that issues which should be a matter of statutory interpretation and, therefore, questions of law, are being classified as questions of fact by the appeal courts. They give the example of the phrase 'other industrial action' in s 238 of the Trade Union and Labour Relations (Consolidation) Act (TULR(C)A) 1992. This section applies if s 238A does not apply, and removes the jurisdiction of the tribunal to see if a dismissal is fair or unfair in cases where the employee was dismissed while taking part in a strike or other industrial action, so long as there are no selective dismissals or selective re-engagement. In *Coates v Modern Methods and Materials Ltd* (1982), the Court of Appeal held that what constitutes 'other industrial action' is a question of fact for the tribunal. This means that a tribunal in one part of the country could come to a totally different conclusion from a tribunal elsewhere, and the decisions could only be appealed if they were perverse. This inconsistency can hardly be said to engender a feeling of fair treatment on the part of complainants.

Smith and Wood's final point is that there has been increasing disapproval of the appellate courts laying down guidelines for tribunals to follow. In the early days of the EAT, that forum laid down guidelines in a variety of cases to establish consistency of approach in the lower tribunals. This was criticised, however, by Lawton LJ in *Bailey v BP Oil (Kent Refinery) Ltd* (1980) and, although later EAT decisions show some guidelines being laid down, this has not been the case recently, although Wood P showed himself to be more accommodating in issuing such guidelines during his presidency. Smith and Wood argue that this relates back to perversity, as without doubt, a tribunal decision which ignored such guidelines would not be a perverse decision within the modern definition and would not be an appealable point of law, so that both (that is, the redefinition of perverse and the restriction on issuing guidelines) together have removed legalism from the employment tribunals. While such an approach does return decision making to the tribunals and does create flexibility, the danger is that it also creates inconsistency and, with it, the potential for a sense of unfairness on the part of complainants.

Notes

———————— # Question 3 ————————

In the past, employment tribunals were overburdened by the number of claims which were presented. There was little in the way of deterrent to a claimant with a claim which had little hope of success and nothing in the way of an alternative to pursuing that claim in a tribunal. Changes introduced since 2000, however, should go a considerable way to reducing the perceived burdens placed on tribunals.

Critically evaluate this statement.

 ## *Answer plan*

This is a nice question asking the student to recount the changes since 2000 and to evaluate the impact of these changes. It is important to note that the question is not just asking about changes to tribunal jurisdiction and powers. It mentions the lack of alternative dispute resolution and therefore also requires a discussion of the introduction of the ACAS arbitration scheme and an analysis of its effectiveness.

The issues to be considered are:

- the introduction of the ACAS arbitration scheme in 2001;
- the changes made by the Employment Tribunals (Constitution and Rules of Procedure) Regulations 2001 and 2004;
- the changes introduced by the Employment Act 2002 (Dispute Resolution) Regulations 2004;
- an evaluation as to whether the changes together will reduce the burden on the tribunal system.

 ———————— # Answer ————————

Employment tribunals were established in 1964 and, since then, their jurisdiction has been steadily increased. They have jurisdiction in respect of all statutory employment rights such as redundancy, unfair dismissal, discrimination claims, etc, and have limited jurisdiction in respect of breach of contract claims. In 1999–2000, there were 100,000 applications made to employment tribunals although three-quarters of those applications were resolved by a conciliation officer from ACAS or by a privately negotiated settlement. There is no evidence that the number of applications to tribunals is falling.

In 1994, the government looked for alternatives to tribunals to resolve employment disputes and examined ways to reduce the number of cases going to a full hearing. This was because of a recognition that the number of applications made to tribunals was increasing and creating an overload. The resultant changes included extending the areas of jurisdiction where a chairperson could solely hear a claim by the Employment Rights (Dispute Resolution) Act 1998. This complemented changes introduced by the TURERA 1993, which allowed the question of whether the tribunal had jurisdiction to hear a claim to be determined without a hearing if the parties so agreed and which also introduced the concept of a pre-hearing review, whereby there is a hearing without witnesses (usually conducted by the chairperson alone). If the pre-hearing review determines that there is no reasonable prospect of success, then a party could be ordered to pay a deposit to enable him or her to pursue the claim to a full hearing. While these measures were intended to reduce the load on tribunals, evidence suggests that in reality this did not happen.

In 2001, the first of a number of reforms was introduced to ease the burden on tribunals. In May of that year, a new ACAS arbitration scheme was introduced as an alternative to a tribunal claim. At present, the scheme only covers unfair dismissal claims. The scheme is an alternative to a tribunal claim and thus, should parties agree to go to arbitration, they must sign an agreement taking the claim out of the tribunal system. An arbitrator's finding is enforceable in the same way as a tribunal decision and an arbitrator has powers to award reinstatement, re-engagement or financial compensation. In addition, arbitration is quicker and less formal than a tribunal.

In addition to the new arbitration scheme, the Employment Tribunals (Constitution and Rules of Procedure) Regulations 2001 were introduced. These gave employment tribunals more teeth and created a statutory duty for the tribunal to consider awarding costs in some cases. First, the amount of the deposit made after a pre-hearing review (discussed above) was increased from £150 to £500. The new regulations create an overriding objective that tribunals deal with cases 'justly' (reg 10). This means that tribunals must ensure that parties are on an equal footing, keep down expense, deal with cases in ways that are proportionate to the complexity of the issues and deal with cases in an expeditious and fair manner. This allows tribunals to move parties on where the issue argued is not difficult and allows parties to argue more fully where issues are more complex. Furthermore, new powers introduced by the 2001 Regulations allow tribunals to strike out any claims or proposed defences on the grounds that they are scandalous, misconceived or vexatious. 'Misconceived' replaces the word 'frivolous' under the old Regulations and appears to give tribunals a much broader category of claims that can be struck out.

The greatest change introduced by the 2001 Regulations is in relation to the costs which can be awarded. Prior to 2001, tribunals had a discretion to award costs of up to £500 where the claim was considered to be frivolous or vexatious. Now tribunals may award costs where either party or the party's representative has acted improperly. In addition, a tribunal must consider awarding costs where parties or their representatives have acted 'vexatiously, abusively, disruptively or otherwise unreasonably, or the bringing of the proceedings by a party has been misconceived' (reg 14). 'Misconceived' includes having no real prospect of success (reg 2). The costs a tribunal can award have been increased to £10,000.

Further changes were made by the Employment Act (EA) 2002. By that Act, the Secretary of State was given the power to issue regulations to cover a number of issues. These changes were introduced by the Employment Tribunals (Constitution and Rules of Procedure) Regulations 2004. First, tribunals have an additional power to award costs against a representative because of the way the representative has conducted the case. Representatives for these purposes only cover representatives who charge for their services. Costs are awarded on the same grounds as above and, as above, are subject to a statutory maximum of £10,000. Secondly, tribunals have powers to determine an extended list of cases without a hearing where both parties consent and waive their rights to a hearing. Thirdly, there is a power for tribunals to strike out weak cases at a pre-hearing review (previously, a tribunal could only require a payment of a deposit if the party continued; it could not prevent the party from continuing). Fourthly, the EA 2002 introduced new statutory disciplinary and grievance procedures which all employers must adopt. The Employment Act 2002 (Dispute Resolution) Regulations 2004 prevent the presentation of claims until the employee has either gone through the statutory grievance procedure or attempted to do so but has been prevented by the employer. In addition, the employer and employee must use the statutory disciplinary procedure. Failure to use the grievance procedure prevents an employee from pursuing a claim in a tribunal. Failure to use the disciplinary procedure may result in either an increase or decrease in compensation, depending on where the blame lies. It should be noted, however, that while an employer's failure to follow the statutory procedures will result in a finding of unfair dismissal, an employer's failure to follow its own procedures over and above the statutory ones will not result in such a finding if the employer can show that the failure made no difference to the final outcome. Finally, a fixed period for conciliation has been introduced. During this time, ACAS is under a duty to conciliate and at the end of the fixed period the duty becomes a discretion. This means that the fixed term can be extended if ACAS feels that a settlement will be reached shortly or ACAS can pass the case to the tribunal service to fix a date for a hearing if it feels that the claim cannot be conciliated.

There have, therefore, been a great many changes since 2000. The question to ask is what impact have these changes had?

The new ACAS arbitration scheme has limitations which have led to criticisms. There are no procedural rules and parties cannot cross-examine witnesses. Arbitrators are not bound by existing law or precedent and, therefore, the provisions of the ERA 1996 which render certain dismissals as automatically unfair are not binding on an arbitrator. The arbitrator can only find that a dismissal is fair or unfair and cannot decide jurisdictional points, such as whether an applicant is an employee or self-employed. In addition, given that the jurisdiction is limited to unfair dismissal, any claim involving unfair dismissal and another claim can only partially be heard by arbitration. Further, if there is an issue regarding whether a dismissal has actually occurred, this must first be decided by a tribunal before ACAS can arbitrate. It is unlikely in these cases that a party would chose two forums to hear his or her claim, preferring to chose one forum that can hear all of the issues.

A further criticism can be levelled in respect of appeals. There is no right of appeal against an arbitrator's decision except in cases where there has been a serious irregularity. The logic behind this is that arbitrators are not bound by existing law. It has to be said, however, that such a restriction on an applicant's rights cannot give the users of arbitration much sense of fairness. It is suggested that the restrictions noted may be a reason why, since its inception, the scheme has only dealt with approximately 50 cases. As such, the scheme is unlikely to relieve the existing burden on employment tribunals.

The changes to the tribunals themselves may, however, lessen the number of cases in the system. The power of the tribunals to order a £500 deposit in a pre-hearing review, in addition to the power to strike out a claim, will reduce the number of cases going to a full hearing. The increase in the amount of costs which can be awarded, including the fact that costs can be awarded against representatives who charge for their services, may act as a deterrent to a claimant with a weak case. Further, the new statutory grievance procedures and the new fixed conciliation periods should, it is suggested, mean that more cases will be settled, either through the employer's own procedures or by conciliation. In addition, the fact that a breach of the employer's disciplinary procedures, over and above the statutory ones, of itself does not render a dismissal unfair where it made no difference to the final decision, will again deter many claimants from pursuing a claim on the basis of procedural unfairness.

The changes are new and their impact is unknown. It is suggested, however, that together they will have the effect of reducing the burden at present experienced by the employment tribunal system.

Notes ————————————————————————————————

_____

_____

_____

_____

_____

_____

_____

_____

_____

_____

_____

——————————— Question 4 ———————————

Since its introduction in 2000, the Human Rights Act (HRA) 1998 has permeated every aspect of employment law. With reference to decided cases to date assess the impact of the Act on the law of private employer and employee.

Answer Plan

This question requires a detailed knowledge of the cases since 2000 which have used the HRA 1998. Students need to know how the HRA has an impact on UK law and in particular the relevant Articles of the European Covention on Human Rights. Merely knowing the cases which have used the Act to date is insufficient. Students need to have sufficient knowledge of the cases to be able to assess the impact of the Act (and therefore the Covention) on employment law. Note also that the question is asking only for the impact in the area of the private not public sector.

The issues to be considered are:

• how the HRA 1998 introduces Convention rights into employment law;

• relevant Convention articles which could impact – in particular, Arts 6, 8, 10, 11 and 14;

• an analysis of case law alleging breaches of Covention rights and incompatiblity of UK legislation;

• an assessment of the impact of the HRA 1998 on employment law.

Answer

The HRA 1998, which gives effect to the European Convention on Human Rights, came into force on 1 October 2000. Since coming into force, claimants can assert Convention rights in UK courts and tribunals but only public sector employees can bring an action against their employers directly by virtue of s 7. Private sector employees have to rely on ss 2, 3 and 6 of the Act. These sections require tribunals to pay heed to the Convention and Strasbourg jurisprudence.

By s 3 of the HRA 1998:

… so far as it is possible to do so, primary and subordinate legislation must be read and given effect in a way which is compatible with the Convention rights.

Section 6 provides:

… it is unlawful for a public body to act in a way which is incompatible with a Convention right.

Section 6(3) provides that courts and tribunals are included in the definition of public authority.

Finally, s 2 provides:

… a court or tribunal determining a question which has arisen in connection with a Convention right must take into account any

(a) judgment, decision, declaration or advisory opinion of the European Court of Human Rights.

Thus while a private individual (as opposed to the state) has no direct obligations under the Covention, courts and tribunals, under ss 2 and 3, must therefore read and give effect to legislation in a way which is compatible with such rights, taking into account Strasbourg jurisprudence. As such, the Act does not create any free-standing rights for employees as there must be an existing right which has to be interpreted in line with Convention rights. Thus, prior to the introduction of the Employment Equality (Religion or Belief) Regulations 2003, given there are no free-standing rights to freedom of religion under Art 9 of the Covention, a private employee could only use the Convention to obtain a remedy for religious discrimination if such a claim could be brought under the Race Relations Act 1976 (for example, under the principle in *Seide v Gillette Industries* (1980)). As such, it is the recent expansion of protection, as required by the UK obligations to Europe, which may increase the impact in the future. In addition, in *Whittaker v P and D Watson (trading as M Watson Haulage)* (2002), the Court of Appeal held that neither an employment tribunal nor the EAT has the power to make a declaration that domestic legislation is incompatible with Convention rights.

Many commentators, at the introduction of the HRA 1998, thought it would significantly impact on employment law. Relevant Convention articles which were thought to produce such impact were:

- Art 6 – the right to a fair trial;
- Art 8 – the right to respect for private and family life;
- Art 9 – the right to freedom of thought, conscience or religion;
- Art 10 – the right to freedom of expression;
- Art 11 – the right to freedom of assembly and association; and
- Art 14 – the right to freedom of enjoyment of Convention rights without discrimination on any ground such as sex, race, colour, language, religion, political or other opinion, national or social origin, association with a national minority, property, birth or status.

As discussed above, the limitation within the Act that such rights are not free-standing means that the anticipated impact has not been so great. Cases to date indicate that where the Act may have the most impact is in respect of Arts 6 and 8 of the Convention.

Article 6 guarantees the right to a fair and public hearing within a reasonable time by an independent and impartial tribunal established by law. The Article has no effect on employer's disciplinary proceedings as the employee will always have a right to apply to an employment tribunal which is independent and impartial. The Article has been used, however, in respect of delay in tribunals. In *Kwamin v Abbey National plc* (2004), the EAT held that excessive delay between the tribunal hearing and the decision rendered the decision unsafe (in that case nearly 15 months after the hearing). The EAT stated that such a proposition was enshrined in the principle of natural justice which was compatible with Art 6. However, in *Bangs v Connex South Eastern Ltd* (2005), the Court of Appeal held that the question of whether a decision is given without reasonable delay *per se* was not a question of law but of fact and therefore could not be appealed to the EAT under s 21 of the Employment Tribunals Act 1996. Only where the delay 'could be treated as a serious procedural error or material irregularity giving rise to a question of law in the proceedings before the tribunal' would it fall under s 21. Such cases, however, would be exceptional – for example, where the delay deprived the party complaining of its right to a fair trial. It is submitted that this decision severely limits the right contained in Art 6. In contrast, in *Teinaz v London Borough of Wandsworth* (2002), the Court of Appeal stated that the right under Art 6 entitles a claimant to an adjournment where, without fault on the part of the claimant, he or she is unable to appear. It is, however, for the claimant to prove the need for such an adjournment.

Article 8 guarantees the right to respect for private and family life, but Art 8(2) places restrictions on the exercise of such rights. This states that there shall be

> no interference by a public authority with the exercise of this right except such as is in accordance with the law and is necessary in a democratic society in the interests of national security, public safety or the economic well being of the country, for the prevention of disorder and crime, for the protection of health or morals, or for the protection of the rights and freedoms of others.

Thus in *X v Y* (2004), it was held that such protection applies only to activity carried out in private and a dismissal when the employer discovered that the employee had been cautioned by the police in relation to sexual activity in a public toilet was not protected by Art 8 as the activity had taken place in public. In *Whitefield v General Medical Council* (2003), a doctor argued that the conditions imposed on his registration by the GMC, which banned alcohol consumption and required submission to random testing for alcohol, were an infringement of his rights under Art 8. The Privy Council held, however, that there was no such interference as he could still enjoy private life without drinking alcohol and further, if there was such interference, it was justified on public safety grounds, since the ban was imposed because of his excessive use of alcohol.

There is an argument that the rights contained in Art 6 and Art 8 may conflict, particularly where one party wants to introduce evidence which may be in breach of the other party's Art 8 rights. In cases involving secretly filmed conduct or those involving medical evidence, the courts have upheld that the right to a fair trial takes precedence over the right to respect for family life (*Jones v University of Warwick* (2003)).

Other Convention rights may impact on employment law. While Art 9 is relevant, it is submitted that until reported cases under the Employment Equality (Religion or Belief) Regulations 2003 start to come through, its actual impact is unknown. Rights under Art 10 (freedom of expression) could have implications for dress codes but, in view of Art 14, rights under Art 10 will not be infringed where the dress code is non-discriminatory. One further provision, however, which has had an impact is Art 11 – the right to freedom of association and assembly.

Wilson and Others v United Kingdom (2002) is a pre-HRA 1998 case but is important because the European Court of Human Rights (ECtHR) held that, by allowing employers to use financial inducements to persuade employees to come out of collective bargaining, UK law was in breach of Art 11. As a result, the Employment Relations Act 2004 has amended the Trade Union and Labour Relations (Consolidation) Act 1992. New ss 145A and B creates rights for workers not to suffer an inducement to prevent them becoming or persuading them to become members of a trade union or to prevent them from taking part in trade union activities (s 145A). Section 145B also gives the worker a right not to be offered an inducement to pull out of collective bargaining. These amendments are a direct result of the Wilson case.

So what has been the impact of the HRA 1998 to date? From the cases so far it seems to be very little. Apart from *Wilson*, the cases seem to conclude that the common law reflects the Convention, or that Convention rights do not apply and thus the tribunal is not required to interpret the law in a way that is compatible. The fact that the Act does not create any free-standing rights has limited its impact, although the recent creation of additional rights such as protection from discrimination on the grounds of religious belief and sexual orientation may see more cases reflecting Convention rights. Hardy, in a paper given at the Society of Legal Scholars Conference in 2001, has suggested that the ACAS arbitration scheme could be an infringement of Art 6 rights and Smith and Wood (Industrial Law, 8th edn, 2003, London: LexisNexis Butterworths) argue that the Article may also be infringed because of the lack of legal aid in employment tribunal claims. Thus, to date the impact is limited but may become considerably more important in the next few years.

Notes

2 Nature of the Relationship

Introduction

Very often, examination papers on employment law contain a question on the nature of an employment relationship. In other words, the examiner is looking for the distinction between independent contractors and employees and the various tests that have evolved over the years to determine whether a person works under a contract of service or a contract for services.

The issues to be considered are:

- the differences between independent contractors and employees;
- the legal consequences of the distinction;
- the tests used to determine whether a person is an employee or an independent contractor.

Questions may be in the form of either essays or problems. Specific issues which students need to be familiar with are:

- the different liabilities an employer has for employees compared to independent contractors;
- how the status of the person may affect terms in the contract;
- how the status of the person affects employment protection rights;
- the control test (*Performing Rights Society v Mitchell and Booker* (1924));
- the organisation test (*Stevenson, Jordan and Harrison Ltd v Macdonald and Evans* (1952));
- the multiple test (*Ready Mixed Concrete (South East) Ltd v MPNI* (1968));
- the irreducible minimum.

It is also important to remember that if the question is a problem type question, it may involve other areas, such as whether the person has a right to sue for an unfair dismissal. It is necessary therefore to establish exactly what the question is asking for. With regard to the above example relating to unfair dismissal, a question on whether the person is an employee and therefore can sue for an unfair dismissal is different from a question asking if the employee in the problem has the necessary qualifying criteria to pursue a claim, as will be seen in Chapter 9, below.

Checklist

Students should be familiar with the following areas:

- the distinction between contracts of service and contracts for services;
- the legal consequences of the distinction;
- the different tests to determine status;
- the 'small businessman' approach;
- the position of casual workers and home workers.

Question 5

'The tasks which people carry out and the contexts in which they do so daily become so much more numerous, more diverse and more sophisticated that no one test or set of tests is apt to separate contracts of service and contracts for services in all cases.' (May J in *The President of the Methodist Conference v Parfitt* (1984)).

To what extent do the courts use one test to determine the nature of the relationship between the parties and what are the consequences of deciding that a person is an employee?

Answer plan

This question is a fairly standard one in this area and breaks down into two parts:

- What are the tests to determine whether there is a contract of service or a contract for services?
- What are the consequences of deciding that a person is an employee?

Answer

For a variety of reasons, which will be discussed below, it is important to determine whether a person is employed under a contract of employment. By s 230(2) of the Employment Rights Act (ERA) 1996:

> ... a 'contract of employment' means a contract of service or apprenticeship, whether express or implied, and (if it is express) whether it is oral or in writing.

By s 230(1) of the ERA 1996:

> ... 'employee' means an individual who has entered into or works under (or, where the employment has ceased, worked under) a contract of employment.

This definition of an employee, although provided by statute, is not, however, helpful as it fails to define what is meant by a contract of service. It is important to note that the definition given by the parties to the relationship is not conclusive and it is the court which determines the status of the parties within the relationship. Thus, the fact that a person is called an employee does not mean that he or she is employed under a contract of employment. Due to the lack of clarity provided by statute, the courts over the years have devised a series of tests to decide if the relationship is one of employer/employee or employer/independent contractor.

In early cases, when employees were less skilled than they are today, the courts used the single test of control. This test arose in the context of vicarious liability and it seemed logical to look at the control an employer exercised over the employees. In *Performing Rights Society v Mitchell and Booker* (1924), McCardie J said: '... the final test, if there is to be a final test, and certainly the test to be generally applied, lies in the nature and degree of detailed control over the person alleged to be a servant.' The question of control was very simple: it meant that the employer controlled not only *when* the work was done but how it was done. As Bramwell LJ said in *Yewens v Noakes* (1880): 'A servant is a person subject to the command of his master as to the manner in which he shall do his work.' While the control test worked well when workers were unskilled, it became apparent that it became more of a legal fiction as the industrial revolution meant that workers became more skilled. In *Hillyer v Governors of St Bartholomew's Hospital* (1909), it was held that nurses were not employees when carrying out operating theatre duties, although a more realistic approach was taken in *Cassidy v Minister of Health* (1951). *Cassidy*, however, shows that control by itself was an insufficient test in a modern industrial society.

Due to the inadequacies of the control test, the courts looked for another test which would reflect the realities of a modern day employment relationship. In *Stevenson, Jordan and Harrison Ltd v Macdonald and Evans* (1952), Denning LJ developed what he called the integration test. He said in the case: '... under a contract of service, a man is employed as part of the business and his work is done as an integral part of the business but, under a contract for services, his work, although done for the business, is not integrated into it but only accessory to it.'

While such a test got round the problems of the control test, Denning LJ never explained what he meant by integration and later judgments regard the question of integration as part of a wider test rather than a test on its own.

The courts realised that, in a modern industrial society, no one factor could be isolated as the determinant of the relationship and, therefore, they developed what is known as the 'multiple test'. This was first propounded by McKenna J in *Ready Mixed Concrete (South East) Ltd v MPNI* (1968). In the case, he looked at a variety of factors, some indicating that the lorry drivers were self-employed, some indicating that they were employees. At the end of this balancing exercise, McKenna J asked himself three questions: (1) Had the employee agreed to provide his skill in consideration of a wage? (2) Was there an element of control exercisable by the employer, and (3) were there any terms in the contract which were inconsistent with it being a contract of service? In the case, the drivers could delegate driving duties and, therefore, although there were factors indicating that they were employees, McKenna J ruled that this term was inconsistent with a contract of service and, therefore, the drivers were self-employed.

While his decision was later criticised, the basis of it (that is, looking at a multitude of factors) was not, and this is the approach of the courts today. Cooke J summarised the approach of the courts in *Market Investigations Ltd v MSS* (1968) when he said that the question to be determined by the court was whether the person was in business on his own account (the small businessman approach). If so, then there was a contract for services.

This then leads to the question of what factors are considered when adopting the multiple test? It is the court which decides the nature of the relationship and not the parties, although what the parties think is a factor that the court will take into account. In *Ferguson v John Dawson Ltd* (1976), a builder's labourer was self-employed. He was injured when he fell off a roof. The employer was in breach of safety duties owed to employees under the Construction (Working Places) Regulations 1966. The employer argued that, as the labourer was self-employed, no duties were owed to him. The Court of Appeal found that the labourer was, in reality, an employee, despite the label the parties had put on the relationship. If there is ambiguity as to the nature of the relationship, Denning MR suggested in *Massey v Crown Life Insurance* (1978) that the label the parties attach to the relationship will be conclusive. This has been doubted and narrowed in the later case of *Young and Wood Ltd v West* (1980) when Stephenson LJ said: 'It must be the court's duty to see whether the label correctly represents the true legal relationship between the parties.'

The small businessman approach summarised by Cooke J in Market Investigations means that the court looks at a variety of factors such as investment, ownership of tools, who bears the risk of loss and who stands to make a profit. Homeworkers and casual workers are particular groups where establishing the nature of the relationship may prove difficult. In both *Airfix Footwear Ltd v Cope* (1978) and *Nethemere (St Neots) Ltd v Taverna and Another* (1984), it was decided that homeworkers were employees – in *Cope*, because work was provided on a regular basis and there was a strong element of control and, in *Taverna*, because, in reality, there was a mutuality of obligations due to the length of the relationship.

By contrast, a case involving casual workers was *O'Kelly v Trust House Forte plc* (1983) where it was held that casual workers were self-employed even though they worked solely for one employer, because there was no obligation for the employer to provide work when they showed up and no obligation on the casuals to offer their services. It was thus the lack of mutuality which led to the decision, despite the clear control exercised by the employer and the fact that it would be difficult to describe a casual worker as being in business on his own account. The House of Lords reached a similar conclusion in *Carmichael and Leese v National Power plc* (1999), in which it was decided that guides employed on a 'casual as required' basis were self-employed. Lack of mutuality of obligations has led to agency workers being classed as self-employed (*Wickens v Champion Employment* (1984), although see *McMeechan v Secretary of State for Employment* (1997)), and trawlermen who entered into separate crew agreements for each voyage were also deemed to be self-employed, despite the fact that they invariably returned to the same employer, again because of the lack of obligation to provide work or services.

The Privy Council highlighted the factors that the court must look to in *Lee v Chung and Shun Chung Construction and Engineering Co Ltd* (1990). The worker was a mason who suffered a back injury while working on a building site. The court looked at whether it could be said that the mason was in business on his own account and said that matters of importance were whether the worker provides his own equipment; whether he hires his own helpers; what degree of financial risk he takes; what degree of responsibility he has for investment and management and whether, and how far, he has the opportunity to profit from sound management in the performance of his task. In *Hall (Inspector of Taxes) v Lorimer* (1992), however, the court stressed that the list of factors should not be gone through mechanically. Upholding a decision of the special commissioners, the court said: 'The whole picture has to be painted and then viewed from a distance to reach an informed and qualitative decision in the circumstances of the particular case.'

More recent cases have talked about the irreducible minimum needed to constitute a contract of employment. In *Carmichael and Leese v National Power plc*, mutuality was seen as the irreducible minimum, while in *Express Echo Publications v Tanton* (1999), the Court of Appeal regarded personal service by the employee to be essential so that the power to delegate job duties was fatal to an employment claim. A later EAT, however, in *Macfarlane v Glasgow City Council* (2001) stated that a limited or occasional power of delegation is not inconsistent with a contract of employment. *Dacas v Brook Street Bureau* (2004) once again puts control firmly at the forefront.

The question which must now be asked is: why is the distinction between employees and independent contractors important? A variety of rights and liabilities apply in respect of employees which do not apply to independent contractors. The major differences are listed below.

An employee pays insurance contributions which are a percentage of his earnings and the employer also makes a contribution. This gives the employee certain benefits in respect of unemployment, sickness and industrial injury as well as state pension rights. An independent contractor pays a flat rate insurance contribution, irrespective of earnings, and has no rights to the benefits mentioned.

An employer must deduct tax at source for his employees and may be committing a criminal offence should he fail to do so (*Jennings v Westwood Engineering* (1975)). The employer is under no such obligation in relation to independent contractors although, in the building industry, the employer is required to deduct tax as if the workers are employees and the workers can then claim tax back if they are genuinely self-employed. This was introduced by the Finance Act 1971 to avoid the notorious 'lump' system which was operating at the time. Criticisms have been raised against this as it provides only for the payment of tax and does not give the workers any other protection.

An employer is vicariously liable for his employees if they cause injury during the course of their employment, while, generally, no such liability exists in respect of independent contractors. In addition, while independent contractors and employees are protected by the Health and Safety at Work etc Act 1974, the employer owes more stringent duties to his employees, supplemented by implied terms in the contract of employment.

The law implies a host of terms into the employment contract and other terms come from sources outside the individual parties' negotiations, such as works rules and collective agreements. By contrast, a court is unlikely to imply terms into a contract between an employer and his independent contractor.

Finally, employment protection legislation – in the form of unfair dismissal and redundancy compensation, time off rights, guaranteed payments and maternity rights – apply only to employees. Independent contractors have no such protection, although *Quinnen v Hovell* (1984) decided that all workers, whatever their status, are protected by the Sex Discrimination Act 1975 and the Race Relations Act 1976 where they are providing personal services, and the rights introduced by the Employment Relations Act 1999 (amending the ERA 1996) apply to workers and not only to employees.

It is therefore possible to say that while the courts use what on the face of it appears to be one test – the multiple test – to decide if a person is an employee, this test involves looking at a whole variety of factors with the aim of deciding whether the person is in business on his own account. Of these factors, control, mutuality of obligations and who bears the financial risk appear to be the most important, although the case of *Lorimer* has stressed that the court should not use the list of factors mechanically but should look at the overall picture. More recent cases are now talking about the irreducible minimum, but what the irreducible minimum is is still unclear. It is important for both parties, however, to know what the legal relationship is. On the part of the employer, he will then know the extent of his liability and, on the part of the worker, he will know what rights he has, both in respect of his employer and in the wider context of welfare benefits and employment protection rights.

Notes

_____

_____

_____

_____

_____

_____

_____

_____

_____

_____

_____

_____

Question 6

Arthur, Ian and Ricky are lorry drivers for East End Ltd, a haulage company. They have all been employed for three years. Employees at the company receive both holiday pay and sick pay. The company states in the contracts that the lorry drivers are self-employed. All the lorry drivers are employed on different terms.

Arthur is paid per delivery although he is guaranteed a minimum of 20 deliveries a week. His lorry is provided by the company, although he must maintain it. He receives no holiday or sick pay. He pays his own tax and national insurance and may substitute another driver if he wishes.

Ian and Ricky are on identical terms. They are paid a minimum weekly wage (which is the equivalent of 20 deliveries) and, after that, per delivery. They use company lorries which the company maintains. They may also substitute a driver, but only with written permission from the company. Ian receives no holiday or sick pay and pays his own tax and insurance. Ricky used to receive his wages net but, recently, the company told him it would be cheaper for both the company and Ricky if he became responsible for his own tax and insurance. Ricky agreed to this.

Last week, Arthur was injured when a badly stacked load on the company premises fell on him. Ian was injured when his brakes failed going down a hill and Ricky was made redundant. The company argues that it has no liability towards any of them as they are all self-employed.

Advise Arthur, Ian and Ricky if they are in fact employees and may therefore claim against the company.

Answer plan

This problem is equivalent to the one addressed in the last question. We have three parties and the issue relating to all three is whether they are, in reality, employees and, in the case of Arthur and Ian, whether they can sue for their injuries and, in the case of Ricky, whether he can claim a redundancy payment.

The issues to be considered are:

- a brief discussion of the tests to determine status;
- a discussion of the multiple test – in particular, the main cases, such as *Ready Mixed Concrete (South East) Ltd v MPNI* (1968); *Market Investigations Ltd v MSS* (1968); *Lee v Chung and Shun Chung Construction and Engineering Co Ltd* (1990); *Hall (Inspector of Taxes) v Lorimer* (1992);
- recent cases talking about the irreducible minimum – *Carmichael and Leese v National Power plc* (1999); *Express Echo Publications v Tanton* (1999); *Macfarlane v Glasgow City Council* (2001); *Dacas v Brook Street Bureau* (2004).
- the effect of tax avoidance on the rights of employees.

——— Answer ———

The issue to be discussed initially in respect of the three parties is whether they are in fact self-employed as their contracts say. It will be seen below that, while the label that the parties attach to the relationship may be a factor considered by the courts, it is by no means conclusive and, therefore, even though the parties are called self-employed, the law may decide that they are employees and are thus entitled to sue East End Ltd.

The original test used by the courts to determine if the relationship was one of employer–employee was the 'control test'. As employees became more skilled, however, it became apparent that the control test, as a single test to determine whether the person was an employee, was inadequate. Denning LJ, in the case of *Stevenson, Jordan and Harrison Ltd v Macdonald and Evans* (1952), developed what became known as the 'organisation integration test' to overcome the problems with the control test. In the case, he said:

> ... under a contract of service, a man is employed as part of the business and his work is done as an integral part of the business but under a contract for services his work, although done for the business, is not integrated into it but only accessory to it.

The problem with the test is that Denning LJ did not define 'integration' and the test never won favour in the courts. The case is important, however, in that it showed a move away from control as the sole determinant.

By the 1960s, the courts realised that a variety of factors needed to be examined to see if the relationship between the parties was one of employment. In *Ready Mixed Concrete (South East) Ltd v MPNI* (1968), McKenna J laid down what is now known as the multiple test. This involved looking at a multiplicity of factors and then asking three questions: first, whether the employee agrees to provide his skill in consideration of a wage; secondly, whether there is an element of control exercisable by the employer; and, thirdly, whether there are provisions in the contract which are inconsistent with it being a contract of employment. Whereas the decision was later criticised, the essence of the test was not. Cooke J, in *Market Investigations Ltd v MSS* (1969), summarised the approach taken by the courts by saying that the question to be determined was whether the person was in business on his own account. Later, cases such as *Lee v Chung and Shun Chung Construction and Engineering Co Ltd* (1990) and *Hall (Inspector of Taxes) v Lorimer* (1992) have given us a list of factors the courts have identified as relevant. More recently, cases such as *Carmichael and Leese v National Power plc* (1999), *Express Echo Publications v Tanton* (1999) and *Macfarlane v Glasgow City Council* (2001) and *Dacas v Brook Street Bureau* (2004) have laid down the irreducible minimum need for a relationship to be one of employment.

In all the cases in the problem, the contracts state that the lorry drivers are self-employed. In *Ferguson v John Dawson Ltd* (1976), a builder's labourer agreed to work as self-employed and was injured when he fell off a roof. No guard rail had been provided, in breach of the duty owed to employees under the Construction (Working Places) Regulations 1966. The employer argued that the worker was self-employed and no duty was owed to him. The Court of Appeal held that the worker was an employee and that the statement as to his status was not conclusive. On the basis of Ferguson, therefore, it would appear that the statement in the lorry drivers' contracts is not conclusive, but may be a factor the court takes into account.

The Court of Appeal, however, has distinguished Ferguson in cases where there has been an agreed change in status. In *Massey v Crown Life Insurance Co* (1978), the worker had been employed for two years as a branch manager. He then agreed to register himself as John L Massey and Associates and his one-man business became the branch manager. The reason for the change was that the employer no longer wanted the administrative burden of deducting tax and insurance contributions and the Inland Revenue agreed to the change in status. When Massey was sacked, he claimed unfair dismissal. The Court of Appeal said that he had no capacity to claim as he was self-employed. Denning MR distinguished *Ferguson* on the basis that, in *Massey*, there was a genuine agreement entered into from which Massey benefited. The agreement was instigated by Massey himself and he could not claim the benefits of self-employment and some time afterward say he was an employee in order to claim unfair dismissal. While this case is of no relevance to Arthur and Ian, it may have a bearing on Ricky's claim as Ricky agreed to become self-employed, having originally been an employee. Massey may be distinguished from Ricky's case, however. While Denning MR was prepared to accept that, in *Massey*, an agreement had been made at the instigation of the worker and the agreement should stand, he also stated 'the parties cannot alter the truth of the relationship by putting a different label on it and use it as a dishonest device to deceive the Revenue'.

Furthermore, in *Young and Wood Ltd v West* (1980), where a worker chose self-employment for tax reasons, Stephenson LJ distinguished *Massey* on two grounds: first, that Massey had two contracts – one as the manager and another for services under a general agency agreement and, secondly, there was a deliberate change in status agreed by the parties. On this basis, it may be possible to argue that, in Ricky's case, the court will not accept the label later agreed by the parties for two reasons: first, it appears that the change is to deceive the Inland Revenue and, secondly, because there is only one contract and not two, as in *Massey*. Should this be the case, the court can look to see the true status of Ricky.

In Arthur's case, there are a variety of factors the court will examine. He is paid per delivery but he is guaranteed a minimum of 20 deliveries per week. This means that he has a guaranteed income every week and this may indicate that he is an employee as per the first condition laid down by McKenna J in *Ready Mixed Concrete*. His lorry is owned by the company although he must maintain it. In the *Lee* case, the court listed a variety of factors to consider when deciding the nature of the relationship. There, the court looked at whether the worker provided his own equipment; whether he hired his own helpers; what degree of financial risk he took; what degree of responsibility he had for investment and management; and how far he had the opportunity to profit from sound management in the performance of his task. In *Lorimer*, the worker was a vision mixer and used equipment provided by the television company which employed him. He was paid gross for his work; he had no long-term contracts with any company; he was responsible for his own pension and sick provision; and none of his money was used in the programmes he mixed. Nor did he stand to make a profit or loss from any of the programmes with which he was involved. The court held that Lorimer was self-employed. If we apply these cases to Arthur's situation – although he is guaranteed a minimum number of deliveries a week which would suggest that there is mutuality of obligations – it is up to him whether he does the work and if he goes above the minimum; therefore, to some extent, he controls how little or how much he does and therefore earns. While he does not own the tools, he has to maintain the lorry, so, to a large extent, he controls the way he earns in that, if he does not invest in adequate maintenance, he will be the loser and not the company. He can delegate his driving duties, so, in a way, he can hire his own workers. Looking at all these factors, and the judgments in *Lee* and *Lorimer*, it would appear likely that the court would hold that Arthur is self-employed, since there appears to be little control on the part of the employer.

One other indication that Arthur is self-employed comes from the judgment of McKenna J in *Ready Mixed Concrete*. The third question McKenna J said had to be asked was whether there were any terms in the contract which were inconsistent with it being a contract of employment. Here, Arthur can delegate driving duties when he wishes without any consultation with the company. Such a term is inconsistent with a contract of employment as such a contract is a personal contract where the employee is taken on for his original skills. Duties cannot be delegated under a contract of employment without the permission of the employer. Furthermore, in *Express Echo Publications v Tanton*, the power to delegate duties was seen as fatal to an employment claim, although the later case of *Macfarlane v Glasgow City Council* stated that a limited power of delegation was not inconsistent with a contract of employment. In Arthur's case, however, there appears to be no limit on his power of delegation, unlike the limit on both Ricky and Ian where they can delegate only with written permission from the company and thus it would appear that Arthur's situation is more like that in *Tanton*.

The term in Arthur's contract is therefore further evidence that he is not an employee but self-employed. As such, he is owed no specific safety duties, but may be able to sue for his injuries under occupier's liability or through the law of negligence.

Ian and Ricky are on identical terms. While their contracts state that they are self-employed, looking at the relevant terms and the judgments in *Lee* and *Ferguson*, it is questionable whether, in reality, this is the case. Both are paid a minimum wage which they appear to get whether or not they work (unlike Arthur who is only guaranteed a minimum number of deliveries if he wants them). The company both provides and maintains the lorries and, therefore, neither Ian nor Ricky have to put in any financial investment. Both can delegate driving duties, but only with the written permission of the company (that is, a limited power of delegation), which means the company has the ultimate say as to who makes the deliveries. While they pay their own tax and insurance, this is only one factor and it is submitted that the factors which indicate that they are employees outweigh this fact. As such, Ian is an employee and the employer owes him a duty to provide safe equipment. The employer has broken this duty and Ian can sue.

It has already been stated that, although Ricky agreed to the change in his status, *Massey* could be distinguished and the parties' statement as to status will be a factor for consideration only and not conclusive. If this is the case, following the arguments above in relation to Ian, Ricky is also an employee. On the face of it, therefore, he is entitled to sue for a redundancy payment. It depends, however, on the reason for the change in status. If the reason was to defraud the revenue, the contract becomes void as it was set up for an illegal purpose. As such, no rights can arise out of it and Ricky has no right to redundancy pay (*Jennings v Westwood Engineering* (1975)). Ricky's innocence or guilt is irrelevant as the contract will be void ab initio because its purpose was illegal rather than it having been established for a valid purpose but illegal in its performance (*Corby v Morrison* (1980)). If, however, Ricky can show that the intention behind the change in status was, for example, administrative convenience for the employer and there was no illegal purpose, then, as an employee, he is entitled to redundancy pay based on his three years' service.

Notes

3 Sources of Contractual terms

Introduction

Many employment law exam papers will contain a question on the sources of the terms in an employment contract. This chapter and Chapter 4, below, will deal with all the terms, although this chapter will be dedicated to those terms which come from sources within the workplace and Chapter 4 will deal with the implied duties.

The issues to be considered are:

- express terms;
- collective agreements as a source of contractual terms;
- the contractual status of works rules – incorporation of disciplinary and grievance procedures;
- the status of the statutory statement;
- custom as a source of contractual terms;
- implied terms.

Although general questions on the different sources of terms do come up, more often, a question will be set on one or two of the sources and will require an answer as to whether a term from a particular source has become part of the individual's contract of employment. This means that a detailed discussion of all the sources is unnecessary. To answer a specific question on this area, students need to be familiar with:

- interpretation of express terms and the process of variation;
- express and implied incorporation of collective agreements;
- the process of incorporation of other documents;
- the relationship between the statutory statement and contractual terms;
- the effect of a custom on the contract;
- the judicial process of implication of terms.

Finally, it is important to note that while sources of terms may be a question in itself, a repudiatory breach of contract on the part of the employer can be a constructive dismissal. Knowledge of this area of the syllabus might, therefore, be required for other questions.

Checklist

Students should be familiar with the following areas:

- judicial interpretation of express terms – in particular, *Johnstone v Bloomsbury Area Health Authority* (1991);
- judicial interpretation of flexibility and mobility clauses;
- what constitutes a variation of terms;
- enforceability of collective agreements between the collective and individual parties – in particular, cases such as *British Leyland (UK) Ltd v McQuilken* (1978); *Joel v Cammell Laird* (1969); *Duke v Reliance Systems Ltd* (1982); *Miller v Hamworthy Engineering Ltd* (1986); *Scally v Southern Health and Social Services Board* (1991); *Henry v London General Transport Services* (2001);
- enforceability of works rules and disciplinary procedures – in particular, *Secretary of State for Employment v ASLEF (No 2)* (1972);
- the status of the statutory statement – particularly the judgment of Browne-Wilkinson J in *System Floors (UK) Ltd v Daniel* (1981);
- the implication of terms by the tests in *The Moorcock* (1889) and *Shirlaw v Southern Foundries Ltd* (1939).

Question 7

Production workers working for Webb Ltd have received a Christmas bonus every year for the last 15 years. During that time, the company has always traded at a profit but, last year, the company traded at a loss and no bonus was paid.

Last week, the company issued a new rule which was posted on the notice board. The rule states that management reserves the right to require any employee to submit to a body search upon leaving the company premises, in order to check that property of the company is not being removed.

All the terms and conditions of employment of production workers working for the company are the product of a collective agreement negotiated between their union and the company, although the agreement has now terminated. One of the clauses in the agreement stated that redundancy selection would be on the basis of LIFO (last in first out). The company now wishes to make five production workers redundant on the basis of 'lack of management potential'.

Advise the company of the contractual implications of these changes.

Answer plan

This question is looking at the implication of terms into an employment contract from three different sources: judicial implication, works rules and collective agreements. The question asks the student to advise the company as to the contractual implications of its actions and thus is asking whether the company can enforce the changes it has introduced against the employees.

Therefore, the issues to be considered are:

- the contractual tests for implication of a term and the test for deciding the content of that term;
- whether works rules are contractual or merely orders from an employer and the consequences of any analysis;
- how far clauses in a collective agreement are appropriate for incorporation into an individual contract of employment;
- the process of incorporation of terms from a collective agreement into an employee's contract;
- the effect on the employment contract of the termination of the agreement at the collective level.

───────── Answer ─────────

The company is seeking advice as to the contractual implications of its actions. If, in each case, the company has lawfully amended the contracts of employment of the production workers, then it can compel the employees to comply with the amended terms. If, however, the company has unilaterally varied the contractual terms, the employees can refuse to comply with the changes and sue for damages should they suffer loss.

In the first situation, the company has paid a bonus for 15 years and now appears to have withdrawn it. If such payment has now become a term of the contract, this unilateral action on the part of the company may be a breach. The question to be asked is: given that it would appear that the contract is silent as to the issue of a Christmas bonus, would the courts imply such a term into the contract and, if so, what would the content of the term be? Implication of terms into a contract allows the court to fill in the gaps where the parties have failed to provide for a situation. In traditional contracts, there has been a presumption against adding in terms the parties have not expressed, but this presumption has not applied in employment contracts. There are two contractual tests which the courts use to imply terms into a contract. The first of these comes from the case of *The Moorcock* (1889) and implies a term because it is necessary to give the contract 'business efficacy'. The second test comes from *Shirlaw v Southern Foundries Ltd* (1939) and is known as the obvious consensus or the 'oh, of course' test on the basis that, if a person asked the officious bystander if such a term should be in the contract, he would reply 'oh, of course'.

Smith and Wood (*Industrial Law*, 8th edn, 2003 London: LexisNexis Butterworths) argue that the old contractual tests have been modified in relation to employment contracts in three ways. First, there are inferred terms which the courts are prepared to imply because they appear reasonable in all the circumstances rather than based on any supposed intention of the parties; secondly, implied duties which apply to all employment relationships; and, thirdly, what the authors describe as overriding terms, that is, terms which are regarded as so important that they will be implied regardless of the parties' intentions. An example of such an overriding term is the duty to ensure the employee's safety which, according to Stuart-Smith LJ in *Johnstone v Bloomsbury Area Health Authority* (1991), is so important that any express contractual term must be read subject to it.

In the case of the Christmas bonus, the first point to consider is whether the courts would hold that this has now become a term of the contract because it appears reasonable in the circumstances. An objective approach to this was seen in the case of *Mears v Safecar Security Ltd* (1982) where the Court of Appeal gave guidance on the implication of terms into the contract. That court said that a broad approach should be taken and a term may be inserted based on all the evidence as to how the parties have worked the contract in the past. Thus, in the case, there was no implied term relating to sick pay, because the employees had never claimed it in the past. This approach can also be seen in *Courtaulds Northern Spinning Ltd v Sibson* (1988) where Slade LJ said that the term the court should imply was one the parties would probably have agreed to if they were being reasonable. As such, a mobility clause was implied into the contract because the employee had always worked on different sites, even though there was no express term requiring him to do so.

For the past 15 years, the employer has paid a Christmas bonus. Given that this has happened for so long, it could be argued that it is reasonable that such payment has become contractual. In fact, it may also be argued that, under *Shirlaw*, the officious bystander would say 'oh, of course' when asked if this has become a contractual term. This ignores, however, the situation when the bonus has been paid. Over the last 15 years, the company has always made a profit and this year it has made a loss. If, therefore, the old contractual tests are used to see if there should be a term relating to bonuses, and the concept of reasonableness is used to define the content of the term, then it could be said that there will be a term that the employees will receive a bonus when the company makes a profit. Thus, if this year the company was in profit, failure to pay the bonus will be a breach of contract and the employees can sue. If, as is the case, the company has made a loss, there will be no breach on the part of the company.

In respect of the new rule the company has recently introduced, the issue to be decided is whether the rules have become contractual. If this is the case, then one party cannot unilaterally alter the terms of the contract and the employees must consent to the change before becoming legally bound. Lord Denning in *Secretary of State for Employment v ASLEF (No 2)* (1972) stated that works rules are 'in no way terms of the contract of employment. They are only instructions to a man as to how he is to do his work'. He reiterated this interpretation in the later case of *Peake v Automative Products* (1978), where it was held that the rule book was non-contractual and only set out the administrative arrangements. On the other hand, given that some employers issue company handbooks with the employee's contracts, and employees often, in these situations, sign acknowledging receipt of the rules, in these circumstances it is likely that the parts of the rules which can be terms become part of the contract between the parties.

In the situation in the problem, there is no evidence of how the rules were originally communicated to the employees. It is safe to presume, however, that it was not done through a company handbook at the time contracts were issued as this new rule has been placed on a notice board, suggesting that this is the method of communication. It is therefore more likely that the court will decide that the rules in this situation are orders from the employer (*ASLEF*) rather than contractual terms. Such an interpretation would, on the face of it, appear to give Webb Ltd *carte blanche*; however, the employer's right to issue and enforce rules is circumscribed by the concept of reasonableness. While the employee is under a duty to obey orders from the employer, this duty extends only to lawful, reasonable orders. In *Talbot v Hugh Fulton Ltd* (1975), the dismissal of an employee for having long hair in breach of the works rules was held to be unfair because the rule did not say what constituted 'long' and, as there was no safety or hygiene risk, the rule was unreasonable. In the case of Webb Ltd, therefore, even though on interpretation of these particular rules it would appear that the company may act unilaterally and change the rules without consultation or agreement, the employees will not be bound to obey the order to submit to a body search if such an order is deemed to be unreasonable. Without evidence of how much the company is losing from thefts, what consultation took place before the introduction of the rule or what alternatives were considered, this rule would not appear to be reasonable and, therefore, the company cannot compel the employees to comply with it.

Collective agreements can be a source of terms of the employment contract. While such agreements are presumed not to be legally binding between the collective parties (s 179 of the Trade Union and Labour Relations (Consolidation) Act (TULR(C)A) 1992), if some of the clauses from the agreement become part of the individual contracts, those clauses are enforceable as contractual terms. Once the clauses are in the individual contracts, their enforceability stems from the contract and not the collective agreement and the fact that the collective agreement between Webb Ltd and the union has now terminated will not affect those terms (*Burroughs Machines Ltd v Timmoney* (1977) and *Whent v T Cartledge Ltd* (1997)). Collective agreements may become part of an employee's contract by express or implied incorporation. On the wording of the question, it appears that there has been express incorporation as all the terms and conditions are stated to be the product of a collective agreement between the union and the employer.

Not all terms of a collective agreement are suitable for incorporation into the individual contract, however. In *British Leyland (UK) Ltd v McQuilken* (1978), it was held that a clause of a collective agreement which stated a policy of offering redundant employees the choice between redundancy and retraining was not intended to create individual rights and, therefore, had not become part of the individual's contract. A similar conclusion was reached in *Young v Canadian Northern Rly Co* (1931) in relation to a redundancy selection policy. On the basis of these authorities, it would appear that the selection policy is not a clause which is appropriate for incorporation at the individual level. It may be, however, that the authorities can be distinguished.

While the policy in *McQuilken* would appear to be inappropriate for incorporation, a distinction between the case at Webb Ltd and *Young* is that the employee in *Young* was not a union member and was relying on the practice that collective agreements applied to all employees. In the case in question, it would appear that all the terms of the production workers have been collectively bargained and that the negotiations at the collective level were obviously intended to bind the individual parties. As such, it may be possible to argue that, based on the intention of the parties and the fact that the provision is specific and relevant to an individual employee, the selection procedure has become contractual, and the five production workers selected contrary to LIFO can sue for a breach of contract.

Notes

_____

_____

_____

_____

_____

_____

_____

_____

_____

_____

_____

Question 8

Despite the fact that collective agreements have a major impact on employees' terms and conditions, often regulating their changing content, their precise relationship with the contract of employment is often unclear and can lead to legal uncertainty as to their precise effect.

With reference to case law, critically evaluate this statement.

Answer plan

This question requires a detailed knowledge of the law relating to collective agreements and their impact on the contract of employment. It also requires the student to evaluate the law and to come to a conclusion as to whether the statement is accurate.

Particular issues to be considered are:

- the definition of collective agreement in s 178 of the TULR(C)A 1992;
- the presumption in s 179 of the TULR(C)A 1992;
- terms which are appropriate for incorporation – in particular, cases such as *NCB v National Union of Mineworkers* (1986), *Young v Canadian Northern Rly Co* (1931);

Alexander v Standard Telephones and Cables Ltd (1990); *Anderson v Pringle of Scotland Ltd* (1998); *Marley v Forward Trust Group* (1986);

- methods of incorporation into individual contracts – in particular, cases such as *NCB v Galley* (1958); *Robertson and Jackson v British Gas Corp* (1983); *Gibbons v Associated British Ports* (1985); *Whent v T Cartledge Ltd* (1997); *Cadoux v Central Regional Council* (1986); *Duke v Reliance Systems Ltd* (1982); *Ali v Christian Salvesen Food Services Ltd* (1997); *Singh v British Steel Corp* (1974); *Henry v London General Transport Services* (2001);

- conflicting collective agreements – in particular, cases such as *Clift v West Riding County Council* (1964) and *Gascol Conversions Ltd v Mercer* (1974).

Answer

Under s 178(1) of the TULR(C)A 1992, a collective agreement is 'any agreement or arrangement made by or on behalf of one or more trade unions or one or more employers or employers' associations and relating to one or more of the matters specified' in s 178(2)'. Collective agreements have two functions: the procedural function, that is, the regulation of the relationship between the employer or employer's association and the trade union; and the normative function, that is, the regulation of provisions for individual employees who are members of the union. Collective agreements govern a large number of employees' terms and conditions of employment, yet there is a statutory presumption that they are not intended to be legally binding (s 179 of the 1992 Act). This, however, is misleading. Section 179 provides that they are not legally binding between the employer and trade union. Should terms of the agreement become terms of the individual employee's contract, then these terms will be legally enforceable by the employee against the employer. There is, however, legal uncertainty as to which terms within a collective agreement are appropriate for incorporation into an individual contract of employment.

In *NCB v National Union of Mineworkers* (1986), Scott J stated that terms which were appropriate for incorporation should be terms such as pay rates, hours of work, etc (the normative terms), whereas terms covering conciliation and other proceedings (that is, procedural terms) were not appropriate for incorporation because they are not intended to be contractually enforceable by employees. Even where an agreement has been expressly incorporated into an individual's contract, this will not incorporate procedural terms. Thus, what is a procedural or normative term is central to the decision of inferring contractual intent. The definition of procedural and normative terms, however, is an area where there is legal uncertainty. This is particularly so in the case of redundancy procedures.

In *Young v Canadian Northern Rly Co* (1931), the Privy Council held that a redundancy selection policy of 'last in first out' was inappropriate for incorporation into individual contracts, yet in *Marley v Forward Trust Group* (1986), a redundancy selection procedure, which was in a personnel manual and which had been expressly incorporated into the individual's contract, was held to be legally enforceable by the employee. The later case of *Alexander v Standard Telephones and Cables Ltd* (1990) again held that a redundancy selection procedure was inappropriate for incorporation, but in *Anderson v Pringle of Scotland Ltd* (1998), the Court of Session held that there was an arguable case that a redundancy selection procedure contained in a collective agreement could become part of the individual's employment contract. While *Marley* and *Anderson* turn on their particular facts, it would appear that in some cases some procedural terms may be apt for incorporation, but in what circumstances remains unclear.

Where the term is normative, then it is appropriate for incorporation, but such a term may be incorporated either expressly or impliedly. Express incorporation is the most straightforward, as the contract of employment will expressly refer to the terms of the agreement. Such reference may include the whole of the agreement, as in *NCB v Galley* (1958), or may refer only to particular terms such as pay or hours, and they will be the only terms to be incorporated. Implied incorporation is more difficult. In this case, the courts look for evidence that both the employer and employee intended the agreement to become part of the contract. In *Joel v Cammell Laird* (1969), the court stated that, in order to be bound by a collective agreement, an employee must have specific knowledge of the agreement, there must be conduct which shows that the employee accepted the agreement and evidence that the agreement has been incorporated into the contract. In *Duke v Reliance Systems Ltd* (1982), the court further held that the employee needed to know of the existence, if not the content, of the term to be incorporated. The case of *Henry v London General Transport Services* (2001) has, however, thrown doubt on some of these decisions. In that case, the court held that an employee was bound by a collective agreement which by custom had become part of his contract. The Employment Appeal Tribunal (EAT) held that for a term to be incorporated by custom, the custom must be reasonable, certain and notorious and it must be presumed that the term supports the intention of the parties. Until *Henry*, notoriety was the reason why custom as a source of contractual terms had fallen into disuse, because movement of workers in a modern society means that fewer workers will be aware of the customs. However, the EAT held that notoriety is not undermined if some employees do not know of it.

While the above appear to give guidance, the law may still be unclear. *Singh v British Steel Corp* (1974) stated that implied incorporation can apply only to union members and, in the case of non-union members, an agreement must be expressly incorporated for the employee to be bound. Furthermore, if an agreement is silent regarding a particular topic, the courts will not imply a term into the agreement (and hence the individual contract) on the basis that the omission must be deliberate (*Ali v Christian Salvesen Food Services Ltd* (1997)). Furthermore, in *Cadoux v Central Regional Council* (1986), a provision of an agreement which had been expressly incorporated was held not to be legally enforceable because the rules could be amended from time to time by the authority. This led the Court of Session to conclude that that part of the agreement was not incorporated because, given that the rules could be unilaterally altered by the council, the parties could not have intended them to be contractually binding. Thus, even where there is express incorporation, legal uncertainty may exist.

Once a term forms part of the contract, it is enforceable between the individual parties and it is irrelevant if one of the parties withdraws from the agreement. This can only affect the relationship between the collective and not the individual parties. In *Robertson v British Gas Corp* (1983), the employer sought to unilaterally withdraw a bonus scheme which had been negotiated by collective agreement. The agreement was no longer in force, but the Court of Appeal held that the bonus scheme was contractual and the employer was in breach of contract. Also, in *Whent v T Cartledge Ltd* (1997), the employer withdrew from a national joint council agreement which regulated the employee's pay and conditions. It was held that the provision that the national joint council rates applied was contractual and the withdrawal of the employer from the agreement had no effect.

The precise relationship between collective agreements and contracts of employment is therefore unclear and thus there is legal uncertainty as to their precise effect. Whereas express incorporation seems simple, the legal uncertainty as to whether a term is appropriate for incorporation means that an employee will not know the precise content of his or her contract. The uncertainty which exists around implied incorporation, including the uncertainty created by Henry, means that often it is only when a case gets to court that both parties will know their responsibilities and rights.

Notes

_____

_____

_____

_____

_____

_____

_____

_____

_____

_____

_____

_____

Question 9

Magic Roundabout Ltd own two factories: one in Leicester and one in Nottingham. Florence and Dougal work in the Nottingham factory. Florence has just suffered a nervous breakdown as a result of family and work pressures and her doctor has ordered a complete rest for six months. Florence has spoken to her employer and it is happy to allow her to take the time off and return to work when she is well. She is worried, however, about her pay during her illness. Florence knows that there was a collective agreement between the NUMCW (National Union of Managers and Clerical Workers) which negotiated a sick pay scheme where the illness lasted up to six months, but does not think there is any such provision in the agreement between her union, the NSWU (National Shopfloor Workers Union) and management. She has asked her shop steward about this and he replied that the omission was due to the fact that the union assumed that the scheme covered the workers in both unions, which is the practice at the Leicester factory.

Dougal was a member of the NSWU but, after an argument with the shop steward, resigned his membership three years ago. Since then, the union has negotiated pay rises and washing time and, although he is not a member of the union, Dougal has had the advantages of these along with the rest of the workforce. The union is now negotiating a new shift system with the management which, if brought into operation, will, he feels, totally disrupt Dougal's domestic life.

Advise Florence as to her entitlement to sick pay and Dougal as to whether he must work the new shift system if it comes into operation.

 ## Answer plan

This question concentrates on incorporation of collective agreements into the individual contract. The first part, although dealing only with one party, raises a variety of issues in relation to incorporation into a union member's contract. The second part deals with the issue of incorporation into a non-union member's contract.

Particular issues to be considered are:

- whether there is an implied term relating to sick pay in all employment contracts;
- methods of incorporation of a collective agreement into an employment contract;
- the effect of a collective agreement negotiated by one union on the contract of a member of another union;
- how far custom and practice can be a source of contractual terms;
- how a collective agreement can become incorporated into the contract of a non-union member.

 # Answer

Florence is concerned about her entitlement to sick pay during her period of illness. Although she will be entitled to statutory sick pay, this is unlikely to be as great as her wage and it is therefore of importance to decide if there is a term in her contract requiring the employer to pay her while she is sick. Given that the employee's consideration under the contract is being ready and willing to perform his or her duties rather than the actual performance, it could be argued that all employment contracts contain a requirement to pay the employee when ill.

This presumption was accepted in *Orman v Saville Sportswear Ltd* (1960) although, as it was a presumption, it could be rebutted from clear evidence that sick pay had never been paid. This position has now been altered by *Mears v Safecar Security Ltd* (1982). In that case, the Court of Appeal clearly stated that there was no presumption that sick pay would be paid and, if there was no express term relating to payment during illness, the tribunal should look to see if there is an implied term. Given the fact that it appears that there is no express term in Florence's contract relating to payment during illness, it is necessary to see if such a term has been implied. Such a term may be implied from the collective agreement or from the parties' conduct.

Collective agreements are agreements negotiated between an employer or employers' association and a trade union. They are defined in s 178(1) of the TULR(C)A 1992 as 'any agreement or arrangement made by or on behalf of one or more trade unions and one or more employers or employers' associations and relating to one or more of the matters specified below'. Section 178(2) lists the specified matters, which include terms and conditions of employment, engagement or termination of engagement of workers, allocation of duties, etc. Such agreements operate at two levels. On the one hand, the agreement will deal with issues pertinent to the collective parties such as negotiation rights. These issues are not important to the individual employee and, therefore, will not become terms of the individual contract. Some clauses, such as those dealing with pay rises, etc, will be relevant to the individual employee and may become incorporated into the individual contract of employment. If such incorporation occurs, the clause from the collective agreement becomes a term of the employment contract and is therefore enforceable as such, despite the termination of the agreement at the collective level (*Burroughs Machines Ltd v Timmoney* (1977) and *Whent v T Cartledge* (1997)).

The two main methods by which collective agreements become terms of the individual's contract are those of express or implied incorporation. Express incorporation occurs where the employee expressly agrees to be bound by collective agreements. In *NCB v Galley* (1958), the employee, by his contract, agreed to be bound by 'such national agreements for the time being in force'. This was held to incorporate the relevant agreement. The statutory statement issued to all employees by s 1 of the Employment Rights Act (ERA) 1996 must state any collective agreements which affect the terms and conditions of employment. This may be sufficient to expressly incorporate such agreements into the individual's contract. In the problem, however, there is no evidence that Florence has expressly incorporated any terms of a collective agreement negotiated by her own union, let alone another and, thus, it is necessary to see whether there has been implied incorporation.

The basis of implied incorporation is that there is evidence that both parties have accepted the agreement as binding. In relation to Magic Roundabout Ltd, it has obviously accepted the agreement as such in the case of the Leicester factory because it is complying with the clause in relation to all the employees. The question which must be asked, however, is has Florence accepted the provision as part of her contract? A problem arises immediately as Florence is not a member of the union which negotiated the agreement. In *Miller v Hamworthy Engineering Ltd* (1986), an agreement on short time, negotiated by a union of which Miller was not a member, and to which he objected, was held not to be impliedly incorporated into his contract. In the problem, however, Florence has not disagreed with the clause in question and wishes to accept it. On the basis of *Joel v Cammell Laird* (1969), she has specific knowledge of the relevant agreement, there is conduct on her part which indicates acceptance of the agreement and, by continuing to work without protest, provides some indication of incorporation into the contract on her part. There is the issue of whether Magic Roundabout wishes the agreement to become part of the contracts of the members of the NSWU at Nottingham. Given that it has accepted that it forms part of the contracts of the NSWU members at Leicester, there is likely to be no problem.

If the collective agreement negotiated by another union does not become part of Florence's contract on the basis of *Miller*, the term relating to sick pay may become part of her contract through custom and practice. In *Sagar v Ridehalgh and Sons Ltd* (1931), a custom allowing the employer to deduct from wages for bad workmanship was held to be a term of the contract. To become a term, a custom must be certain, notorious and reasonable. In the case of sick pay at Magic Roundabout, the term relating to sick pay is probably certain as it is part of a collective agreement. It is notorious in the sense that it applies to all the employees at the Leicester factory and at least to the members of the NUMCW at Nottingham. Furthermore, given that it gives payment to employees when they are sick, it is reasonable.

There is an issue as to precisely when the custom becomes a term. Smith and Wood (*Industrial Law*, 8th edn, 2003) argue that there are three propositions: first, the custom has become notorious; secondly, where it is so well established that the employee must have accepted employment subject to it; and, thirdly, where the practice grew up while the employee was employed and the employee accepted benefits under it. While it is unlikely that Florence could argue on the basis of the first two propositions, the agreement was negotiated while she was in employment and if other terms in a collective agreement negotiated by the NUMCW have applied to her in the past, then by custom and practice so will this term.

A further argument relating to both the collective agreement and custom comes from the case of *Henry v London General Transport Services Ltd* (2001). In this case, there was a custom whereby collective agreements were incorporated into all employees' contracts, whether union members or not. The Court of Appeal, upholding the EAT, held that the custom was 'reasonable, certain and notorious' and, as such, a collectively agreed pay reduction was implied into every employee's contract. The EAT held that such incorporation could not be undermined by showing that some individuals did not know of the practice or did not intend or wish it to apply to them. On this argument again, the provision of the collective agreement which applies to members of both unions at Leicester may apply in the same way at the Nottingham site, given that this is the impression of the union. In order to establish this, Florence would have to provide evidence that it has been the case in the past to establish a custom which is 'reasonable, certain and notorious' and, on the basis of *Henry*, it would be irrelevant that some employees did not know of the custom and did not want the provision as part of their contracts.

There is one further point on which there is no evidence in the problem but which may be the case. If there is a negotiation agreement between the two unions so that any collective agreement negotiated by the NUMCW is also negotiated on behalf of the NSWU (for example, because only the NUMCW is recognised by Magic Roundabout), then the agreement will be treated in relation to Florence as if it had been negotiated by her union, and will be part of her contract by implied incorporation, as argued above.

Dougal resigned from his union membership three years ago but, since then, has had the advantages of any negotiations conducted by the union, such as pay rises and washing time. He is now concerned about a disadvantageous term negotiated by the union.

The position of non-unionists and the enforceability of collectively negotiated provisions in their contracts is unclear at the moment. Kahn-Freund argued that such agreements could become part of the non-unionist's contract by implied incorporation through the conduct of accepting such agreements in the past – a method he described as a 'crystallised custom'. Some of the cases, however, do not support this view. In *Singh v British Steel Corp* (1974), the facts were similar to the problem in that Singh had resigned from his trade union membership and later argued that the new shift system negotiated by the union did not become incorporated into his contract. It was held that his original terms stood, although it could be argued that this appears to be based on a concept of agency and Singh had withdrawn the agent's authority, a concept which does not appear to find favour with the courts today (*Burton Group Ltd v Smith* (1977)). Likewise, in *Young v Canadian Northern Rly Co* (1931), it was held that a redundancy selection procedure negotiated collectively did not become part of a non-unionist's contract, although, again, it could be argued that in *Young* the term itself was inappropriate for incorporation into any individual contract. These cases would appear to support the proposition that incorporation of a collective provision into the contract of a non-unionist cannot happen impliedly and there must be express incorporation. This is further supported by *Miller v Hamworthy Engineering* above, which concluded that an agreement negotiated by one union did not become a term in the contract of a member of another union.

Dougal's case may be distinguishable from Singh, however. He resigned from the union three years ago, but since then has accepted advantageous negotiated clauses into his contract. If his resignation suggests that he does not wish the union to negotiate on his behalf, his subsequent conduct in accepting collective bargains may suggest otherwise. If this is the case, then on the basis of Kahn-Freund's crystallised custom, should the final negotiations change the shifts, Dougal will be bound and refusal to comply will be a breach of contract. Moreover, as already discussed in relation to Florence, *Singh* and *Miller* may now be limited by *Henry v London General Transport Services*. If it can be established that there is a custom which is 'reasonable, certain and notorious' that implies collective agreements into the contracts of all employees, Dougal will be bound by the new shift system if negotiated and, on the basis of *Henry*, this will be in spite of his objections. The fact that in the past, since his withdrawal from the union, he has accepted advantageous terms negotiated by the union may lend weight to this argument. If, on the other hand, *Singh* is followed, then the negotiations at the collective level will not alter the term relating to hours in his contract and he does not have to work the new shift system. One thing Dougal should be aware of, however, is that, in Singh, the fact that all the other employees had accepted the new shifts meant that Singh's dismissal was fair under some other substantial reason.

_____

_____

_____

_____

_____

_____

_____

_____

_____

_____

_____

_____

Question 10

Pete, Mark and Pauline work for Walford Engineering Ltd, a firm manufacturing rides for fairs.

During the last two years, there have been periods of short-time working. Two years ago, there was an industrial dispute and all the workforce were put onto a four day week for the period of the dispute, which lasted from February to March. Six months later, another dispute occurred which lasted for five months from September to January, and, again, the workforce were put onto a four day week. In both cases, the two unions at the factory, the CMU and the SWU, agreed to the cuts. In September last year, the CMU agreed that, in the event of future disputes, it would accept a three day working week if it became 'economically necessary'. This agreement was stated to be binding in honour only.

Last month, there was another dispute and the company put the workforce on a three day working week for a month. Both Pete, a member of the CMU, and Mark, a member of the SWU, are claiming four days' pay.

Pauline works as a typist in the typing pool at the factory. She started work four weeks ago. Last week, she fell ill and will be off work for a total of three weeks. Her statutory statement says that she is entitled to sick pay after two weeks of illness but her contract, which was sent to her home during her illness, states that sick pay will be paid only after three weeks of illness. In addition, when she applied for her job, the advertisement said that the position was that of 'personal assistant/typist', however, the title of the job on her contract is 'typist'. She feels that she would not have taken the job if she had known that it would only involve typing.

Advise Pete and Mark as to the likely success of their claims and Pauline in relation to her sick pay and the nature of her job.

Answer plan

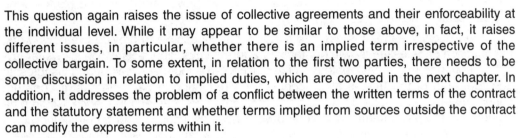

This question again raises the issue of collective agreements and their enforceability at the individual level. While it may appear to be similar to those above, in fact, it raises different issues, in particular, whether there is an implied term irrespective of the collective bargain. To some extent, in relation to the first two parties, there needs to be some discussion in relation to implied duties, which are covered in the next chapter. In addition, it addresses the problem of a conflict between the written terms of the contract and the statutory statement and whether terms implied from sources outside the contract can modify the express terms within it.

The issues to be considered are:

- the implied term in relation to payment during lay-off;
- how far conduct on the part of the employee can vary contractual terms;
- the implication of collective agreements into individual contracts;
- the effect at the individual level of a collective agreement stated to be binding in honour only;
- which prevails when there is a conflict between the statutory statement and the written contractual terms;
- how far terms from documents such as advertisements can be implied into the contract.

Answer

Pete and Mark have in the past accepted a four day working week when there has been an industrial dispute. This is evidenced by the fact that they are both only suing for four days' pay in relation to the last four week lay-off. Generally, at common law, there is an implied duty to pay wages but not to provide work (*Collier v Sunday Referee Publishing Co Ltd* (1940)). This, however, is only a general proposition.

In some cases, there is a duty to provide work where, for example, the employee needs to develop his skill or where the work must be done to earn the wage, as in the case of piece workers (*Devonald v Rosser and Sons* (1906)). The implied duty to pay may be ousted by an express term in the contract (*Hulme v Ferranti Ltd* (1918)) or the practice of the industry may imply a term that there is no pay during lay-off and this will oust the general duty (*Puttick v John Wright and Sons (Blackwall) Ltd* (1972)).

The first question to ask in relation to Pete and Mark is whether there is a duty to pay during lay-off. In the past, both have accepted a four day week when there has been an industrial dispute. Whereas the general duty is to pay, this does not apply when the failure to pay wages is outside the control of the employer. In *Browning v Crumlin Valley Collieries* (1926), Greer J held that the duty did not apply when the employer had to close down the colliery when a land fault necessitated urgent repairs. In the case of Walford Engineering, it appears that the industrial disputes render it impossible to provide work for five days. If such impossibility is proved and further work cannot be provided for the last working day of the week, then, under the authority of *Browning*, it would appear that there is no breach of contract on the part of the employer and Pete and Mark will be unsuccessful in their claims.

If, on the other hand, it is deemed that it is not impossible to provide five days' work, the question to be asked is whether there is a term in their contracts which allows for lay-offs without pay. In the past, both men have accepted a four day week during disputes. In addition, both of the unions also accepted the reduction in pay, although it does not appear that this was done by collective agreement, merely an acquiescence. Could it be argued that the past conduct of Pete and Mark has now implied a term in their individual contracts that there will be a shorter working week when there is a dispute? It appears that until the recent lay-off, there were only two occasions in the past when there was a four day working week, although it lasted *in toto* for five months. In implying terms into the employment contract, the courts do not tend to rely on the old contractual tests of business efficacy or obvious consensus, but rather what is a reasonable term in all the circumstances. In *Courtaulds Northern Spinning Ltd v Sibson* (1988), a mobility clause was implied into the employee's contract because he had been mobile between two sites during the relationship. Slade J said: 'The court merely has to be satisfied that the implied term is one which the parties would probably have agreed if they were being reasonable.' Thus, it may be argued that because of the acceptance of the four day week without protest in the past, this has now become an implied term in both the parties' contracts.

A further argument which the employer may put forward is that lay-off without pay has now become a custom. It is submitted, however, that to show that a practice has become a custom and implied into the contract, it must be certain, general and reasonable. Smith and Wood (*Industrial Law*, 8th edn, 2003) state that this can occur in one of three ways. Either the custom is so notorious that there is judicial notice of it, or it is so well established that the employee must have accepted employment subject to it (*Sagar v Ridehalgh and Sons Ltd* (1931)), or the practice grew up while the employee was employed and he impliedly accepted it, although du Parcq LJ said, in *Marshall v English Electric Co Ltd* (1945), that mere continuance at work may not be enough to signify acceptance as it may be caused by other factors such as a fear of dismissal. This is re-emphasised in *Samways v Swan Hunter Shipbuilders Ltd* (1975).

Given that the practice in the problem has only been happening over the past two years, it would appear that the only way it could have become a custom and thereby implied into Pete and Mark's contracts is the fact that it arose during their employment and they have accepted the deductions. Given *Samways*, however, it would be possible to argue that their acceptance of the shorter week was due to a fear of losing their jobs and not because they accepted that they were contractually bound to do so.

Even if there is a term in both of their contracts, previous deductions have been in relation to one day's pay and the disputed deduction is in relation to two days' pay. Pete's union, the CMU, has agreed to a three day week where there is a dispute if this is 'economically necessary'. The agreement is stated to be 'binding in honour only' but this will have no effect on the enforceability of the term if it has become a term of the individual's contract.

Where there is no express incorporation of a collective agreement at the individual level, it is possible that the agreement may be impliedly incorporated. From *Joel v Cammell Laird* (1969), it appears that for implied incorporation into a union member's contract, there must be knowledge of the agreement, conduct on the part of the employee which shows he accepts the agreement and some indication of incorporation into his contract. *Duke v Reliance Systems Ltd* (1982) adds that the employee must have knowledge of the existence of the term if not its content and, in *Jones v Associated Tunnelling Co Ltd* (1981), the EAT held that the fact that an employee continues to work does not imply assent to a change in terms, particularly if the change does not have immediate effect. In relation to Pete, therefore, if he is aware of the agreement made by his union and of the existence of a term relating to unpaid lay-off, the term will be part of his contract. Unless he can show that the three day week was not economically necessary, he will be unable to sue for the loss of four days' pay. Mark, on the other hand, is not a member of the CMU. Even if he has varied his contract so that the employer is entitled to put him onto a four day week, by *Miller v Hamworthy Engineering Ltd* (1986) he is not bound by the negotiations of another union. As such, Walford Engineering is in breach of contract by deducting two days' pay and his claim will be successful. *Henry v London General Transport Services Ltd* (2001) can be distinguished in Mark's case as he is a member of a union which has, in the past, negotiated with the employer and which, in the case of the three day week, has not done so. On these facts, it is unlikely that a tribunal will find that there is a custom that the CMU negotiates on behalf of all of the employees, including those who belong to a different union.

In Pauline's case, there is a discrepancy between her statutory statement and her contract in relation to sick pay. Although all employees should receive a statutory statement of terms and conditions within eight weeks of starting their employment, the statement is not contractual but merely evidence of what the terms of the contract are.

Browne-Wilkinson J in *System Floors (UK) Ltd v Daniel* (1981) said of the statement: 'It provides very strong *prima facie* evidence of what were the terms of the contract between the parties, but does not constitute a written contract between the parties.' Such an interpretation, however, does not help Pauline. While in some cases the courts have accepted that the statement does comprise the contractual terms, this is usually where there is no further written document and where the employee has signed the statement itself and not merely a receipt (*Gascol Conversions Ltd v Mercer* (1974)). We have no evidence of whether Pauline signed the statement itself. If she did, it may be possible to argue that by sending different terms in a later document, the employer is attempting a unilateral variation and there is no conduct on the part of Pauline which shows acceptance of the change. If, on the other hand, she has signed nothing or merely a receipt acknowledging that she has received the statement, then, relying on the judgment of Browne-Wilkinson J above, her contractual terms will prevail and she will not be entitled to sick pay during her illness.

Pauline is employed as a typist according to her contract, but the advertisement for the job described the post as personal assistant/typist. The normal contractual rule is that an express term cannot be overridden by an implied term (*Deeley v British Rail*

Engineering Ltd (1980)). In *Johnstone v Bloomsbury Area Health Authority* (1991), Stuart-Smith LJ stated that an express term relating to hours was subject to the implied duty to ensure the employee's safety, although Browne-Wilkinson VC in the same case stated that the exercise by the employer of his right to ask for extra hours over and above the obligatory ones was subject to the implied duty in relation to safety, so leaving the contractual principle intact. Whether *Johnstone* is seen as an attack on the normal contractual principle or not, it is unlikely in Pauline's case that a court would allow the written express term to be overridden by a term implied from an advertisement (*Deeley*) and, as such, Pauline is employed as a typist only.

Notes

4 Implied Duties

Introduction

In this text, implied duties are those terms implied into every contract of employment. The word 'duties' is used to distinguish the questions in this chapter from implied terms discussed in Chapter 3. By implied term, this text means terms implied into a specific individual contract because that is what the parties would have expressed if they had thought about it. On the other hand, implied duties are in every contract of employment, irrespective of the parties' intentions, and can normally only be ousted by an express term. The majority of student texts split the duties into those of the employer and those of the employee. Examination questions may, however, mix the two areas and therefore it would be unwise to know one group of duties but not the other. In addition, this area impacts on others. Breach of these duties may constitute a repudiatory breach and thus a constructive dismissal, and so be relevant to questions on unfair dismissal. Sexual harassment may be a breach of the duty of mutual respect as well as an infringement of the Sex Discrimination Act (SDA) 1975. As such, knowledge of this area will form a good foundation for a variety of questions which may come up on an examination paper.

General issues which the student needs to understand are therefore:

- the personal nature of the employment contract;
- the duties of the employer;
- the duties of the employee;
- remedies for a breach of an employment contract.

Although breach of one of the implied duties may form the basis of other claims, it is important to see exactly what the question is asking for. If it is only on the area of such duties, a discussion of unfair constructive dismissal is not going to gain any marks. Detailed knowledge of the duties is therefore needed for specific questions on this area.

In particular, students need to be familiar with:

- whether there is a duty to provide work;
- the duty to pay wages;
- whether there is a duty to indemnify;
- the duty of mutual respect;
- the duty to ensure the employee's safety;
- the duty of co-operation;
- the duty to obey lawful, reasonable orders;
- the duty to exercise reasonable care and skill;

- the duty not to accept bribes or secret commission;
- the duty not to disclose confidential information;
- the duty not to work for a competitor;
- the ownership of inventions.

It can be seen from the list above that this is a vast area which is expanding. Recent decisions have suggested that some of these duties are overriding ones and students should be aware of these developments.

Checklist

Students should be familiar with the following areas:

- the discussions in relation to the duty to provide work and the expansion of the exceptions in *Turner v Sawdon* (1901);
- issues relating to the payment of wages: itemised pay statements, the concept of normal working hours, deductions from pay under the Employment Rights Act (ERA) 1996, payment during sickness and payment during lay-off;
- whether a duty to indemnify exists;
- the expansion of the duty of mutual respect;
- the specific aspects of the safety duty – in particular, safe place of work, safe system of work, safe plant and materials and competent employees;
- how far the duty of safety is an overriding one since *Johnstone v Bloomsbury Area Health Authority* (1991);
- the employee duty of co-operation and the effect of a breach since *Ticehurst v British Telecommunications plc* (1992);
- what constitutes reasonable orders;
- the duty of confidentiality – that is, not to work for a competitor or disclose confidential information;
- aspects of trust and confidence, such as working with reasonable care and the duty not to accept secret payments;
- judicial expansion of the employer's responsibility since *Johnstone v Bloomsbury Area Health Authority* (1991), *Scally v Southern Health and Social Services Board* (1991) and *Spring v Guardian Assurance* (1994).

 ——————————**Question 11**——————————

Ironsides Ltd is a company manufacturing sheet metal. Last year, the company placed the workforce on a four day week in an attempt to reduce costs while maintaining productivity. Work in the factory is arduous and involves a lot of heavy lifting of sheets of metal each weighing between 40 kgs and 60 kgs. Workers are advised to lift such sheets in pairs but are unsupervised in their work. Management provides waist belts to reduce the risk of injury. The belts are available on request, but, as the company knows, they are rarely worn in practice.

Len has worked for Ironsides for nine months and has complained to management that the change to a four day week has created additional safety risks on the shop floor. Management has not followed up these complaints. Len, in fact, strained his back when he first started work in a lifting accident, an event of which the management is aware, but Len never wears a waist belt.

Two months ago, as no assistance was readily available, Len attempted to lift a 60 kg sheet of metal unaided and, in doing so, slipped a disc in his back. Due to his previous injury, this recent accident will lead to him having future back problems. Len has now resigned from his job and wishes to sue Ironsides for compensation.

Advise Len.

Answer plan

This question deals exclusively with the employer's duty to ensure the employee's safety. Do not be swayed by the issue of the four day week and the effect on the contract. It does not say that the workers' pay has been reduced and, furthermore, Len has worked for the majority of his contract with Ironsides on a four day week and thus will have accepted any consequent effect on his pay. The four day week is, however, pertinent to the safety issue.

Particular points to discuss are:

- the general duty to ensure the employee's safety;
- the individual nature of the duty;
- the provision of a safe system of work;
- whether the duty is active or passive;
- defences to a common law claim.

Answer

There is a duty implied in every contract of employment that the employer shall take reasonable steps to ensure the employee's safety. The duty is based in negligence under *Donoghue v Stevenson* (1932), in that an employee is a neighbour of his employer as a result of the proximity of the relationship. As such, the employer must take reasonable care to ensure that his acts or omissions do not cause foreseeable injury to his employees. In other words, he must act as a reasonable employer.

If an injury is not foreseeable, for example, because the state of medical knowledge is such that it is not known that a particular disease or injury can result from a particular practice, the employer will not be liable (*Down v Dudley Coles Long* (1969)). Once the knowledge becomes available, however, the employer must do all that is reasonable to protect the employees (*Baxter v Harland and Wolff plc* (1990)).

The employer is only under a duty to act as a reasonable employer; therefore, in some circumstances, the cost of total protection may be outweighed by the fact that the risk of the injury happening is slight and it would not be serious should it occur. In *Latimer v AEC* (1953), after its factory was flooded, an employer put down sawdust on the wet floors to keep the factory open rather than close down until the floors had dried out. It was held that it was not liable for the injury to one of its employees who had slipped on an uncovered part of the floor, because the action of keeping the factory open was reasonable in the circumstances. It is also reasonable to assume that the employee has some common sense and will look after his or her own safety in certain circumstances (*O'Reilly v National Rail* (1966)).

In *Wilsons and Clyde Coal Co v English* (1938), the House of Lords identified three specific aspects of the duty: safe system of work, safe plant and materials and reasonably competent fellow employees. In addition, a fourth aspect can be added: that of the provision of a safe place of work. The employer has to comply with all aspects of the duty to escape liability, although he may raise a defence to reduce or negate such liability.

Len worked for Ironsides for nine months and, during the majority of that time, he has been on a four day week. Ironsides owes Len a duty to take reasonable steps to protect him against foreseeable injury. In particular, given that the injury has been caused by the way Len does the job, the question to be asked is whether Ironsides is in breach of the specific aspect of the duty to provide a safe system of work. Furthermore, given that Ironsides knows of Len's previous injury, there is the question of whether it should have taken extra care as Len was more vulnerable than other employees.

Len has slipped a disc which has caused back problems. Given that the job involves heavy lifting, it could be argued that a slipped disc is a reasonably foreseeable injury. Ironsides has, however, advised the men to lift in pairs and provided waist belts for the workers to reduce the risk of injury. On the face of things, it would appear that Ironsides is taking reasonable precautions to prevent the occurrence of injuries such as Len's.

There are various issues which should be raised, however. Len has complained to management that the four day week is causing safety risks, but nothing has been done. Given that the aim of the four day week is to maintain production but to reduce costs, this would imply that the same amount of output is required in a shorter space of time. Failure to investigate complaints about safety can lead to a finding against the employer. In *Franklin v Edmonton Corp* (1966), the employee had complained to the employer that the brakes on his lorry were defective, but the employer did not investigate the complaint. It was held that the employer was liable for the employee's injuries sustained in an accident when the brakes failed. Thus, the failure to investigate Len's complaint may constitute a breach of duty on the part of Ironsides.

In addition, there is the question of whether the duty owed by Ironsides is active or passive. In other words, will it have complied with its duty by merely providing safety equipment or should it have done more? It appears that, if the risk of injury is obvious to the employee and the injury is not likely to be serious if it occurs, the duty is passive and the employer must merely provide the equipment and leave it up to the individual employee to use it if he wishes (*Qualcast (Wolverhampton) Ltd v Haynes* (1959)). On the other hand, if the risk is not obvious, or the injury would be serious, then the employer must do more by insisting that safety precautions are taken and supervise to see that this is happening (*Berry v Stone Manganese Marine Ltd* (1972)). Ironsides advises that lifting should be done in pairs but does not supervise the employees to check that the advice is followed. It provides waist belts but does nothing to ensure that they are worn and knows that they are rarely worn in practice. If the duty owed is active, therefore, Ironsides is in breach.

It could be argued that the risk is obvious to the employees. However, the dangers of lifting alone may not be obvious and, furthermore, the reduction to a four day week with no reduction in productivity may mean that it is impossible to find another worker to help lift the sheets of metal at certain times. In other words, it is the fault of the employer that the job cannot be performed safely. Furthermore, it would appear from Len's injury that the potential damage can be serious. The employer knows that the workers do not use the waist belts and knew from Len's complaints that the reduction in the working week was creating safety risks. Even if it is held that the duty was passive when there was a five day week, the employer should have emphasised the dangers when the week was reduced and at least tried to ensure that the belts were worn and lifting was done in pairs. It is likely, therefore, that the courts would find that, in the circumstances, the duty was active and that Ironsides is in breach.

If this is not the case in relation to the workforce generally, the court may find that Ironsides owes a greater duty to Len. In *Paris v Stepney Borough Council* (1951), a worker, who had one eye, was blinded when a piece of metal fell off a bus he was cleaning and fell into his good eye. It was held that although the employer was not under a common law duty to provide goggles for all the employees, goggles should have been provided for Paris. He was more vulnerable than the others because, given that he had only one eye, any potential injury was likely to have more serious consequences. This demonstrates that the duty is owed to employees individually and, if the employer has a particularly vulnerable employee, the duty owed to that individual may be higher than that owed to the other employees. In this case, Ironsides knows that Len has previously strained his back. It could be argued, therefore, that, by analogy with Paris, Len is now more vulnerable as any subsequent injury is likely to have more serious consequences given that his back is already weakened. As such, even if the duty is passive in relation to the rest of the workforce, the duty will be active in relation to Len, and Ironsides should have checked that he was lifting correctly and insisted that he wore a waist belt. The failure to do this means that Len can sue for a breach of the implied duty.

Ironsides may be able to raise a defence to reduce or even negate its liability. The first of these is that of causation – that is, the injury was not caused by the employer's breach of duty. On the facts, however, it would seem this is not open to Ironsides to argue. Len's first injury was presumably caused by his not wearing a waist belt. His second injury was caused by his not wearing a belt and having to lift the metal single-handedly, and has been exacerbated by his first injury. As such, causation has been established. Ironsides may try to argue *volenti non fit injuria* to negate the claim. While such a defence is in theory available, it rarely succeeds in employment cases. There are two reasons for this. First, knowledge of the risk by the employee is not sufficient to establish consent (*Smith v Baker and Sons* (1891)). Secondly, consent must be freely given and this will rarely be the case in an employment situation where the employee is acting under orders or where he is not in a position to refuse to do the act in question.

A final defence which may be available to Ironsides is that of contributory negligence. This is not a complete defence since the Law Reform (Contributory Negligence) Act 1945 but reduces the employer's liability to such an extent as the court thinks is 'just and equitable having regard to the plaintiff's share in the responsibility for the damage'. It appears that this may apply to Len as he knew of the advice in relation to lifting and he knew of the existence of the belts but never wore one. The courts, however, may be prepared to expect a lower standard of care from the employee in relation to his own safety. This appears to be the case in relation to breach of statutory duty in this area. In *Caswell v Powell Duffryn Associated Collieries Ltd* (1940), both Lord Atkin and Lord Wright stated that in considering the standard the employee must achieve in relation to his own safety, regard must be had to the conditions under which he works and that long hours, fatigue and constant repetition can lead to a slackening of concentration. While Lord Tucker, in *Staveley Iron and Chemical Co Ltd v Jones* (1956), doubted whether this more lenient test applied to common law actions, Lord Reid declined to decide one way or the other. If the more lenient test does apply to Len's claim, the fact that he was completing five days' production in four days will have a bearing on the court's decision and may lead to a finding that there is no contributory negligence. If, on the other hand, the more lenient test does not apply to common law claims, then it could be argued that Len, particularly after his first accident, has been negligent towards his own safety in that the wearing of a belt would have reduced the seriousness of his injury, as would getting help to lift the metal. As such, the damages he will be awarded will be reduced by what the court feels is just and equitable.

Notes

Question 12

Riskit, Duck and Dodge have worked at Lax Ltd for 10 years. Riskit and Duck work in the machining room at one of the two sites operated by the company. Riskit has to cut two inches off a metal bolt. The correct method, as he knows, is to use a milling machine to file it off. Since this process is rather lengthy, Riskit decides to use a circular saw. During this process, the blade of the saw disintegrates along with part of the bolt. Metal fragments shower from the machine and bolt and, while taking evasive action, Riskit injures his head on the corner of the saw table. One of the fragments flies into the eye of Duck, who had left his machine at the other end of the factory in order to fill in his pools coupon jointly with Riskit.

Dodge works at the other site of Lax Ltd, which is five minutes away from the main site. The finishing machine on which Dodge works has broken down and will take two months to mend. As a result, Lax Ltd has closed down the factory and has laid off Dodge for two months without pay. Lax Ltd argues that without the machine there will be a build up of unfinished products which it cannot sell or store.

Advise Riskit and Duck whether they may claim compensation from Lax Ltd, and Dodge whether he is entitled to payment of wages during the two month lay-off.

Answer plan

This question is dealing with two separate implied duties: the duty to ensure the employee's safety, and the duty to pay wages. While the first part may seem similar to the question above, it is, in fact, different. The question in relation to one party is whether there is a complete defence to the employee's claim and, in relation to the second, whether any duty is owed at all.

Particular points to raise are therefore:

- the general duty to ensure the employee's safety;
- the duty to provide a safe system of work;
- the duty to provide safe plant and materials;
- defences to a claim;
- the duty to provide reasonably competent fellow employees;
- vicarious liability;
- the duty to pay during lay-off.

Answer

The employer is under an implied duty to ensure his employees' safety. The duty arises under *Donoghue v Stevenson* (1932), in that, because of the proximity of the relationship between employer and employee, the employer must take reasonable care to ensure that his acts or omissions do not cause the employee foreseeable injury. The standard is that of a reasonable employer and should the employer do all that is reasonable, he will not be liable for any injury sustained by the employee (*Latimer v AEC* (1953)).

In *Wilsons and Clyde Coal Co v English* (1938), the House of Lords identified specific aspects of the duty. One of these aspects is the duty to provide a safe system of work; another is the provision of safe plant and materials. In relation to Riskit, it is necessary to see if one or both of these aspects of the duty have been broken.

Riskit injures his head when the blade of a saw disintegrates while sawing a bolt. Riskit, however, knows that he should use a milling machine to cut the two inches off the bolt. It would appear therefore that Riskit has been told the correct and safe way of performing the job and chooses an unsafe way. While one of the aspects of the duty to provide a safe system of work is training and supervision, Riskit has worked for the company for 10 years and appears to be experienced. Even if the employer supervised his work at the beginning, he should know and observe the correct method of cutting the bolt after 10 years. In addition, the employer is entitled to assume that the employee will take some responsibility for his own safety (*Smith v Scott Bowyers Ltd* (1986)) and is entitled to assume that the employee has a modicum of common sense (*Lazarus v Firestone Tyres and Rubber Co Ltd* (1963)). As such, it is unlikely that the court will find that Lax Ltd is in breach of its duty to provide a safe system of work.

While Riskit is using the saw, the blade disintegrates and causes injury to both Riskit and Duck. While the employer is under a duty to provide safe plant and materials, breach of this duty depends on the employer's knowledge (*Davie v New Merton Board Mills* (1959)). Once the employer knows of a defect, if he does nothing to protect his employees, he will be in breach. In *Taylor v Rover Car Co* (1966), the employee was using a chisel which was badly hardened and which shattered causing him injury. A chisel from the same batch had shattered previously without causing injury. It was held that the employer was in breach of duty because, given the previous incident, it should have known that the batch was faulty and withdrawn it from use. Here the cause of the injuries was the saw blade. If Lax Ltd knew that the blade was dangerous (for example, because another one from the same supplier had disintegrated), then, by analogy with *Taylor*, it could be argued that Lax Ltd is liable to Riskit. A similar conclusion would be reached if the reason the saw blade shattered was because of lack of maintenance by the employer (*Bradford v Robinson Rentals Ltd* (1967)). If, however, Lax Ltd can show that it was the misuse of the blade which caused it to disintegrate, then there will be no breach on the part of the employer. In this case, however, if there is a hidden defect, by the Employers' Liability (Defective Equipment) Act 1969 any defect attributable to the negligence of a third party will be deemed to be attributable to the negligence of the employer. Thus, by statute, Lax Ltd will be liable and will be able to recover any compensation paid to Riskit from the manufacturer.

Even if it is held that Lax Ltd is in breach of the common law duty in relation to Riskit, there are two defences that Lax Ltd could raise. The first is lack of causation – that is, the employer's breach of duty did not cause the employee's injury. Riskit was wrongly using a circular saw. If he had used the correct method to cut the bolt, no injury would have been sustained. It could also be argued that the action he took to avoid the fragments and the injury to his head was not foreseeable. If this is successful, then the injury was caused by Riskit and not the breach of duty and, as such, Lax Ltd can negate its liability (*Horne v LEC Refrigeration Ltd* (1965)).

Alternatively, Lax Ltd may raise the defence of contributory negligence under the Law Reform (Contributory Negligence) Act 1945. Such a defence will reduce the employer's liability, as damages will be reduced to reflect the proportion of the blame which can be attached to the employee's own negligence. In *Bux v Slough Metals* (1973), the employer was held to be in breach of his common law duty when he provided goggles for the employees but did not ensure that they were worn. Damages were reduced by 40%, however, because of the employee's own negligence in failing to wear the goggles. Thus, even if the employer is in breach, it can be argued that Riskit's negligence in using the saw in the first place contributed to his injury and damages should be reduced accordingly.

Fragments from the saw hit Duck in the eye. Duck may be able to claim compensation from Lax Ltd in one of two ways. First, he could argue along similar lines to Riskit – that is, that Lax Ltd is in breach of the duty to provide a safe plant and materials. The success or otherwise of this line of argument is demonstrated above. Conversely, Duck could argue that Lax Ltd had not provided him with a reasonably competent fellow employee in that it was due to Riskit's negligence that Duck was injured in the first place. The basis of the liability under this head is again knowledge. If Lax Ltd had no idea that Riskit was using unsafe methods, there will be no breach of duty (*Coddington v International Harvester Co of Great Britain* (1969)). On the other hand, if Lax Ltd did have this knowledge, then a breach will have occurred (*Hudson v Ridge Manufacturing Co Ltd* (1957)).

Should Duck not succeed in establishing a breach of the primary duty, he may be able to establish that Lax Ltd is vicariously liable for Riskit. Vicarious liability arises when the employee injures someone by his or her negligence while within the course of employment. 'Course of employment' appears to mean while the employee is doing an authorised act in an authorised manner or an authorised act in an unauthorised manner (*Limpus v London General Omnibus Co* (1862)). It does not cover acts specifically forbidden by the employer (*Conway v George Wimpey* (1951)) but may do if such an act benefits the employer (*Rose v Plenty* (1976)). The House of Lords, however, has recently redefined the common law definition of 'course of employment'. In *Lister v Helsey Hall Ltd* (2001), their Lordships held that the correct approach to determine whether an employee's act is committed during the course of his or her employment is to concentrate on the relative proximity between the nature of the employment and the act committed. As such, a boarding school was vicariously liable for the sexual abuse of boys by a school warden because the nature of his employment meant that he had close contact with the boys and this created a sufficiently close connection between the acts of abuse and the work he was employed to do to make it fair to hold the employer liable. On this wider definition of course of employment, it can be argued that as Riskit is employed to cut bolts and he injures someone while doing that incorrectly, there is a sufficiently close connection between his employment and the wrongful act to establish vicarious liability. Even under the narrower definition of course of employment prior to *Lister*, Riskit is authorised to cut the bolt. The employer cannot argue that he is only authorised to cut the bolt with the milling machine. Once the authorisation has been given, the employer cannot then limit the way the employee performs that authorised act (*Limpus*). As such, Lax Ltd is vicariously liable for Riskit.

Again, the employer may have a defence. Duck is injured when coming over to Riskit to complete his pools coupon. As such, is the injury to Duck a foreseeable consequence of the negligence of either Lax or Riskit? It is reasonably foreseeable that, if the saw blade disintegrates, an employee will be injured because the saw is in the workplace. It could be argued, therefore, that given that some injury is foreseeable, the injury to Duck is a natural consequence and thus liability is established. It may be possible, however, for Lax to argue contributory negligence on the part of Duck.

Dodge has just been informed that he will be laid off for two months without pay. While generally there is no duty on the employer to provide work, there is a duty to pay wages (*Collier v Sunday Referee Publishing Co Ltd* (1940)). This is the consideration the employer provides under the contract and breach of the term is repudiatory. There are two situations when the duty will not apply. First, as the duty is implied, it can be overridden by an express term (*Hulme v Ferranti Ltd* (1918)) or a term implied by custom (*Puttick v John Wright and Sons (Blackwall) Ltd* (1972)), although the right to lay-off without pay may only be exercised for a reasonable length of time (*Dakri (A) and Co Ltd v Tiffen* (1981)). Secondly, the duty will not be implied when the failure to provide work is outside the control of the employer. In *Browning v Crumlin Valley Collieries* (1926), a colliery had to close down when a land fault necessitated repairs. Greer J held that the employer was not under a duty to pay the laid off employees because the reason for the lay-off was totally outside his control.

In the case of Dodge, there appears to be no term in the contract allowing a lay-off without pay and, thus, the general implied duty will apply unless Lax Ltd can show that the lay-off is totally outside its control. In this case, it appears that the reason Lax Ltd has closed down the factory is because it does not want to stockpile unfinished articles. In other words, work is possible but inconvenient to the employer. In *Devonald v Rosser and Sons* (1906), an economic recession was held not to be sufficient reason to lay-off piece workers without pay. This would suggest that the situation facing Lax Ltd does not fall within the exception in *Browning* and therefore the employer is under a duty to pay Dodge. Should it be held that the duty is not applicable, Dodge will be entitled to a guaranteed payment under ss 28 to 32 of the Employment Rights Act (ERA) 1996.

Notes

Question 13

Vanessa worked for Dodgey Investment Consultants for four years. She was entitled to a bonus calculated according to the annual profits of the company. By virtue of this arrangement, Vanessa should have received £1,000 for the year ending 31 December. However, mistakenly, she was paid £2,000. Vanessa, being unaware of the mistake, paid for a £2,000 holiday for herself and her room-mate with the money.

Under a 'garden leave' clause in her contract, Vanessa was entitled to be paid wages during her one-month notice period, although she was under no obligation to work. Vanessa was given one month's notice to terminate her contract, but at the end of the month she received no pay (when she should have received £1,500) because the company had discovered its mistake in overpaying the bonus and wished to recoup the bonus and a sum of £500 they had paid out in damages to a client of Vanessa to whom Vanessa had given bad investment advice. Just before she was given her notice, Vanessa signed a document saying that she would repay any monies owed to the company on the termination of her employment.

Advise Vanessa as to her legal position in contract and under the ERA 1996.

Answer plan

This question is essentially dealing with the employer's duty to pay wages, but is also looking at the remedies an employee may have when payment is not forthcoming. As such, it brings in actions under the ERA 1996. Many employment law courses cover the ERA 1996 under the duty to pay wages and that is why it is part of a question under implied duties. Vanessa's 'garden leave' clause is important because it means that her employer will pay her at the end of the leave rather than pay her wages in lieu of notice.

Particular issues to be considered are therefore:

- whether the employee owes a duty to indemnify the employer;
- when the employer is entitled to recover an overpayment of wages;
- what constitutes a legal deduction under s 13(1) of the ERA 1996;
- which deductions are excluded by s 14;
- what is a deduction;
- what constitutes wages.

Answer

The question asks for advice to be given to Vanessa on both her contractual rights and her rights under the ERA 1996. As such, the question will be dealt with in two parts.

In relation to her contractual claim, the employer is arguing that Vanessa owes £1,000 in respect of the overpaid bonus and a further £500 to repay damages the employer has incurred due to Vanessa's negligence. In relation to the overpayment of the bonus,

Vanessa was unaware that she had been overpaid and, in fact, spent the money as soon as she received it. In *Avon County Council v Howlett* (1983), an employee who was off sick was inadvertently overpaid. When the employer attempted to recover the overpayment, the employee argued on the basis of estoppel by representation. In other words, the employee had relied on the representation by the employer that he was entitled to the money and had altered his legal position as a result (that is, he had spent the money). The defence succeeded, but the later House of Lords case of *Lipkin Gorman v Karpnale Ltd* (1992) said that future cases based on *Howlett* should be dealt with not on the basis of estoppel, but on the general defence of change of position in the law of restitution. These decisions, however, are on the basis that the employee does not realise that an overpayment has occurred.

If the employee, on realising that there has been an overpayment then spends the money, this will constitute theft under s 5(4) of the Theft Act 1968. In Vanessa's case, she was unaware that she had been overpaid by £1,000 in relation to the bonus. On the basis of *Howlett* and *Lipkin*, she altered her legal position by buying a holiday. As such, Dodgey Investment Consultants is not entitled to recover the £1,000 and Vanessa can sue for recovery as she does not legally owe it the money. The agreement she signed prior to leaving will not cover this overpayment.

In relation to the £500 that the company has paid out in damages to Vanessa's client, this may be recoverable if there is an implied duty in the contract that the employee will indemnify the employer against loss incurred due to the employee's negligence. *Harmer v Cornelius* (1858) is said to be the authority for the proposition that the employee owes the employer a duty of care. As such, should the employee be in breach of the duty, this would give the employer the right to sue for damages. In the case of *Janata Bank v Ahmed* (1981), an employee was successfully sued by his employer for the recovery of £34,640 which the employer had lost due to the employee's failure to exercise proper care and skill as implied by his contract. In the case of Vanessa, it would appear that the employer is arguing breach of contract. In some circumstances, an employer will join the employee as joint tortfeasor under the Civil Liability (Contribution) Act 1978. In the problem, this has not occurred and Dodgey Investments is now trying to recover damages it has already paid. In other words, it is claiming an indemnity from Vanessa.

The leading case in this area is *Lister v Romford Ice and Cold Storage Co Ltd* (1957) where the House of Lords clearly held that the implied duty to indemnify the employer against damage caused by the employee's negligence exists. The case, however, has been severely criticised. The main basis of the criticism is that given that the employer has to pay damages because he is vicariously liable for his employee (and given that although liability arises through notional control of the employee by the employer, the principal rationalisation of vicarious liability is that the employer (or his insurers) has the financial ability to pay damages), creating a right of indemnity is inconsistent. In *Lister* (1957), the employee tried to argue that there was a further implied term in the contract that the employer will ensure that the employee is insured against such liability before the right of indemnity can arise, but this was rejected by the House of Lords.

There have been attempts to avoid the decision in *Lister*. In *Harvey v RG O'Dell Ltd* (1958), it was held that the indemnity did not arise when the employee was doing work he was not normally employed to do but when he was helping his employer. This decision has been criticised by Jolowicz (The Master's Indemnity – Variations on a Theme (1959) 22 MLR 71 and 189), however, in that it gives a very narrow view of what the employee is employed to do. Another way of avoiding *Lister* can be seen in *Jones v Manchester Corp* (1952) where the Court of Appeal held that a hospital board was not entitled to an indemnity from a young inexperienced doctor who had caused injury to a patient through his negligence because the board was at fault in failing to adequately supervise him. This stems from the common law rule that a contribution can be claimed from a joint tortfeasor if that tortfeasor is not wholly innocent, as opposed to being liable through principle rather than action (as in most cases of vicarious liability). While this does not prevent the court from apportioning damages under the Civil Liability (Contribution) Act 1978, it prevents the contractual claim arising.

In the problem, Vanessa has worked for the company for four years. There is no evidence that she is inexperienced, as in Jones, and it is unlikely that a court would feel that she needed supervision unless there was evidence of problems in the past. As such, it would appear that the only reason that the employer has had to pay the £500 is because of the imposition of vicarious liability rather than any negligence on the company's part and thus Jones will not apply. This means that, given that the right of indemnity does apply though it is rarely enforced, Dodgey Investments will have a contractual claim to recover the £500 if the loss was caused by Vanessa's negligence.

It would appear, therefore, that the company has no contractual right to the £1,000 overpayment but does have a contractual right to the £500. The question which must now be asked, however, is whether the money was deducted correctly.

The Wages Act 1986 (now the ERA 1996) was brought in to deal with deductions from wages made incorrectly by employers. It gives employment tribunals jurisdiction over deductions which contravene the Act. The issue of legal entitlement to the money deducted is irrelevant. The Act merely lays down an administrative structure of how and when the employer can deduct. Section 13(1) of the ERA 1996 states that the employer cannot make a deduction from the wages of an employee unless the deduction is required or authorised by statute, required or authorised by a provision in the employee's contract, or agreed to previously by the employee in writing before the deduction was made. Section 14, however, contains a list of exceptions to s 13(1), and s 14(1)(a) and (b) covers deductions in respect of an overpayment of wages or expenses.

'Wages' is defined by s 27 of the ERA 1996 and includes 'any fee, bonus, commission, holiday pay or other emolument referable to his employment' (s 27(1)(a)). As such, it would appear from the problem that the overpayment of the £1,000 was an overpayment of wages for the purpose of s 14 of the Act. At one time, it was thought that if the employer had no contractual right to recover the overpayment, s 14 did not apply (*Home Office v Ayres* (1992)). This has now been overruled, however, and even though Dodgey Investments does not have a contractual right to recover, Vanessa cannot use the tribunal jurisdiction under the Act but must use the contractual jurisdiction (*Sunderland Polytechnic v Evans* (1993)). In relation to the deduction of the £500, however, the situation is different. Vanessa was under a 'garden leave' clause. While the decision in *Delaney v Staples (trading as De Montfort Recruitment)* (1992) states that wages in lieu of notice are damages for a breach of contract and therefore not wages for the purposes of the Act, Vanessa will be paid at the end of the period although there is no requirement to work. As such, her final payment will be wages under s 27(1)(a). A further point is that, in reality, Vanessa received no money whatsoever rather than a reduction in money. Can a total failure to pay constitute a deduction for the purposes of the Act? The Court of Appeal in *Delaney* stated that a non-payment was a 100% deduction and therefore fell within the tribunal jurisdiction. The House of Lords did not hear this point on appeal and it therefore appears that this is still the law. Vanessa has thus suffered a deduction from her wages. The question must therefore be asked: did the deduction comply with s 13(1)?

There is no requirement to deduct the sum by statute, nor is there evidence that Vanessa's contract allowed such a deduction. Vanessa did, however, sign a document allowing the deduction to be made just before she was given notice. Until the early 1990s, such an agreement would have meant that the Act had been complied with but, in *Discount Tobacco and Confectionery Ltd v Williamson* (1993), the Employment Appeal Tribunal (EAT) held that such an agreement had to be signed before the event causing the deduction and an agreement signed after the event but before the deduction was made did not comply with s 13(1). Here, Vanessa signed the agreement after she gave the bad advice and caused the company loss. Therefore, the deduction is in breach of s 13(1) and can be recovered.

Notes

Question 14

Tony is employed as a lecturer by Tinseltown University. Due to the extreme tightness of the scheduling at examination times, Tony, along with many other members of staff, has to work both evenings and weekends to ensure that all the examination scripts are marked in time for the requisite Examination Board meetings. This particular year, Tony and a few other staff have refused to work evenings and weekends marking the scripts, because of the pressure this causes to their families. This refusal has led to a disruption to the Examination Board meeting schedule and to the University as a whole. The University has now responded by consulting your firm of solicitors as to whether it can deduct a percentage of these lecturers' wages for their action, or even refuse to pay them any wages at all. The lecturers involved have refused to sign an undertaking to the University that they will not take such action again in the future.

Advise Tinseltown University.

Answer plan

The last question in this chapter brings together a variety of issues and shows that questions on the contract of employment sometimes involve both interpretation of contractual terms as well as implied duties.

Particular issues to be considered are:

- how far an employee can be required to perform duties which are reasonably incidental to his main job duties;
- the interpretation of flexibility clauses;
- the implied duty on the employee to obey all lawful reasonable orders of his employer;
- how far there is an implied duty in all contracts of employment that the employee will not disrupt the employer's business – in particular, a discussion of *Secretary of State for Employment v ASLEF (No 2)* (1972) and *Ticehurst v British Telecommunications plc* (1992);
- whether the employer can deduct a proportion of an employee's wage – in particular, *Sim v Rotherham Metropolitan Borough Council* (1986), distinguishing *Wiluszynski v London Borough of Tower Hamlets* (1989);
- whether the action in the problem is industrial action;
- whether the proposed deductions must comply with the ERA 1996.

Answer

The problem deals with a variety of different contractual issues and each will be discussed separately.

The first issue to raise is the content of the lecturers' contracts. While many contracts of employment list specific job duties, this is not definitive and the courts have long recognised that an employee can be asked to perform functions which are not listed as main duties but which are reasonably incidental to the job. One of the implied duties in the contract of employment is that the employee is required to obey all lawful reasonable orders issued by the employer and failure to do so is a breach of contract. The starting point to determine if the order is reasonable is the contract itself and, therefore, if the requirement to work evenings and weekends is a contractual one, the lecturers are in breach of the duty to obey reasonable orders and the University has an action for damages.

It is likely that a lecturer's contract would be specific in relation to the duties that the job entails. Even if marking examination scripts is not particularly mentioned, part of a lecturer's job will be the assessment of students and, as such, the marking of examination scripts would, without doubt, be seen as reasonably incidental to the job. It appears from the problem, however, that the lecturers are not refusing to perform this function, but are refusing to do so in the evenings and at weekends. If the contracts specify when the lecturers work and evenings and weekends are not mentioned, then it could be argued that there is no breach on the lecturers' part so that the expectation on the part of the University is unreasonable and there is no requirement on the part of the employees to comply (*O'Brien v Associated Fire Alarms Ltd* (1968)). On the other hand, if there is a flexibility clause within the contract, in particular, relating to the hours the lecturers are required to work, it would then be up to the court to determine whether the requirement to work evenings and weekends at certain times of the year is within the ambit of the clause and therefore a reasonable order on the part of the University. If the court holds that the order is reasonable, the lecturers will be in breach of their implied duty.

If the court holds that the requirement to work evenings and weekends is not part of the contract, it is possible that the lecturers are still in breach because their action is disrupting the University. There is an implied duty in the contract that the employee shall serve the employer faithfully and it could be that an insistence on following the terms of the contract to the letter could be a breach of this duty. This proposition was first mentioned in the famous case of *Secretary of State for Employment v ASLEF (No 2)* (1972). In that case, ASLEF was conducting a work-to-rule whereby the employees were strictly adhering to the rule book, but in a way which was causing total disruption to the railway system. The Court of Appeal held that the employees were in breach of contract. Lord Denning MR said that if an employee took steps to wilfully disrupt his employer's undertaking, he would be in breach of contract. Buckley LJ said that there was an implied term in all contracts that an employee should serve his employer faithfully and promote the employer's commercial interests.

The leading case is now *Ticehurst v British Telecommunications plc* (1992). In this case, a manager, who was also a union official, took part in industrial action, first by way of a go-slow and work-to-rule and finally by going on strike. The employers wrote to all employees saying that if they did not fully comply with their contracts, they would be considered to be in breach of contract and sent home without pay until they were prepared to work normally. Ticehurst refused to sign an undertaking that she would work normally and was therefore sent home without pay. The case arose when the employee sued for her lost wages on the basis that she was willing to work and the employer had refused to allow her to do so. She won at first instance but lost on appeal. The Court of Appeal held that Ticehurst had demonstrated, by refusing to sign the undertaking, that she had withdrawn her goodwill. The Court of Appeal held that there was a breach of the implied term to serve the employer faithfully. Ralph Gibson LJ said that such a term was necessary in the contract of a manager who was in charge of other employees and who had to exercise discretion in giving instructions to others and supervising their work. He continued:

The term is breached ... when the employee does an act, or omits to do an act, which would be within her contract ... not in the honest exercise of choice or discretion for the faithful performance of her work but in order to disrupt the employer's business or to cause the most inconvenience that can be caused.

Although the case involves a manager, Smith and Wood (*Industrial Law*, 8th edn, 2003 London: LexisNexis Butterworths) suggest that this is not central to the issue, but that the discretion enjoyed by an employee and the exercise of that discretion is.

Given that in modern conditions, and almost certainly in respect of the contracts in the problem, the job is unlikely to be exhaustively defined, action disrupting the employer's business is likely to be a breach of the duty to serve the employer faithfully. The problem in question, however, can be distinguished from both *Ticehurst* and *ASLEF* in that, in both of the cases, there was an intention on the part of the employee to cause inconvenience to the employer. In the case of the lecturers, this intention appears to be missing in that they are concerned about the effect of the work on their families rather than embarking on a deliberate attempt to cause disruption. A counter-argument may be raised, however, that once the lecturers knew of the disruption, they should do what is necessary to avoid it and the refusal to sign the undertaking demonstrates an intention on their part to withdraw goodwill and so cause inconvenience to the employer. If this is the interpretation put upon their actions by the court, their refusal will be seen as a breach of their duty to serve the employer faithfully. Should the action of the employees be a breach of either the express terms of the contract or the implied duties within it, the next question to be asked is whether the University can deduct all or part of their wages. If the part of the duties not performed is discrete and quantifiable, the employer can refuse the amount of wages representing that part. In *Sim v Rotherham Metropolitan Borough Council* (1986), a deduction of part of a teacher's salary for refusing to cover for absent colleagues as part of industrial action was upheld (see also *Miles v Wakefield Metropolitan District Council* (1987)).

There is a divergence of opinion on the reasoning behind these decisions. In *Sim*, Scott J held that the employee could sue for his full wages subject to the employer's right of set-off representing the duties not performed. In *Miles*, the House of Lords said that the employee had not provided consideration for a certain part of his duties. Such arguments apply when the refusal to perform can be identified as a discrete part of the whole of the duties, but causes problems where the action is more general, as in the case of a go-slow or a work-to-rule. While the employer could still deduct a reasonable sum, the cases of *Wiluszynski v London Borough of Tower Hamlets* (1989) and *Ticehurst* appear to show that if the employer makes it clear that he will not accept defective performance, he can refuse to pay all the wages even if the employee has worked. On the basis of both cases, however, if the employer permits the defective performance (for example, by allowing the employee to continue working), he may have waived his rights (*Bond v Cav Ltd* (1983)). In *Wiluszynski*, it was made clear in the judgment that the employer could not be expected to discover all the employees taking part in industrial action and refuse them entry, given the number of employees the council employed. In *Ticehurst*, those refusing to sign the undertaking were sent home.

In the problem, the lecturers could be said to be conducting a go-slow. If the aim of this is to disrupt the employer's business then, on the basis of *ASLEF* and *Ticehurst*, it could be argued that they are in breach of contract. As such, the employer may be entitled to deduct part of their wages, if the duties are discrete and identifiable, or the whole of their wages for the requisite period, even if they eventually perform the work, as long as the University has made it clear it will not accept defective performance. There seems no evidence on the facts, however, that this is the case. Nor does it appear that the University has prevented the lecturers from continuing to work and, on the basis of *Bond*, this may mean that the employer has waived his right to deduct.

If the right to deduct exists, the final question to be asked is whether such deduction must comply with the provisions of s 13(1) of the ERA 1996. A deduction from wages cannot be made unless it is authorised by statute, authorised by the employee's contract or the employee has agreed to the deduction in writing before it is made. *Discount Tobacco and Confectionery Ltd v Williamson* (1993) states that such agreement must take place before the event which led to the deduction and thus any agreement obtained from the lecturers now could not authorise a deduction in respect of past action but could cover future action. The provisions of s 13(1), however, do not apply to deductions listed in s 14 and this includes deductions in respect of industrial action. Once a deduction in respect of industrial action has been made, the tribunal has no jurisdiction under the Act to query whether the deduction represents the loss to the employer (*Sunderland Polytechnic v Evans* (1993)). While industrial action has not been given a statutory definition, definitions of strike and lock out in s 235(4) and (5) of the ERA 1996 suggest that a breach of contract is not necessary, but the motive behind the action must be to compel the employer. If the aim of the lecturers' refusal to mark in the evenings and at weekends is to force the University to alter the examining schedules, their action may be taken to be industrial action. As such, any deductions from wages will fall within s 14 and the tribunal will have no jurisdiction under the ERA 1996 in respect of them. If the action is not industrial action, however, any deduction now in respect of past action will infringe s 13(1) unless it is authorised by the employees' contracts.

Notes

_____

_____

_____

_____

_____

_____

_____

_____

_____

_____

_____

5 Discrimination

Introduction

Discrimination is an area which recently has rapidly expanded. It has been affected greatly by European Court decisions and is an area where a complainant not only has rights under national law but may also have rights under European law in the form of the Equal Treatment Directive (76/207/EEC). Both discrimination and equal pay, discussed in Chapter 6, are areas where European law has probably had the greatest impact and, to answer questions on these topics, it is necessary to understand the relationship between national law and European law and how far an individual in a Member State can enforce European law in the national courts. For the purposes of ease, most employment law courses deal with the general topic of discrimination rather than separate it out into the different types of discrimination, and that approach has been adopted here. Until 2001, the Sex Discrimination Act (SDA) 1975 and the Race Relations Act (RRA) 1976 were very similar. However, changes made to the SDA in 2001 by the Sex Discrimination (Indirect Discrimination and Burden of Proof) Regulations and changes made to the RRA in 2003 by the Race Relations Act 1976 (Amendment) Regulations created differences between the two Acts. The introduction of the Employment Equality (Religion or Belief) Regulations and the Employment Equality (Sexual Orientation) Regulations, both 2003, meant that these and the RRA were very similar, leaving the SDA standing out as different. However, changes to the SDA brought about by the Employment Equality (Sex Discrimination) Regulations 2005 have now, to a large extent, aligned the legislation again. In addition, the Disability Discrimination Act 1995 is different again from the other pieces of legislation. Originally, it had no concept of indirect discrimination, although changes made by the Disability Discrimination Act 1995 (Amendment) Regulations 2004 introduce such a concept; it is based on the duty to make reasonable adjustments and thus is different from other definitions. It should also be noted that the Sex Discrimination (Gender Reassignment) Regulations 1999, the Part-Time Workers (Prevention of Less Favourable Treatment) Regulations 2000 (as amended) and the Fixed-Term Employees (Prevention of Less Favourable Treatment) Regulations 2002 may all be included in questions in this area.

In any problem question on sex or race discrimination, the starting point should always be to identify the relevant legislation (RRA, SDA etc) and then the type of discrimination which has occurred, because this will then lead on to whether a potential defence exists, The next stage is to identify the specific act of discrimination committed and finally any defence, if one is available. Furthermore, if the employer is an organ of the state, be aware of the possibility of a claim under a Directive, in addition to any claim under national law.

For questions on the area of discrimination, general issues which the student needs to understand include:

- the relationship between national and European law in this area;
- the concept of discrimination;
- direct discrimination;
- indirect discrimination;
- victimisation;
- harassment;
- post-termination discrimination;
- the acts of discrimination;
- the role of the commissions;
- genuine occupational qualifications;
- genuine occupational requirements;
- exceptions to the legislation;
- enforcement and remedies.

Questions in this area may come in the form of either essays or problems, and problem type questions will often include different types of discrimination.

In particular, therefore, students should be familiar with:

- the definitions of discrimination under each piece of legislation;
- the burden of proof;
- the concept of continuing acts;
- the comparator in a direct discrimination claim;
- the definition of indirect discrimination;
- the limitations in a victimisation claim;
- the statutory definition of harassment;
- what constitutes post-termination discrimination;
- the specific acts of discrimination;
- genuine occupational qualifications;
- genuine occupational requirements;
- remedies and how compensation is assessed.

Finally, given the impact of European law, no student should attempt a question in this area without a knowledge of the major cases in the European Court of Justice (ECJ) and their impact on national law.

Checklist

Students should be familiar with the following areas:

- the concept of discrimination – in particular, cases such as *James v Eastleigh Borough Council* (1990) and *Showboat Entertainment Centre v Owens* (1984);

- the burden of proof in particular cases, such as *Khanna v MOD* (1981); *King v Great Britain China Centre* (1991); *Zafar v Glasgow City Council* (1998); and the changes made in 2001 and 2003;
- the necessary comparison in direct discrimination and the impact of *Webb v EMO Air Cargo (UK) Ltd* (1994) ECJ, (1995) HL;
- the enforceability of the Equal Treatment Directive – in particular, in cases such as *Marshall v Southampton and South West Hampshire Area Health Authority (No 2)* (1993); *Foster v British Gas plc* (1991); *Doughty v Rolls Royce plc* (1992); *Francovich v State of Italy* (1992); *Marleasing SA v La Comercial Internacional de Alimentacion SA* (1992);
- the elements of indirect discrimination and, in particular, cases such as *Enderby v Frenchay Health Authority* (1994); *Jones v University of Manchester* (1993); *Bilka-Kaufhaus GmbH v Weber von Hartz* (1987); *Hampson v DES* (1989); *Cobb v Secretary of State for Employment and Manpower Services Commission* (1989); *Falkirk Council v Whyte* (1997); *London Underground v Edwards (No 2)* (1998); *R v Secretary of State for Employment ex p Seymour-Smith and Perez* (1999) ECJ, (2000) HL;
- problems of interpretation of the specific acts of discrimination;
- problems of interpretation in the genuine occupational qualifications;
- the statutory definition of harassment;
- genuine occupational requirements;
- potential conflicts between the Employment Equality (Religion or Belief) Regulations 2003 and the Employment Equality (Sexual Orientation) Regulations 2003;
- changes made by the Disability Discrimination Act 1995 (Amendment) Regulations 2004;
- principles in the award of compensation in particular cases, such as *City of Bradford Metropolitan County v Arora* (1989); *AB v South Western Water Services Ltd* (1993); *Deane v Ealing London Borough Council* (1993);
- the impact of European law on legislation – in particular, the effect of *Marshall (No 2)* above and the earlier Marshall decision (1986); *R v Secretary of State for Employment ex p EOC* (1994); *R v Secretary of State for Employment ex p Seymour-Smith and Perez* (1999) ECJ, (2000) HL;
- the impact of the Human Rights Act (HRA) 1998;
- the Part-Time Workers (Prevention of Less Favourable Treatment) Regulations 2000 (as amended) and Fixed-Term Employees (Prevention of Less Favourable Treatment) Regulations 2002.

Question 15

Alexis, Crystal and Blake work for Dynasty Products Ltd. Alexis has just discovered that she is pregnant. She was due to go on a two-month training course in two weeks' time, but Dynasty has now refused to send her, saying that it will be wasted because, shortly after she returns, she will be on maternity leave. Another employee is now being sent in her place. The company has said that it would treat a man on long-term sick leave in the same way.

Crystal applied for a promotion recently. During her interview, she was asked about her childcare arrangements and about her husband's new job 100 miles away. In the end, no one interviewed was offered the promotion because the post was frozen as a result of cutbacks. Crystal has now learned that the interview panel had decided before the post was frozen that she would not be offered it, because Dynasty assumed that the family would be moving shortly because of her husband's job.

Blake works on the shop floor. He has objected because women on his shift can leave half an hour earlier on a Friday than the men in order to do their shopping. The women are not paid for this half an hour but Blake feels he should be given the opportunity to leave early.

Advise Alexis, Crystal and Blake whether they may pursue claims under the SDA 1975 against Dynasty Products Ltd.

Answer plan

This question deals with allegations of direct sexual discrimination and, as seen in previous questions, the easiest way to approach it is to deal with each party individually. In the case of all the parties, it looks unlikely that a genuine occupational qualification exists so it is a waste of valuable time to discuss this issue.

Particular issues to be considered are:

- the burden of proof;
- the definition of direct discrimination;
- the problems in s 5(3) of the SDA 1975 and the impact of *Webb v EMO Air Cargo (UK) Ltd* (1994);
- denying access to promotion, training or transfer, or any other benefits, facilities or services in s 6(2)(a);
- the problems caused by *Thorn v Meggit Engineering* (1976) and whether *Brennan v Dewhurst Ltd* (1984) can apply;
- whether assumptions can be discriminatory;
- the problems caused by *Peake v Automative Products* (1978) and the effect on the problem of *MOD v Jeremiah* (1980).

——————————————Answer——————————

In the case of all three parties, any potential claim against Dynasty Products Ltd will be of direct sexual discrimination. The definition of direct discrimination is found in s 1(1)(a) of the SDA 1975 and occurs when a woman, on the grounds of her sex, is treated less favourably than a man. This is perhaps misleading, however, because the Act further protects against discrimination on the grounds of marital status (s 3) and applies equally to men (s 2). Until the Sex Discrimination (Indirect Discrimination and Burden of Proof) Regulations 2001, the burden of proof in sex discrimination cases was on the party alleging discrimination, although the courts acknowledged that this was a heavy burden and, in *Khanna v MOD* (1981), it was held that the action of the employer could lead to a *prima facie* presumption of discrimination which caused the burden to shift to the employer to show some reason other than the sex or marital status of the employee for his actions. This approach was approved by the Court of Appeal in *Baker v Cornwall County Council* (1990) and, in *King v Great Britain China Centre* (1991), Neil LJ said that:

> ... a difference in treatment and a difference in race (or gender) will often point to the possibility of discrimination. In such circumstances, the tribunal should look to the employer for an explanation and, if one is not forthcoming or is inadequate, it is legitimate to infer discrimination has occurred.

This statement was approved by the House of Lords in *Zafar v Glasgow City Council* (1998). The Sex Discrimination (Indirect Discrimination and Burden of Proof) Regulations 2001 altered the burden of proof in sex discrimination claims. The 2001 Regulations inserted s 63A into the SDA 1975, which provides that where a complainant proves facts from which the tribunal could conclude, in the absence of an adequate explanation from the respondent, that the respondent has committed an act of discrimination, the tribunal shall uphold the complaint unless the respondent proves that he did not commit the act. Thus, the Regulations impose a statutory duty on the tribunal to shift the burden of proof where the complainant establishes a *prima facie* case of discrimination.

While s 1(1)(a) talks of less favourable treatment, the question to be asked is 'less favourable than what?'. This is answered by s 5(3), which requires a tribunal to consider the treatment of the complainant and compare it to that of a person of the opposite sex where 'the relevant circumstances ... are the same or not materially different'. This means that, in the case of all the parties in the problem, it must be shown that their treatment was different from that of a person of the opposite sex whose circumstances were the same or not materially different, and the reason for the different treatment was the complainant's sex. Should this be proved to the satisfaction of the tribunal, the employer's motive for his actions is irrelevant (*Grieg v Community Industries* (1979)). In *James v Eastleigh Borough Council* (1990), the House of Lords said that the question to ask was 'Would the complainant have received the same treatment but for his or her sex?'. If the treatment would have been different if the complainant's sex were different, discrimination has occurred and the reason for that discrimination is irrelevant. On the other hand, if the employer shows that he would have treated both sexes in the same way, there is no discrimination. In *Home Office v Coyne* (2000), Coyne complained of sexual harassment, but her complaint was not dealt with for two years and she was eventually dismissed. The Court of Appeal held that for a complaint to lie, she had to show that but for her sex, the complaint would have been dealt with. In that case, however, there was no evidence that the Home Office would have dealt with a complaint by a man in a more favourable way and thus her complaint failed. It is submitted that this is a narrow interpretation of the law and allows a bad employer to escape liability on the basis that he treats all employees equally badly.

In the case of Alexis, she has been turned down for training because she is pregnant. Alexis may be the victim of direct discrimination in that no provision, criterion or practice is being imposed by the employer, and the treatment is on a one-to-one basis; thus, the claim is not one of indirect discrimination. The potentially discriminatory act is refusing her access to training in s 6(2)(a). To establish a claim, Alexis must prove that, due to her sex, she has been treated less favourably than a man whose circumstances are the same or not materially different (s 5(3) and *James v Eastleigh Borough Council* (1990)). It is obvious that Alexis cannot compare her treatment to that of a man in the same circumstances as men cannot get pregnant!

Until recently, however, tribunals looked to see if the employer would treat a man who was on long-term sick leave in the same way, on the basis that such circumstances were not materially different (*Hayes v Malleable WMC* (1985)). This comparison was questionable since the case of *Webb v EMO Air Cargo (UK) Ltd* (1995). In that case, Webb was taken on as a maternity leave replacement but, shortly afterwards, discovered that she too was pregnant and would therefore be unable to work for the whole of the absent employee's maternity leave. Prior to discovering her pregnancy, EMO had told her that she would be kept on when the absent employee returned. On discovering her pregnancy, however, EMO dismissed Webb, arguing that a man who required long-term sick leave would have been treated in the same way. Webb alleged sex discrimination, but lost her claim in the tribunal, the Employment Appeal Tribunal (EAT) and the Court of Appeal. On appeal to the House of Lords, the case was referred to the ECJ, on the basis that the ECJ had recently decided a series of cases (for example, *Dekker v VJV Centrum* (1991)) which held that less favourable treatment on the grounds of pregnancy was direct discrimination and a breach of the Equal Treatment Directive. The ECJ in *Webb* ruled that termination of a contract on the grounds of pregnancy was sex discrimination as pregnancy was a condition which only affected women and that comparison with a man on long-term sick leave was an inappropriate comparison as pregnancy is not an illness. The House of Lords upheld the ruling on the basis that Webb was on an indefinite contract.

In Alexis's case, her contract has not been terminated; rather, she has been denied a place on a training course. If she had been dismissed because of her pregnancy, she would have been protected by s 99 of the Employment Rights Act (ERA) 1996 which makes such dismissals automatically unfair. Alexis's problem is that the SDA 1975 requires a comparison. While it appears to be the case that, if an English statutory provision can be construed to give effect to European law, this is the approach the courts will take, the position was unclear if the statute predated the Directive. In the ECJ case of *Marleasing SA v La Comercial Internacional de Alimentacion SA* (1990), it was stated that national courts, in applying national law, should interpret it in such a way to achieve the result required by the Directive, whether national law predates the Directive or not. Lord Keith, hearing Webb's appeal in the House of Lords, stated that this was the case. As such, given that later cases have stated that unfavourable treatment on the grounds of pregnancy is sex discrimination per se, so removing the need for a comparator (for example, *Hardman v Mallon trading as Orchard Lodge Nursing Home* (2002)), then Dynasty's argument that it would treat a man on long-term sick leave in the same way is irrelevant.

Therefore, in relation to pregnancy, the comparison required by s 5(3) will be ignored and the only reason that Alexis has not been selected for her training course is her pregnancy and, thus, her sex has caused the less favourable treatment and an action for direct discrimination will lie. Given that it is an action for direct discrimination, Dynasty will have no defence.

Crystal was interviewed for a promotion but was not offered the post because the interview panel assumed she would be moving because of her husband's new job. Crystal's case raises a variety of issues. First, it must be decided what is the less favourable treatment. If Crystal argues that it is not getting the promotion, she may have problems because no one was promoted because the post was frozen. In *Thorn v Meggit Engineering Ltd* (1976), a woman was rejected for a job because of her sex but in the end no one was appointed. The tribunal held that there had been no sex discrimination as she had not been treated less favourably than a man because a man did not get the job. This can be contrasted with the case of *Roadburg v Lothian Regional Council* (1976) where, in similar circumstances, a woman was refused a job which was offered to a man, but then the post was frozen and so no one actually took up the job. In that case, it was held that there was discrimination in that the less favourable treatment was not being offered the job in the first place. Thus, to choose the lack of an offer may not lead to a finding of discrimination despite the fact that the reason for the refusal to make an offer was because of a sex-based assumption – that is, that her husband is the breadwinner and therefore she will move with his job (*Horsey v Dyfed County Council* (1982)). As no man was offered the promotion, Crystal will not satisfy s 5(3).

Crystal may, however, be able to argue that the interview itself was where the less favourable treatment occurred. In *Gates v Wirral Borough Council* (1982), it was held that asking questions about childcare arrangements of women, when the same questions were not asked of men, was discriminatory. In *Saunders v Richmond-upon-Thames Borough Council* (1978), it was held that questions in an interview for a golf professional, such as 'are you blazing a trail for women', were not discriminatory when not asked of men. In *Brennan v Dewhurst Ltd* (1984), a girl applied for a job as a butcher's assistant but was turned down for the job because of her sex. The post was then frozen and no one was appointed. She was successful in her claim for direct discrimination on the basis that the interview was the incident of discrimination in that the questions made it clear that the employer did not want to appoint a woman and, therefore, her action lay under s 6(1)(a) (arrangements for determining who shall be employed) rather than s 6(2)(a). Crystal was asked questions about her husband and her childcare arrangements. If men were also interviewed and were not asked similar questions, she can argue less favourable treatment on the grounds of her sex, given that it appears that they had no intention of appointing her in the first place. The Equal Opportunities Commission (EOC) has argued that such questions should not be asked until the job is offered. This makes sense, in that, if the men were asked the same questions, it would be difficult to show less favourable treatment. The point, of course, is that it is the answers to the questions that will influence the employer because, even in today's society, the majority of childcare responsibilities will still fall to women.

Blake feels that he is receiving less favourable treatment in that he has to work an extra half an hour on Fridays. Section 6(2)(a) covers discrimination in access to benefits, facilities or services. In *Peake v Automative Products* (1978), Mr Peake claimed discrimination on the basis that women were allowed to leave five minutes early every day to avoid the rush to leave when the factory closed. In the EAT, Peake won his case, Phillips J saying that 'benefit' in s 6(2)(a) 'meant no more than advantage'. The Court of Appeal, however, overruled the EAT, Lord Denning MR stating that rules for safety and good administration could not be discriminatory and that Peake's claim was de minimis. The case caused some criticism as it suggested that motive was relevant in direct discrimination and a later Court of Appeal, in *MOD v Jeremiah* (1980), overruled the first part of the decision but upheld it on *de minimis*. In Blake's case, the difference between his situation and Peake is five minutes a week, albeit that, in Blake's case, it all happens in the one day. How far the courts will invoke the de minimis principle is unclear. In *Birmingham City Council v EOC* (1989), the House of Lords held that deprivation of choice is sufficient to constitute less favourable treatment and, in *Gill v El Vino Co Ltd* (1983), Eveleigh LJ said:

> I find it very difficult to invoke the maxim de minimis non curat lex in a situation where that which has been denied to the [claimant] is the very thing that Parliament seeks to provide, namely, facilities and services on an equal basis.

On the basis of these cases, it would appear that *de minimis* is unlikely to succeed. There is one important difference between Blake's case and *Peake*, however. In *Peake*, the women were paid for the five minutes: in Blake's case they are not paid for the time off. In *Jeremiah*, men were required to work in dirty conditions, for which they were paid extra, but the women were not so required. It was held that forcing men to work in such conditions was discriminatory and it was irrelevant that they received extra pay; an employer cannot buy the right to discriminate. On this authority, the fact that the women do not receive pay is irrelevant. The lack of choice is because of Blake's sex (*James v Eastleigh Borough Council*) and should the courts reject *de minimis*, which seems likely, Blake will be successful in his claim for direct discrimination.

Notes

Question 16

Northbury Health Authority has recently advertised internally for a supervisor to take charge of domestic staff. Deirdre, who is 36, worked for the health authority full-time as a supervisor until five years ago when she left to have children. Until that time, she had worked for the health authority for 10 years. She now works part-time as a domestic auxiliary to fit in with her children, and is prepared to work to job share. She is not interviewed for the job because the authority tells her the post is not open to part-time staff, nor can the job be shared.

The health authority has recently dismissed Harvinder, a Sikh, from his job as mortuary attendant. The reason for his dismissal, according to personnel, is that he cannot wear a protective surgical cap when attending post-mortems because of his turban and his long hair. He has been frequently warned about this and had taped some of the conversations with personnel secretly, in case of such an eventuality. The discovery of the tapes coincided with his dismissal, although the authority claims that the tapes had no bearing on their decision to dismiss.

Advise Northbury Health Authority.

Answer plan

This question covers both sex and race discrimination. Again, it is easier to deal with each party separately and identify the type of discrimination first and the act of discrimination which may have been committed.

Particular issues to be considered are:

- the requirements for an actionable indirect discrimination claim;
- what constitutes a provision, criterion or practice – comparing cases such as *Holmes v Home Office* (1984); *Clymo v Wandsworth London Borough Council* (1989); *Falkirk Council v Whyte* (1997);
- the defence of justifiability and, in particular, cases such as *Bilka-Kaufhaus GmbH v Weber von Hartz* (1987); *Hampson v DES* (1989); *Cobb v Secretary of State for Employment and Manpower Services Commission* (1989);
- the acts of discrimination in s 6 of the SDA 1975 and s 4 of the RRA 1976;
- the concept of racial discrimination;
- the meaning of 'can comply' in *Mandla v Dowell Lee* (1983);
- the concept of victimisation – in particular, *Aziz v Trinity Street Taxis* (1988).

Answer

This question deals with a variety of issues in relation to discrimination claims. By s 63A of the SDA 1975, introduced by the Sex Discrimination (Indirect Discrimination and Burden of Proof) Regulations 2001, where a complainant proves facts from which the tribunal can conclude, in the absence of an adequate explanation from the employer, that an act of discrimination has occurred, the tribunal must uphold the complaint unless the respondent proves he did not commit the act. Thus, the 2001 Regulations impose a statutory duty on the tribunal to shift the burden of proof where the facts establish a *prima facie* case of discrimination.

Deirdre is at present employed part-time, but worked full-time for the authority before she had her family and is prepared to job share. The authority has told her that the job is not open to part-time staff nor can it be job shared. To establish a *prima facie* case, Deirdre must convince the tribunal that the facts give rise to a *prima facie* case of discrimination. The type of discrimination that Deirdre must try to establish is indirect discrimination (s 1(1)(b) of the SDA 1975) in relation to access to opportunities for promotion (s 6(2)(a)).

By s1(1)(b), indirect discrimination occurs where the employer applies a provision, criterion or practice: which he applies or would apply equally to a man; which puts or would put women at a particular disadvantage when compared with men; which puts her at that disadvantage and which the employer cannot show to be proportionate means of achieving a legitimate aim. This definition was introduced by the 2005 Regulations. There are considerable differences between this definition and the original definition in the 1975 Act. The previous definition required the complainant to show that: the employer was imposing a condition or requirement which applied equally to both sexes; the proportion of women who could comply with the condition or requirement was considerably smaller than the proportion of men who could comply; the employer could not justify the imposition of the condition or requirement irrespective of sex; and it was to the complainant's detriment that she could not comply.

The differences are immediately apparent. The phrase 'provision, criterion or practice' is wider than the more restrictive 'condition or requirement'. The woman no longer has to show a difference in the proportions of men and women affected. The defence of justifiability remains the same.

At present, there are few cases under the amended definition but, given that the old definition was more restrictive, any set of facts which would have satisfied the previous definition will most certainly satisfy the new. Given the paucity of cases, we can look to see if Deirdre would have been successful under the old law and assess the likelihood of her success under the new.

The old 'condition or requirement' was interpreted as meaning something that was necessary for the job (*Perara v CSC (No 2)* (1983)). This interpretation meant that if an employer merely expressed a preference, then he was not imposing a condition or requirement – a view expressed as unfortunate by the Court of Appeal in *Meer v Tower Hamlets* (1988). In *Falkirk Council v Whyte* (1997), however, the EAT held that if a factor described as a preference was in reality the deciding criterion in who was offered a job or promotion, it was a condition or requirement. Under the previous definition, therefore, it is clear that working full-time is a necessary requirement for the supervisor's job because she is told that she cannot apply because she is part-time and that the job cannot be job shared. Thus, full-time working would be classed as a condition or requirement pre-2001 and most certainly would be a provision, criterion or practice under the amended section.

Secondly, Deirdre must show that working full-time puts women at a particular disadvantage. This will involve some consideration of a comparative group. While *Holmes v Home Office* (1984) decided that the imposition of full-time working was indirectly discriminatory to women, *Kidd v DRG (UK)* (1985) demonstrated that it is necessary for Deirdre to choose the correct comparative group. In *Pearse v Bradford Metropolitan District Council* (1988), one of the requirements of eligibility to apply for the post of senior lecturer in a college was that the applicants had to work full-time. Pearse argued that the requirement was discriminatory and produced statistics that out of all the academic staff, 21.8% of women worked full-time compared with 46.7% of men. The EAT held that the wrong comparative group was used. The group should have been those academic staff eligible to apply for a senior lectureship due to qualifications and experience. On this comparison, there was little difference in the proportions and therefore no discrimination. A similar wrong choice of comparative group was seen in *Jones v University of Manchester* (1993). In establishing the comparative group, therefore, Deirdre must choose those at the workplace who are qualified to apply for the post of supervisor. If, when looking at this group, the proportion of women working part-time is considerably smaller than the proportion of men working part-time, she will have established the second requirement for an indirect discrimination claim. That is the provision of full-time working puts women at a particular disadvantage and this is supported by *London Underground v Edwards (No 2)* (1998), the Court of Appeal upheld the EAT in finding that a difference of just under 5% constituted indirect discrimination, this must now be subject to the ECJ decision in *R v Secretary of State for Employment ex p Seymour-Smith and Perez* (1999) where, although the court held that it was up to Member States to determine the relevant difference, the court did not feel that a difference of less than 10% indicated indirect discrimination. The ECJ added, however, that a smaller, persistent and constant disparity over a long period of time could indicate discrimination. This interpretation was adopted by the House of Lords when it decided *ex p Seymour-Smith* in February 2000.

The third requirement Deirdre must establish is that the imposition of the provision is not proportionate means of achieving a legitimate aim. This defence available to the employer is the same as that under the old law and has had a chequered history. In *Steel v UPOW* (1978), Phillips J stated that the employer had to establish that the condition was necessary and not merely convenient to establish the defence. This stringent test was watered down by the Court of Appeal in *Ojutiku v Manpower Services Commission* (1982) in which it was said that whether the employer was justified in imposing the requirement depended on whether his decision 'would be acceptable to right thinking people as (having) sound and tolerable reasons for doing so'. The ECJ in *Bilka-Kaufhaus GmbH v Weber von Hartz* (1987) stated that the employer had to show 'objectively justified' grounds and the employer had to show that the factors which have a disparate effect 'correspond to a real need on the part of the undertaking, are appropriate with a view to achieving the objectives pursued and are necessary to that end'. *Hampson v DES* (1989) stated that to show that a condition is justifiable 'requires an objective balance to be struck between the discriminatory effect of the condition and the reasonable needs of the party who applies that condition'. Wood J in *Cobb v Secretary of State for Employment and Manpower Services Commission* (1989) said:

It was for the tribunal ... to carry out the balancing exercise involved, taking into account all the surrounding circumstances and giving due emphasis to the degree of discrimination caused against the object or aim to be achieved – the principle of proportionality.

In Deirdre's case, therefore, the employer must establish an objectively justified reason for the imposition of the provision that only full-time staff can apply for the job. From the facts, it would appear that the authority feels that the job can only be adequately performed full-time. This is indicated by the refusal to consider job sharing.

Despite *Holmes*, above, this may be justifiable in relation to certain types of job. In *Clymo v Wandsworth London Borough Council* (1989), the EAT held that the refusal of an employer to allow a woman to job share a managerial post was not discriminatory, in that full-time working was an inherent characteristic of the job rather than a condition or requirement. If such an argument can be validly raised in respect of a supervisor's job, then the requirement that the job be performed full-time will not be discriminatory. This, however, is not the only argument put forward by Northbury. The authority is refusing part-timers the opportunity to apply for the post, whether such workers are prepared to work full-time or not. What the authority appears to have done is to make an assumption that because Deirdre works part-time at present, due to her childcare responsibilities, she cannot work full-time. Northbury is therefore making assumptions based on Deirdre's sex. Such assumptions are discriminatory (*Horsey v Dyfed County Council* (1982)) and therefore the provision that the applicants must work full-time at the time of their application is not justifiable.

The final hurdle for Deirdre is to show that she has been put at a disadvantage. Under the old law a woman had to show she had suffered a detriment. Detriment was not defined by the SDA, but Lord Brandon, in *MOD v Jeremiah* (1980), said that it meant no more than 'putting under a disadvantage'. In this case, Deirdre has suffered a disadvantage when compared to men because she cannot apply for a promotion due to the provision or criterion imposed by the authority. She is unable to apply for the supervisor's job because of the provision that the job must be worked full-time and not job shared. Although there is no longer the additional hurdle that she has suffered a detriment because she cannot comply with the provision of full-time working, in this particular case, that is the reason why she has been put at a disadvantage. As such, under the old law, Deirdre would be likely to succeed in an indirect discrimination claim. As such Deirdre will have made out her *prima facie* case and the tribunal must uphold the complaint unless the employer can show sex is not the reason for the provision.

Harvinder has been dismissed ostensibly because his turban and long hair mean that he cannot wear the surgical cap when attending post-mortems. Harvinder, however, may be able to argue that the real reason for his dismissal is that he taped the warnings he received and therefore he has been the subject of victimisation. If we look at the reason given by Northbury first, it would appear that the authority is imposing a provision that surgical caps should be worn during post-mortems.

The Race Relations Act 1976 (Amendment) Regulations 2003 created the same burden of proof as the SDA. This means that should Harvinder establish a prima facie case of race discrimination, the burden will shift to Northbury to put forward another reason for his treatment. In addition, the 2003 Regulations introduced a new definition of indirect discrimination. By s1(1)(b) of the RRA 1976, indirect discrimination occurs when: the employer applies a provision, criterion or practice which he applies or would apply equally to a person not of the same race or national or ethnic origins as Harvinder; the provision, criterion or practice puts or would put persons of the same race or national or ethnic origins as Harvinder at a particular disadvantage when compared with other persons; the employer cannot show the provision, criterion or practice to be a proportionate means of achieving a legitimate aim and the provision, criterion or practice puts Harvinder at a disadvantage.

Harvinder can argue that a provision, criterion or practice is being applied, in that it is necessary for his job as a mortuary attendant that he wears a protective surgical cap when attending post-mortems. The House of Lords in *Mandla v Dowell Lee* (1983), decided that Sikhs were a race within the meaning of the Act. The provision that those attending post-mortems must wear surgical caps is likely to put Sikhs at a particular disadvantage when compared to other races who do not wear turbans. It may also be possible for Harvinder to argue that he is also suffering indirect discrimination under the Employment Equality (Religion or Belief) Regulations 2003. The definition of indirect discrimination is virtually identical to that under the RRA 1976. Jurisprudence under the European Covention on Human Rights, however, interpreting Art 9 of the Convention and to which employment tribunals must have regard under the HRA 1998, suggests that if an employee knows of employer requirements before taking a post, the Article will not uphold their rights (for example, to dress in a particular way due to religious beliefs) as the employee knew the requirements and still took the job (*Kontinnen v Finland* (1996)). In Kontinnen, the Commission held that, given the conflict, the employee was free to leave his job and held that he was not dismissed because of his religious beliefs but because he refused to work the hours required by his employer. On the same basis, it is argued that Harvinder will have no claim for discrimination on the grounds of religion as he freely took the job knowing the dress requirements.

If Harvinder is successful in showing indirect race discrimination, the authority may have a defence if it can show that such a provision is a proportionate means of achieving legitimate hygiene aims and that alternatives will not work (*Singh v Rowntree Mackintosh Ltd* (1979)). This will require the tribunal to balance the aims of the employer with the rights of Harvinder. In *Saint Matthias Church of England School v Crizzle* (1993), a tribunal held that the needs of the Church of England School to have a headmaster who was a communicant outweighed the discriminatory impact on the complainant who was Asian and a Christian but a non-communicant.

Harvinder may have an alternative claim of victimisation under s 2 of the RRA 1976. This occurs when a person has been treated less favourably because he or she has brought proceedings under the Act, has given evidence in such proceedings, done anything under or by reference to the Act or has alleged that the discriminator has contravened the Act, unless that allegation is false and made in bad faith. The Court of Appeal, in *Cornelius v University College, Swansea* (1987), has said that it is the conduct listed above which is the basis of a victimisation claim and not the complainant's race. Harvinder taped his interviews with personnel and once this was discovered he was dismissed. To show that he was the subject of victimisation, he must show that the reason for his dismissal was that he taped the interviews to use in evidence in a race discrimination claim and that it was because of the potential use of the tapes that his dismissal occurred – in other words, that a person who taped such interviews for another purpose would not have been dismissed.

In the leading case of *Aziz v Trinity Street Taxis* (1988), a person was dismissed for secretly recording conversations he intended to use in discrimination proceedings. The employer argued that the reason for his dismissal was the fact that he had taped the conversations and not because of their eventual use. Given that the employer argued that anyone who had made such tapes would have been dismissed, the Court of Appeal held that there was no victimisation. Given Aziz, Harvinder would have to prove that the reason for his dismissal was, by s 2(1)(c), the fact that he was going to use the tapes in discrimination proceedings. This means that he must show that it was the discovery of the tapes that led to his dismissal, not the problem with the surgical cap, and that it was because of the eventual use of the tapes and not the fact that the tapes were made. On the facts, this may be difficult, given the number of warnings he has received in relation to his head wear during post-mortems. It appears, therefore, that this is the true reason for his dismissal and that the authority may have the defence of justification to defeat an indirect discrimination claim.

Notes

Question 17

Annie and Bet work for Mike's Fashions Ltd, a shop selling factory seconds. Bet feels aggrieved because she wishes to wear trousers to work as the shop gets very cold in the winter. Mike refuses to let her do this, saying that skirts are more feminine and look smarter. Bet feels that she can look smart in trousers, particularly as the male assistants wear jumpers under their suits in cold weather, which Mike does not prevent, despite the fact that he has said how untidy it looks.

Annie has recently been dismissed by Mike. The reason for her dismissal was her refusal to obey an order not to serve customers from a particular area in the town where the shop is situated. The inhabitants of this area are predominantly Asian. Mike argues that the reason for his order is that the majority of customers from the area are bad payers. Annie feels that there is no evidence to support Mike's contentions.

Ravinder has just been refused a job by Mike. She was concerned when she was asked questions at the interview such as 'Can you handle British money?' and 'Can you use a telephone?'. She has since learned from a friend that a white applicant was given the job and that, given that some of the suppliers are racist, Mike had probably done her a favour by not appointing her.

Advise Bet, Annie and Ravinder.

Answer plan

This is another question which mixes sex and race discrimination. In all the cases, the type of potential discrimination which has occurred is direct discrimination and students should therefore be aware that the defence of justification has no application.

Issues which need to be considered are:

- the definition of direct discrimination in s 1(1)(a) of the SDA 1975 and s 1(1)(a) of the RRA 1976;
- the meaning of racial grounds – in particular, *Showboat Entertainment Centre v Owens* (1984);
- the comparator in s 5(3) of the SDA 1975;
- the specific acts of discrimination in s 6 of the SDA 1975 and s 4 of the RRA 1976;
- the relevance of motive.

Answer

All the parties in the problem have potential discrimination claims against Mike's Fashions Ltd. In all the cases, the allegations will be of direct discrimination which, if proved, will mean that the employer will have no defence. There seems no argument on the facts that a genuine occupational qualification (GOQ) exists in any of the situations.

Bet is aggrieved by Mike's refusal to let her wear trousers. For a direct discrimination claim, it is necessary to show that the complainant was treated less favourably than a man, whose circumstances are the same or not materially different, and that the reason for her less favourable treatment was her sex or marital status. In order to establish her claim, Bet must show that she was discriminated against in that she suffered a detriment within the meaning of s 6(2)(b).

The meaning of 'less favourable treatment' and 'detriment' was discussed by the Court of Appeal in *Peake v Automative Products Ltd* (1978) in which it was decided that allowing women to leave five minutes earlier than men was not discriminatory on the de minimis principle. The EAT in *Schmidt v Austicks Bookshop Ltd* (1977) held that restrictions on clothing, in that women had to wear overalls and could not wear trousers, were not discriminatory, partly because the employer applied rules to all employees in that men were not allowed to wear T-shirts, and partly because details of the rules on dress had to take into account the differences between the sexes and the Act did not prevent those differences being taken into account. In Bet's case, it would appear that some dress code is in force for the male assistants as the facts say that they wear suits, albeit that they now wear jumpers under their suits, a practice Mike does not like but does not prevent. However, in *Department for Work and Pensions v Thompson* (2004), the EAT held that, in the context of a requirement for staff to dress in a professional and businesslike way, if that could be achieved by allowing some flexibility, the fact that one sex was given that flexibility and the other sex was not could lead to discrimination. Thus, if Bet feels that the men have some flexibility in the dress code which is not afforded to females, she may have a claim of direct discrimination.

The problem in Bet's situation lies with the meaning of detriment and the de minimis principle. Bet has been prevented from wearing trousers. If the men are not subject to dress codes, it could be argued that she has been treated differently, but has she been treated less favourably and suffered a detriment within s 6(2)(b)? In Jeremiah, Lord Brandon described detriment as meaning putting under a disadvantage, but in Schmidt, Phillips J held that there was no detriment to the complainant since detriment must have something serious or important about it. Furthermore, in *De Sousa v Automobile Association* (1986), a racist comment by a manager was held not to constitute discrimination because it was difficult to find the disadvantage to the employee who had merely suffered distress. Even if Bet is successful in showing a detriment, she may be caught by the de minimis principle. Peake survived the later case of *MOD v Jeremiah* (1980) on de minimis and there is uncertainty as to the scope of the defence and the extent to which technical discrimination may be ignored. In Jeremiah, Brightman LJ suggested that differentiation per se is not necessarily discrimination, although in *Birmingham City Council v EOC* (1989), the House of Lords held that deprivation of choice (as is happening in Bet's case) was sufficient to constitute less favourable treatment.

A Northern Ireland High Court case may help Bet. In *McConomy v Croft Inns Ltd* (1992), it was held to be discrimination to bar a man from a pub for wearing earrings. While the court accepted that rules of decency can dictate dress codes, it went on to say that in today's conditions, it was not possible to say that circumstances were different between men and women as regards the wearing of jewellery and other personal items. Bet may be able to argue that this case shows that, in today's society, forbidding women from wearing trousers denies them a choice (*Birmingham City Council v EOC* (1989) and

Department for Work and Pensions v Thompson (2004)) and therefore subjects them to a detriment which has been caused because of their sex.

Annie has been dismissed. The question which must be asked is what is the reason for her dismissal? Mike argues that it was her refusal to obey an order, but she refused because she feels that the order was racist. It may be possible for Annie to argue that she has been the victim of direct racial discrimination. In order to do this, Annie must show that she has been treated less favourably on racial grounds, the less favourable treatment being her dismissal (s 4(2)(c)).

In *Showboat Entertainments Centre v Owens* (1984), the Court of Appeal, confirming the earlier decision of *Zarczynska v Levy* (1979), decided that the basis for discrimination under the RRA 1976 is wider than that under the SDA 1975. In that case, the applicant, a white man, was dismissed as the manager of an amusement centre when he refused to obey an order to exclude young blacks. It was held that s 1(1)(a) covered all cases where an employee was treated less favourably on racial grounds even if the race in question was that of another person. As such, Annie can argue that the reason for her dismissal was racial grounds and thus sue for racial discrimination. It is irrelevant that Mike thinks that the inhabitants are bad payers, even if there were evidence to support this belief (which, on the facts, does not appear to be the case). In a direct discrimination claim, motive and intention are irrelevant.

In *R v CRE ex p Westminster City Council* (1985), the withdrawal of a job offer to a black applicant was held to be discrimination despite the fact that the reason had been that the employer feared industrial unrest if the appointment went ahead. In *James v Eastleigh Borough Council* (1990), the council argued that it did not intend to discriminate against Mr James. The Court of Appeal had upheld this argument, concluding that there was no discrimination because the council's intentions had been to benefit pensioners and not discriminate against men. This reasoning was overruled by the House of Lords which reaffirmed that the test in direct discrimination was an objective one and required a tribunal to ask the question 'would the complainant have received the same treatment but for his sex (race)?'. If the answer is 'no', discrimination has occurred and the intention and motive is irrelevant.

Ravinder has not been offered employment. While the facts do not expressly say so, there is an inference that the reason is her race, given the comment by her friend. Ravinder has to prove facts from which inferences can be drawn that she has been treated less favourably on racial grounds. Once a tribunal is satisfied that she has established a prima facie case, the burden shifts to the employer to show that the less favourable treatment was not on racial grounds (*University of Huddersfield v Wolff* (2004)). Unreasonable treatment of itself is not sufficient, even if there is nothing else to explain it (*Bahl v Law Society* (2004)). Likewise, a tribunal must find that subjectively racial considerations were in the mind of the discriminator (*Bahl v Law Society*). Given the facts in the problem, it is suggested that Ravinder could establish a prima facie case that her treatment was on racial grounds and that such considerations were in the mind of Mike's Fashions Ltd.

Ravinder may be able to argue less favourable treatment under two sub-sections of the RRA 1976. It would appear that she was asked some particularly offensive questions when she was interviewed. By s 4(1)(a), discrimination can occur in the arrangements for determining who shall be employed. By comparison with cases in the field of sex discrimination, such as *Brennan v Dewhurst Ltd* (1984), it would be possible for Ravinder to argue that the less favourable treatment was the questions asked at the interview if the same questions were not asked of white applicants. In addition, Ravinder was not offered the job. Section 4(1)(c) specifies less favourable treatment in refusing or deliberately omitting to offer employment on racial grounds.

Given that it is likely that Ravinder has established a *prima facie* case, Mike must show that Ravinder's race was not a factor in his decision. In *Owen and Briggs v James* (1982), it was held that the applicant had suffered race discrimination when she was not offered a job. The employer's argument, that there could only be discrimination if race was the only factor involved, was rejected by the Court of Appeal. The fact that race is an important factor is sufficient. In *Nagarajan v London Regional Transport* (1999), it was held that the employer had to show on the balance of probabilities that the treament was not significantly influenced by racial considerations.

The facts suggest that race was a factor Mike took into account when he refused Ravinder a job, particularly since her friend has told her that some of the suppliers are racist. Furthermore, even if Mike did not appoint her because he was worried for her, this is irrelevant. It has already be seen above that motive and intention are irrelevant in a direct discrimination claim (*James v Eastleigh Borough Council* (1990)). In *Grieg v Community Industries* (1979), the employer dismissed a girl when the only other female left. The employer's argument that he had dismissed her for her own good was rejected. Once the discriminatory act has occurred, the reason behind the act is irrelevant. As such, should Ravinder show that the reason she was not offered the job was her race, she will have a claim against Mike's Fashions Ltd.

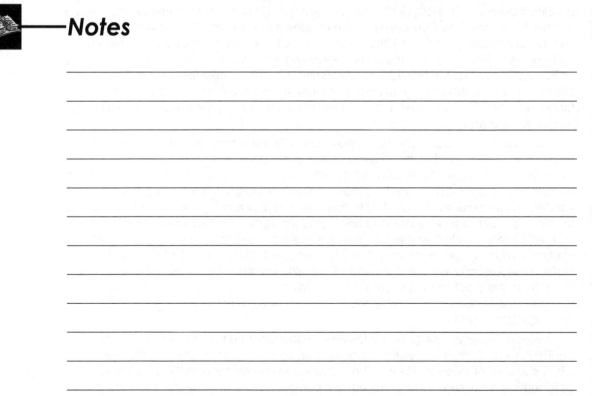

Notes

_____

_____

_____

_____

_____

_____

_____

_____

_____

_____

_____

Question 18

Until the Employment Equality (Sex Discriminations) Regulations 2005, changes made to the Sex Discrimination Act, the Race Relations Act and the Disability Discrimination Act since 2001, in addition to the introduction of protection against discrimination on the grounds of religious belief or sexual orientation, means that there is greater protection against discrimination on some grounds than others.

Critically evaluate this statement.

Answer Plan

This question is asking the student to look at the changes made to the major pieces of anti-discriminatory legislation and to compare and contrast them. It also requires the student to evaluate whether there is greater protection against discrimination on some grounds compared to others; therefore, merely listing the changes is not sufficient to answer the question.

The issues to be discussed here are:

- the main changes to the SDA 1975 in 2001;
- the changes made to the RRA 1976 in 2003;
- the rights under the Employment Equality (Religion or Belief) Regulations 2003;
- the rights under the Employment Equality (Sexual Orientation) Regulations 2003;
- changes made to the DDA 1995 in October 2004;
- a comparison between the different rights.

Answer

While the first modern piece of anti-discriminatory legislation preventing discrimination in employment was the Equal Pay Act (EPA) 1970, the first statute to cover both contractual and non-contractual discrimination in employment was the SDA 1975. Not only did this Act provide protection during employment, it also provided protection against discrimination in selection procedures. Furthermore, it provided protection against discrimination not just on the grounds of sex but also on the grounds of marital status. While amendments were made by the Sex Discrimination (Amendment) Act 1986 to ensure compliance with the Equal Treatment Directive 1976 (76/207/EEC), the fundamental tenets of the Act, as enacted in 1975, remained the same until 2001. Thus, the concepts of direct discrimination, indirect discrimination and victimisation were unaltered until 2001. The only major amendment until then was the introduction of protection against discrimination on the grounds of gender reassignment in 1999. This, however, did not alter the basic concepts of the Act.

The RRA 1976 used the SDA as its model and thus embodied the same concepts of direct and indirect discrimination and victimisation. Throughout, the two pieces of legislation were almost identical in their wording, the only differences being that the SDA protected against discrimination on the grounds of sex or marital status, the RRA providing protection against discrimination on the grounds of colour, race, nationality or ethnic or national origins. The only major difference between the two Acts was that protection under the RRA arises where the employer on racial grounds treats a person less favourably, whereas under the SDA protection is afforded where 'on the grounds of her sex' an employer treats a person less favourably. This difference still exists and its significance is seen in cases such as *Showboat Entertainment Centre v Owens* (1984), where an employee who was dismissed for refusing to obey a racist order was held to have been racially discriminated against as the RRA did not require the actions of the employer to have anything to do with the race of the complainant, only to have been on racial grounds. Thus, treating a person less favourably because they associate with people of a different race would also be actionable. A complainant dismissed for refusing to obey a sexist order would have an action only if he or she could also show the action was based on his or her sex.

While this difference still existed, until the changes which began in 2001, only two other significant differences existed. The first was as a result of statutory interpretation in the case of *Coote v Granada Hospitality Ltd* (1998). In the earlier case of *Adekeye v Post Office* (1997), it was held *inter alia* that Ms Adekeye had no race discrimination claim under the RRA in respect of actions taken post-termination, as the legislation only protected those who were employees or those under a contract to personally perform services (s 78(1)). However, in *Coote*, after referral to the ECJ, the EAT held that an ex-employee could bring a claim of post-termination victimisation under the SDA. The reasoning behind this can be seen in the Court of Appeal decision in *Rhys-Harper v Relaxion Group plc* (2001), which applied *Adekeye* and distinguished *Coote*. The court said that Art 6 of the Equal Treatment Directive required national legislation to protect ex-employees from victimisation on the grounds of sex after the relationship had ended. As such, there was only protection for post-termination acts under the SDA and not the RRA and this itself was limited only to victimisation. The House of Lords (2003) increased the protection by saying that there was protection under all the legislation for post-termination acts of discrimination where the post-termination act has a substantive connection with the employment relationship. The second difference was in respect of remedies. Since 1996, it has been possible to claim damages in an indirect sex discrimination claim, but this is only the case in an indirect race discrimination claim where the discrimination is intentional. This remains the case even after statutory amendments.

So while some differences existed, on the whole the legislation gave much the same protection. Amendments to the legislation, which began in 2001, then saw a great divergence in the Acts.

The first amendments were made to the SDA by the Sex Discrimination (Indirect Discrimination and Burden of Proof) Regulations 2001, introduced to implement the Burden of Proof Directive (97/80/EC). As the title suggests, these regulations amended the burden of proof in sex discrimination claims and gave a new definition of indirect discrimination, thus creating on the face of them two major differences between the RRA and the SDA. In respect of the burden of proof, the Regulations inserted s 63A into the SDA; this provides that where a complainant proves facts from which the tribunal could conclude, in the absence of an adequate explanation from the respondent, that the respondent has committed an act of discrimination, the tribunal shall uphold the complaint unless the respondent proves that the actions were not based on the complainant's sex. While this appeared to create a difference in the burden of proof between a sex discrimination and a race discrimination claim, in practice the differences were not as great as they appeared. In the decision of *King v Great Britain China Centre* (1991), Neil LJ said that:

> ... a difference in treatment and a difference in race will often point to the possibility of discrimination. In such circumstances, the tribunal should look to the employer for an explanation, and if one is not forthcoming or is inadequate, it is legitimate to infer discrimination has occurred.

This was approved by the House of Lords in *Zafar v Glasgow City Council* (1998). While the amended SDA created a statutory duty on tribunals to shift the burden to the respondent if a *prima facie* case was established, and *King* only gave tribunals a discretion to do so, in reality the differences which existed until amendments made to the RRA in 2003 were probably not that great.

The major difference between the two pieces of legislation in 2001 was in the new definition of indirect discrimination in the amended SDA. The RRA still contained the old definition, which required the complainant to show that (a) the employer had imposed a condition or requirement; (b) the proportion of the complainant's racial group who could comply with the condition or requirement was considerably smaller that the comparative group; (c) the condition or requirement was not justified irrespective of race, and (d) it was to the complainant's detriment because he or she could not comply with the condition or requirement. This definition had caused a number of problems: in particular, the definition of 'condition or requirement' (*Perara v CSC* (1983), the definition of the comparative group (*Jones v University of Manchester* (1993)) and the definition of 'considerably smaller' (*Fulton v Strathclyde Regional Council* (1986), *London Underground v Edwards (No 2)* (1998) and *R v Secretary of State for Employment ex p Seymour-Smith and Perez* (1999)). By contrast, the definition in the SDA required the complainant to show that (a) the employer has applied a provision, criterion or practice; (b) the provision etc was to the detriment of a considerably larger proportion of women than men; (c) the application of the provision was not justified; and (d) the provision etc was to her detriment. While not appearing to diverge greatly, the words 'provision, criterion or practice' are considerably wider than the more restricted 'condition or requirement' and, arguably, by 2001 it was easier to show indirect discrimination under the SDA than the RRA.

Changes made to the RRA by the Race Relations Act 1976 (Amendment) Regulations 2003 were as a result of the Race Relations Directive 2000 (2000/43/EC). However, the Directive applies only to discrimination on the grounds of race or national or ethnic origin as opposed to the wider grounds of the RRA, which also include colour and nationality. As such, the regulations amend the RRA only with respect to those grounds in the Directive and not on the wider grounds, creating differential protection within the Act itself. The changes discussed below therefore apply only when the ground for the claim is race or ethnic or national origin. For claims based on colour or nationality, the unamended RRA still applies.

The first change introduced by the 2003 Regulations is a harmonisation of the burden of proof. While this is to be welcomed, as noted above, the amendments introduced in 2001 probably did not have as great an effect as first thought in that in practice the amendments to a large extent reflected judicial practice since *King v Great Britain China*

Centre. Other amendments to the RRA, however, show a large gap between protection afforded to victims of discrimination based on race or national or ethnic origin when compared to victims of sex discrimination or discrimination on the grounds of colour or nationality. The definition of indirect discrimination in the RRA reflects to a large extent the definition in the Directive. This, however, is distinctly different from the definition in the Burden of Proof Directive. Although the definition in both the SDA and the RRA talked about the employer applying a 'provision, criterion or practice', this was the only similarity. Compared with the definition in the SDA noted above, the RRA goes on to say 'the provision, criterion or practice puts those in the same racial group as the complainant at a particular disadvantage compared to others of another racial group; the employer cannot show the provision etc to be a proportionate means of achieving a legitimate aim and the provision etc puts the complainant at a particular disadvantage.'

The implications of the differences were clear. First, while there was still a need for a victim of sexual discrimination to have a comparative group and show differences in proportions, this was not the case under the RRA. Problems in identifying the right comparative group and establishing statistical evidence have already been noted, including the problems of interpretation of 'considerably larger'. None of these problems appeared to apply to the definition under the RRA. In addition, a complainant under the RRA merely had to show he or she was put at a particular disadvantage, whereas under the SDA there was still a requirement for the complainant to show a detriment. The defence available to an employer also looked very different. In reality, however, this was probably not be the case. The defence under the original definition had already been interpreted in line with the ECJ ruling in *Bilka-Kaufhaus GmbH v Weber von Hartz* (1987) on which the RRA defence is based; therefore, cases under the SDA and RRA are interpreted in the same way.

Other differences, however, were apparent. While both pieces of legislation specifically covered certain post-termination discrimination, the RRA contained a statutory definition of harassment which was not found in the SDA. By s 2A of the RRA, harassment occurs when there is unwanted conduct which has the purpose or effect of violating a person's dignity or creating an intimidating, hostile, degrading, humiliating or offensive environment. The Act further states that the perception of the complainant is particularly important. The differences here were also apparent. In addition to a specific definition of harassment, it appeared that the tribunals are required to take the subjective not objective view in a harassment claim and, further, there is no need for a comparator. Both of these points caused considerable case law in sexual harassment claims (*Stewart v Cleveland Guest Engineering* (1994); *British Telecommunications plc v Williams* (1997); *Driskel v Peninsula Business Services Ltd* (2000); *Pearce v Governing Body of Mayfield Secondary School* (2003).

The 2003 Regulations also partially repeal s 4(3) of the RRA which deals with genuine occupational qualifications (GOQs) and a new exception of genuine occupational requirement (GOR) is introduced. This allows an employer to recruit if it can be shown that, having regard to the nature of the employment or the context in which it is being carried out, being of a particular race or of a particular ethnic or national origin is a genuine and determining occupational requirement and it is proportionate for that requirement to be applied in that particular case. The existing GOQs apply where the claim is based on colour or nationality. It can be agued that the GOR exemption is much narrower than the GOQ exemption in the original RRA and SDA and thus affords greater protection for victims of certain types of race discrimination.

The amendments noted above could arguably be said to have given greater protection to victims of race discrimination where the basis of that discrimination is race or ethnic or national origins. The change in the burden of proof, the wider definition of indirect discrimination, the narrower exemption of GOR and the statutory definition of harassment all lead to this conclusion. As noted, however, the original wording of the RRA 1976 still applies to those discriminated against on the grounds of colour or nationality. As such, the burden is still on the complainant, the 1976 definition of indirect discrimination applies, there is no statutory definition of harassment and the GOQ exemption is wider.

In respect of sex discrimination claims, a different (and arguably more restricted) definition of indirect discrimination, no statutory definition of harassment and the wide exemption of GOQs again lead us to the conclusion that by 2003 the RRA offered more protection in a lot of cases than the SDA.

As the Commission for Racial Equality (CRE) said in *Which Way Equality* (2002), commenting on changes to the RRA:

> There will be two definitions of indirect discrimination; two definitions of harassment; two definitions of genuine occupational qualifications; two burdens of proof; and, effectively, two classes of equality.

If we add to this the differences between the SDA and RRA, it could be argued that by 2003 there were three different classes of equality, all of which offered less or more protection depending on the ground for discrimination.

The Employment Equality (Sex Discrimination) Regulations 2005 have now aligned the legislation and although there is no concept of a genuine occupational requirement in the SDA, the two Acts are once again virtually identical. The problem still remains, however, that the amended RRA is restricted in its application and thus it can still be said that protection against discrimination on the grounds of colour or nationality is still more limited than protection for discrimination on other grounds.

Notes ————————————————————

Question 19

Lyndsay works for ACME Engineering. She began work as an accounts secretary four months ago. Since the beginning, she has been the subject of unwelcome advances from Tom, the company accountant. These have consisted of unwanted remarks concerning the way she dresses. Yesterday evening, after working late, Tom put his arm around Lyndsay's waist and said, 'Come on love, it's obvious you're fair game.' Lyndsay was then subjected to a particularly humiliating assault.

On arriving at work the next morning, Lyndsay reported the assault to the works manager, who informed her that a one-off incident gave her no cause for complaint. He also said that should she decide to take the matter further, he would have no choice but to mention Lyndsay's liberal attitude to matters of a sexual nature.

Advise Lyndsay whether she may take any action against the company.

Answer plan

This question looks short but it is requiring students to discuss a number of different issues. In Lyndsay's case, there is the question of sexual harassment under the SDA 1975 and whether the time of the assault means that she has no claim. Her treatment by the works manager could also potentially be direct discrimination or victimisation and both need to be discussed, as does vicarious liability on the part of the employer.

Particular issues to be considered are therefore:

- the definition of direct discrimination in s 1(1)(a) of the SDA 1975 – in particular the 'but for' test in *James v Eastleigh Borough Council* (1990) and *Coyne v Home Office* (2000);

- the definition of 'subjecting to' in s 6(2)(b) of the SDA 1975 and, in particular, *Burton v De Vere Hotels* (1996) and its subsequent overruling by the House of Lords in *Pearce v Governing Body of Mayfield Secondary School* (2003)

- the new statutory definition of harassment and to aid interpretation a discussion of the old law – in particular, *Porcelli v Strathclyde Regional Council* (1985); *Snowball v Gardner Merchant* (1987); *Bracebridge Engineering Ltd v Darby* (1990); *Insitu Cleaning Co Ltd v Heads* (1995); *Stewart v Cleveland Guest Engineering Ltd* (1994); *Wileman v Minilec Engineering Ltd* (1988); *Reed and Bull Information Systems Ltd v Stedman* (1999); *British Telecommunications plc v Williams* (1997); *Driskel v Peninsula Business Services Ltd* (2000); *Pearce v Governing Body of Mayfield Secondary School* (2003);

- whether the action by the works manager was a detriment or victimisation under s 4 – in particular, *Aziz v Trinity Street Taxis* (1988) and *Nagarajan v London Regional Transport* (1999);

- whether the time of the assault is relevant – in particular, *Waters v Commissioner of Police of the Metropolis* (2000) and *Chief Constable of Lincolnshire v Stubbs* (1999);

- vicarious liability of the employer under s 41 of the SDA 1975 – in particular, *Jones v Tower Boot Ltd* (1997) and *Waters* and *Stubbs* (above);

- the burden of proof in s 63A.

Answer

Lyndsay may have a claim for direct sex disrimination. In order for her claim to be successful, she would have to show that she has been treated less favourably on the grounds of her sex (s 1(1)(a) of the SDA 1975). In addition, she will have a claim under the new harassment provisions in S4A SDA.

Prior to changes introduced by the Employment Equality (Sex Discrimination) Regulations 2005, in order to claim sexual harassment, a complainant argued direct discrimination and that she had suffered a detriment under s 6(2)(b) of the SDA. This often proved difficult. In the early days of sexual harassment claims, it was thought that the detriment had to be a contractual detriment, however *Porcelli v Strathclyde Regional Council* (1986) stated that sexual harassment *per se* constituted the detriment for the purposes of the Act. To aid interpretation the Equal Opportunities Commission produced a Code of Practice which defines Sexual Harassment as 'unwanted conduct of a sexual nature, or other conduct based on sex affecting the dignity of women and men at work' and although not binding, the Code was relied upon in cases such as *Wileman v Minilec Engineering Ltd* (1988) and *British Telecommunications plc v Williams* (1997). *Williams* also established that there was no need for a comparator in a sexual harassment claim but the House of Lords in *Pearce v Governing Body of Mayfield Secondary School* (2003) stated that this was the wrong approach and the fact that the conduct was gender specific did not prove that the reason for the conduct was sexed-based. This seemed to clarify a number of decisions, some of which stated that there was no need for a comparator (*Williams* above and *Institu Cleaning Co Ltd v Heads* (1995) and others which said the normal test in *James v Eastleigh Borough Council* (1990) applied (*Stewart v Cleveland Guest Engineering Ltd* (1994) and *Driskel v Peninsula Business Services Ltd* (2000)). In other words after *Pearce*, a complainant had to show that 'but for' her sex she would not have been subjected to the harassment thus requiring the need for a male comparator. The re-introduction of a male comparator in this area was seen as unfortunate by many academic writers. A further problem with the use of s 6(2)(b) in the area of sexual harassment was that the complainant had to show that she had been 'subjected to' a detriment. While the phrase was given a broad interpretation in *Burton v De Vere Hotels* (1996), this was overturned in the House of Lords decision in *Pearce*, thus causing more difficulties for complainants alleging sexual harassment.

In October 2005 the Employment Equality (Sex Discrimination) Regulations 2005 introduced a new s 4A into the SDA. The section provides that a person subjects a woman to harassment when:

(a) On the ground of her sex, he engages in unwanted conduct that has the purpose or effect–

(i) of violating her dignity, or

(ii) of creating an intimidating, hostile, degrading, humiliating or offensive environment for her,

(b) he engages in any form of unwanted verbal, non-verbal or physical conduct of a sexual nature that has the purpose or effect-

(i) of violating her dignity, or

(ii) of creating an intimidating, hostile, degrading, humiliating or offensive environment for her, or

(c) on the ground of her rejection of or submission to unwanted conduct of a kind mentioned in paragraph (a) or (b), he treats her less favourably than he would treat her had she not rejected, or submitted to, the conduct."

Section 4A(2) states that the conduct shall be regarded as harassment, if having regard to all the circumstances, including in particular the perception of the woman, it should reasonably be considered as having that effect.

There are a number of things to note about the new definition. First, it is clear that harassment does not have to be intentional as it is sufficient that the conduct has an effect on the complainant. Second, the definition talks about 'on the ground of her sex' which means it is still limited to the complainant's sex and not the wider 'on the grounds of' found in other legislation. Third, while the conduct will only be regarded as harassment if in all the circumstances it should reasonably be regarded as having that effect – that is there is an objective element. However, the tribunal is particularly directed to take into account the perception of the complainant. Fourth, if the complainant suffers an unpleasant atmosphere because she has rejected or accepted sexual overtures this can also constitute harassment.

How will the new definition benefit Lyndsay's claim? The question states that Lyndsay has been the subject of unwelcome advances from Tom therefore his conduct has been unwanted. He put his arm around Lyndsay's waist which was unwanted physical conduct of a sexual nature. He then subjected her to 'a particularly humiliating assault'. Such action would have the effect of violating her dignity at least and creating an intimidating, degrading and humiliating environment for her and appears to have done so in the problem as she has reported the incident to the work's manager. Although he told her he would have to mention her liberal attitude to matters of a sexual nature, should she take the matter further, this is irrelevant if Lyndsay feels that her dignity was violated etc. because of Tom's actions. As such it is likely that a tribunal will hold that Lyndsay has suffered sexual harassment.

When Lyndsay complains to the works manager, she is told that she has no claim. However, Lyndsay may therefore have two further potential claims in respect of the action by the works manager. She may be able to argue that the failure to do anything constituted a detriment (s 1(1)(a)) or that she has suffered victimisation.

In *Home Office v Coyne* (2000), a complaint of sexual harassment was not dealt with by a manager and Coyne argued that the failure to deal with the complaint caused her to suffer a detriment and was thus sex discrimination. The Court of Appeal held that Coyne had to show that, but for her sex, the complaint would have been investigated. There was no evidence to suggest that the Home Office would have dealt with a complaint by a man more favourably and thus Coyne had not shown that the failure to deal with her complaint was on the grounds of her sex. On this basis, if the works manager argues that he would have treated any complaint by ignoring it, whether from a man or a woman, Lyndsay will not be able to prove the lack of investigation constituted a detriment she suffered because of her sex.

However, Lyndsay may be able to argue that she has suffered victimisation under s 4 of the SDA 1975. Victimisation occurs when a person is treated less favourably because he or she has brought proceedings under the Act; has given evidence in such proceedings; has done anything by reference to the Act or has alleged that the discriminator has contravened the Act. *Aziz v Trinity Street Taxis* (1988) makes it clear that it is the doing of one of the acts in s 4 which is the basis of the claim and not the sex of the person. *Nagarajan v London Regional Transport* (1999) further establishes that the motive of the discriminator is irrelevant if the action was significantly influenced by her sex. Thus, if Lyndsay can show that the reason the works manager failed to do anything was because she was alleging sexual harassment, and if her complaint had been about, for example, her hours of work, it would have been investigated, she may be able to pursue a claim of victimisation.

Her claims are in relation to the actions of two employees. This raises the issue of the vicarious liability of the employer. Section 41 states that an employer shall be liable for the acts of its employees during the course of their employment unless the employer can show that it took all reasonable steps to prevent the unlawful acts being perpetrated. In the race discrimination case of *Jones v Tower Boot Ltd* (1997), a claim under the equivalent provision in the RRA 1976, it was originally argued that the phrase 'in the course of employment' should be interpreted in the same way as at common law – that is, the employee is doing an authorised act in an authorised way or an authorised act in an unauthorised way. On this interpretation, it was held that an employer was not liable for the severe racial harassment of an employee because such harassment would not be an authorised act or an unauthorised way of conducting an authorised act. This initial decision was severely criticised on the basis that the more serious the harassment, the less likely that the employer would be held liable. The Court of Appeal in *Jones* reversed the decision, stating that the course of employment had to be given its ordinary meaning, that is, the act was committed by the employee whilst at work.

While this is a much more sensible interpretation, the question which must be asked is where does this leave Lyndsay? While it appears that the sexual comments by Tom occur during working hours, the problem states that the assault took place after they had been working late and it is the assault which the works manager will not investigate. In *Waters v Commissioner of Police of the Metropolis* (1997), the Court of Appeal held that a female police officer who felt that she had been victimised because she had complained about a sexual assault committed by a fellow officer at a party outside of working hours had no claim for victimisation, because the original assault had not taken place during the course of employment. In other words, a victimisation claim could only be upheld if the employer was legally liable for the original act. While the employer was held to be liable in negligence by the House of Lords on appeal (2000), this restriction on 'course of employment' was seen as unfortunate. The decision was limited before the appeal by *Chief Constable of Lincolnshire v Stubbs* (1999), which held that an employer was liable under s 41 for sexual harassment suffered by a female at a work-related party held outside working hours because the party was pre-arranged and linked to the employer. On the basis of this, it can be argued that, as the assault on Lyndsay took place while she and Tom were working late on the employer's premises, the assault was committed during the course of Tom's employment and thus ACME is liable under s 41.

Notes

6 Equal Pay

Introduction

Equal pay is an area which often comes up on examination papers since, like discrimination in Chapter 5, it is an area where European law has had a great impact. To answer questions in this area, students need to understand the relationship between European law and national law and, in particular, the enforceability of European law in the national courts. It is necessary, therefore, to understand fully the applicability of Art 141 of the EC Treaty and the Equal Pay Directive (75/117/EEC) and recent decisions of the European Court of Justice (ECJ) affecting the interpretation of national law.

For questions in this area, general issues which the student needs to understand are:

- the different routes to equal pay under the Equal Pay Act (EPA) 1970;
- the two possible routes to equal pay under European law;
- who constitutes a valid male comparator;
- the different procedures to claim equal pay;
- how the tribunal decision is applied;
- the defence available to the employer on a like work or work rated equivalent claim;
- the defence available to an employer on an equal value claim.

Although this area can lend itself to essay type questions, it is more common to have problems and, thus, it is important that students understand the steps involved in an equal pay claim.

In particular, students should be familiar with:

- the implied equality clause in the contract;
- the operation of s 1(2) of the EPA 1970;
- the definition of a 'male comparator' in s 1(6);
- the definition of 'like work' in s 1(4) and 'work rated equivalent' in s 1(5);
- the importance of cases such as *Hayward v Cammell Laird Shipbuilders* (1988) and *Pickstone and Others v Freemans plc* (1988);
- the problems with the equal value route to equal pay;
- the defence of genuine material difference/factor;
- the difference between the EPA 1970 and a claim under Art 141 of the EC Treaty;
- recent ECJ decisions which have impacted on the interpretation of the EPA 1970.

Finally, given the impact of European law on this area, any answer will almost certainly discuss the Treaty Article, the Directive and ECJ decisions made thereunder. A detailed knowledge of this area is therefore essential to answer an examination question fully.

Checklist

Students should be familiar with the following areas:

- the operation of *Pickstone v Freemans plc* (1988) on the choice of the route to equal pay;
- the choice of comparator – particularly, *Ainsworth v Glass Tubes and Components* (1977), *McCarthys v Smith* (1980); *Scullard v Knowles* (1996); *Lawrence v Regent Office Care* (2002); *Allonby v Accrington and Rossendale College* (2004);
- the different components in a like work claim – particularly cases such as *Capper Pass Ltd v Lawton* (1977) and *Coomes (Holdings) Ltd v Shields* (1978);
- the operation of s 1(5) and the guidance given in *Eaton v Nuttall* (1977);
- the importance of *Hayward v Cammell Laird Shipbuilders* (1988) and *Murphy v Bord Telecom Eireann* (1988);
- the definition of a genuine material difference – in particular, *Clay Cross (Quarry Services) v Fletcher* (1979); *Rainey v Greater Glasgow Health Board Eastern District* (1987); *Jenkins v Kingsgate Clothing Productions Ltd* (1981); *Strathclyde Regional Council v Wallace* (1998);
- the genuine material factor defence in equal value claims and the effect of *Enderby v Frenchay Health Authority and Secretary of State for Health* (1994); *Ratcliffe v North Yorkshire County Council* (1995); *British Road Services v Loughran* (1997);
- actions under Art 141 (formerly 119) – in particular, *Defrenne v SABENA* (1976); *Garland v British Rail Engineering Ltd* (1982); *Rinner-Kühn v FWW Spezial Gebäudereiningung GmbH* (1989); *Barber v Guardian Royal Exchange Assurance Group* (1990); *Barry v Midland Bank plc* (1999);
- actions under the Directive – in particular, cases such as *Marshall v Southampton and South West Hampshire Area Health Authority* (1986); *Marshall (No 2)* (1991) and (1993); *Foster v British Gas plc* (1991);
- time limits – in particular, *Biggs v Somerset County Council* (1996); *Preston v Wolverhampton Health Care NHS Trust* (2001); *Margorrian v Eastern Health and Social Services Board* (1998);

————————— Question 20 —————————

Dot, Lou and Pauline work for Midshire University.

Dot is a secretary. She feels that her work is of equal value to the computer technicians who work on a different site from her. She feels that her qualifications and experience are similar to those of the technicians. Dot works 9 am to 5 pm and has six weeks' holiday a year. The technicians work 12-hour shifts (because they need to be available when part-time classes run in the evenings) and get four weeks' holiday a year. Dot receives £5.50 per hour. The technicians receive £7 per hour.

Lou is a cleaner. She claims that her job is of equal value to that of the caretakers at the same site. There is no difference in the number of hours worked by the cleaners and the caretakers, but the caretakers receive £1 an hour more than the cleaners. All the cleaners are women apart from one man. All the caretakers are male.

Pauline is a cook. She feels that her job is of equal value to that of the University administrative assistants in terms of qualifications and experience. The administrative assistants earn £1,500 per annum more than Pauline, although Pauline gets free meals and free transport, provided by the University, to and from work. Midshire says that to increase Pauline's pay would involve restructuring the pay scales of all the catering staff both on the main campus and in the halls of residence and this would involve a great deal of extra administrative work.

Advise Dot, Lou and Pauline.

Answer plan

This question raises a variety of preliminary issues in an equal pay claim and also involves a detailed discussion of possible defences. All the parties are claiming that their jobs are of equal value and, given the special procedure in such claims, it is worth briefly describing the procedure in relation to all the parties, before discussing each individual case.

Particular issues to be considered are therefore:

- the procedure in an equal value claim;
- the definition of a male comparator in s 1(6) of the EPA 1970;
- what are common terms and conditions within the section and, in particular, *Leverton v Clywd County Council* (1989) and *O'Sullivan v Sainsbury plc* (1990);
- the exclusivity of the routes in s 1(2) and the effect of *Pickstone v Freemans plc* (1988);
- the meaning of pay within Art 141;
- the term by term approach in s 1(2) and the effect of *Hayward v Cammell Laird Shipbuilders* (1988);
- the defence in s 1(3) and, in particular, *Clay Cross (Quarry Services) v Fletcher* (1979), *Rainey v Greater Glasgow Health Board Eastern District* (1987); *Strathclyde Regional Council v Wallace* (1998).

Answer

All the parties in the problem wish to claim equal pay with their male colleagues. In all cases, the parties are arguing that their jobs are of equal value to those of the men. The equal value route was introduced into the EPA 1970 by the Equal Pay (Amendment) Regulations 1983 after the case of *Commission of the European Communities v United*

Kingdom (1982), when the ECJ held that the original Act did not satisfy the principle of equal pay for work of equal value contained in the Equal Pay Directive. Prior to the change in the legislation, the only two ways in which a woman could claim equal pay was by showing that she was on 'like work', that is, work which was the same or broadly similar to that of her male comparator (s 1(4)), or that she was on 'work rated equivalent' to that of her male comparator (s 1(5)). While the second route appeared to satisfy the purpose of the Directive, in reality, a woman can only use s 1(5) if her employer has conducted a job evaluation scheme (JES) and there is no statutory requirement that employers do so. This meant that until 1984, when the Regulations came into force, in the vast majority of cases, a woman could only claim equal pay if she was on the same or similar work. The 1983 Regulations sought to remedy this defect and created a third route to equal pay, that of equal value, now contained in the amended s 1(2) of the 1970 Act.

The Regulations introduced a new procedure, contained in s 2A of the Act, and a new defence for equal value claims, and all three parties in the problem will have to use this procedure. Briefly, after conciliation, the tribunal will decide if there are grounds for an equal value claim. If there are not, it will dismiss the claim and must do so if a JES has given the complainant's job a different value, unless the JES is discriminatory (*Neil v Ford Motor Co* (1984)). If the tribunal thinks that there are grounds for the claim, the employer must raise his defence. If the defence is upheld, the claim will be dismissed. If the defence is rejected or not raised, the tribunal may commission an independent expert who will assess both the complainant's job and that of her male comparator and report back to the tribunal. The tribunal will then make a finding based on the report, although it is not conclusive or binding on the tribunal (*Tennants Textile Colours Ltd v Todd* (1989)). In the past, a major criticism of the procedure was the length of time the procedure entailed. Changes introduced by the Equal Pay Act 1970 (Amendment) Regulations 2004 now reduce considerably the length of time a claim will take. If the tribunal does not appoint an expert, it will make a decision as to whether the work is of equal value. The changes envisage in this situation that a claim should take 25 weeks. Where an expert is appointed, the claim should take 37 weeks. Also, until recently, where the complainant was successful in an equal pay claim, the tribunal could only award back pay for two years (s 2(5)). Decisions such as *Levez v TH Jennings (Harlow Pools) Ltd* (1999) (ECJ) and the ECJ and House of Lords decisions in *Preston v Wolverhampton Health Care NHS Trust* (2000) (ECJ) and (2001) (HL) questioned the compatibility of s 2(5) with European law. As such, the Equal Pay Act 1970 (Amendment) Regulations 2003 amend s 2(5) allowing back pay to be claimed for up to six years before the institution of proceedings (s 2ZB(3)).

In each case, the woman must find a male comparator to start her equal pay claim. The definition of the male comparator is contained in s 1(6). Such a comparator is a man employed by her employer or an associated employer of her employer, and employed at the same establishment, or at a different establishment in Great Britain where common terms and conditions are observed for that class of employee. It is the responsibility of Dot, Lou and Pauline to find their own comparator and not the responsibility of the tribunal (*Ainsworth v Glass Tubes and Components* (1977)).

We will turn first to Dot's situation. She wishes to claim equal pay with the computer technicians and therefore it is necessary to see if one of the technicians will fall within the definition of male comparator in s 1(6). Without doubt, the technicians are employed by her employer, but they work at a different site from her and therefore at a different establishment. This means that she must show that common terms and conditions of employment are observed. In *Leverton v Clywd County Council* (1989), a nursery nurse employed by the county council compared herself to higher paid clerical workers at other establishments, also employed by the council. She worked 32.5 hours a week and had 70 days' holiday a year. Her comparator worked a 37 hour week and had about 20 days holiday a year. All the council employees were employed on terms derived from a collective agreement known as the 'purple book'. Both the EAT and the Court of Appeal held that she had no valid comparator because two important terms, hours and holidays, were fundamentally different. The House of Lords, however, took a wider view of common terms and conditions. Lord Bridge held that the test in s 1(6) did not mean a comparison of the terms of the contract of the woman with those of the comparator, but to see if there are general terms which apply across the establishments operated by the employer, covering a wide range of employees, but where there will be variations among individuals. His Lordship felt that a collective agreement applying to all employees was the paradigm of common terms and conditions contemplated by the section.

We have no evidence in Dot's case that the terms and conditions of non-academic staff have been negotiated by a collective agreement. If there is such an agreement, and if it applies across all the establishments and is not just applicable to the site where Dot works, by *Leverton*, she has a valid comparator and, given that it does not appear that the University has a defence in her case, the tribunal could appoint an independent expert to assess the two jobs. On the other hand, if there is no such agreement, then it would appear that the tribunal will be required to analyse the individual terms to discover a broad similarity. In contrast to the earlier decisions in *Leverton*, in *O'Sullivan v Sainsbury plc* (1990), it was held that there were common terms when holiday, sick provisions and maternity provisions were common. Given the vast difference in hours and holidays in Dot's case, in the absence of a collective agreement covering herself and the technicians at the other site, it is unlikely that she has a valid comparator within s 1(6) and her claim will therefore fail.

Lou is a cleaner and claims that her work is of equal value to that of caretakers. There is no mention that there are no caretakers working at the same establishment as Lou; therefore, the question of common terms and conditions does not arise. The route of equal value is found in s 1(2)(c) of the Act. The section starts with the words 'where a woman is employed on work which, not being work in relation to which para (a) or (b) above applies'. In other words, an equal value claim can be pursued if the work in question is not like work (s 1(2)(a)) or work rated equivalent (s 1(2)(b)). The interpretation of s 1(2)(c) was the question for the courts in *Pickstone v Freemans plc* (1988). In this case, the applicant sought equal value with a comparator doing a different job, but there was a man doing the same job as her. Until the case reached the House of Lords, it was successfully argued that the interpretation of s 1(2)(c) meant that if a man was doing like work or work rated equivalent, the applicant could not bring an equal value claim using another male comparator and that the equal value route existed only if no like work or work rated equivalent route was available (although the Court of Appeal upheld the applicant's claim on the basis of Art 141). Thus, because Mrs Pickstone had a man doing like work, she was unable to compare herself to another man doing totally different work on an equal value claim. The House of Lords held that this was a misinterpretation of s 1(2)(c). On true construction of the Act, the starting point was for the applicant to choose her male comparator. It was after this that s 1(2) applied and if her chosen comparator was doing like work, her route lay under s 1(2)(a), and if he was doing work rated equivalent, her route was under s 1(2)(b). If neither of those applied, she could claim equal value. In this case, Mrs Pickstone had chosen a comparator who was doing a totally different job from her and where no JES existed; thus, she could pursue an equal value claim. To construe the section any other way would mean that the employer could place a man doing the same work as women and defeat any possible equal pay claims. This would frustrate the purpose of the Act. Following this decision, it is irrelevant in Lou's case that one man is doing like work to her. If she chooses a caretaker as her male comparator, given that the work is different and there is no JES, she can claim that her work is of equal value and the procedure described above will start. It is her choice of comparator which determines her route to equal pay and not the route which determines the comparator.

Pauline is also arguing that her work is of equal value to a man doing another type of job. Again, if the comparator falls within the definition in s 1(6), Pauline is not prevented from pursuing her claim if there are male cooks (*Pickstone*). The University, however, may try to argue on two points. First, although the administrative assistants earn more money than Pauline, she gets non-cash benefits in terms of free meals and transport. How far can these non-cash benefits be taken into account when assessing the pay differential? Art 141 describes pay as 'the ordinary, basic or minimum wage or salary and any other consideration, whether in cash or in kind, which the worker receives, directly or indirectly, in respect of his employment from his employer'. In *Hayward v Cammell Laird Shipbuilders* (1988), the applicant claimed that her work was of equal value to her male comparators. She, however, received non-cash benefits which they did not and the employer argued that, by reference to the definition of pay in Art 141, the court was obliged to look at the pay package as a whole and put a cash value on the non-cash benefits. The House of Lords disagreed, saying that s 1(2) stated that if a woman showed that she was entitled to equal pay, the term in the woman's contract which was less favourable than that of the man should become as favourable, and any beneficial term in his contract, not contained in the woman's, should be included in her contract. In other words, the court should not do a whole pay package approach, but a term by term comparison. Thus, the fact that Pauline receives extra non-cash benefits does not prevent her cash pay being equalised to that of the administrative assistants.

The University has attempted to raise a defence, however. In relation to an equal value claim, the employer has a defence if he can show that the difference in pay is due to a genuine material factor which is not the difference of sex and which may be a material difference between her case and his (s 1(3)(b)). In relation to a like work or work rated equivalent claim, the factor must be a genuine material difference. This means that all the factors which have been held to be material differences in like work or work rated equivalent claims will also be defences to an equal value claim, but that the defence is wider in an equal value claim and factors which are not material differences will be included.

Originally, market forces could not be raised as a genuine material difference (*Clay Cross (Quarry Services) v Fletcher* (1979)). However, there was a major revision of the defence in *Rainey v Greater Glasgow Health Board Eastern District* (1987), where the House of Lords held that the restriction of the defence in *Fletcher* was unfortunate and that the defence could include objectively justified grounds which were connected with economic factors affecting the efficient carrying on of the employer's business. In *Rainey*, therefore, there were objective reasons for putting new male entrants on a higher rate (because of the need to expand the service) and objectively justified administrative reasons for not increasing the pay of one group of NHS employees whose pay was determined by the Whitley Council. Thus, if the University can show an objectively justified reason for the difference in pay, the defence will be made out. In *Enderby v Frenchay Health Authority and Secretary of State for Health* (1994), the ECJ ruled that different bargaining structures *per se* were not objectively justified factors allowing a difference in pay where the disadvantaged group is almost exclusively women. Therefore, if there are different pay bargaining structures within the University, this in itself is not a defence if the different structures predominantly disadvantage women. Whether the court would accept the argument raised by the University about the extra administrative work is debatable. In *Rainey*, a shortage of prosthetists led to the health authority bringing in private practitioners to meet demand.

In addition, if the applicant had been successful, this would have created an anomaly for one group of NHS workers on the Whitley Council grades, an anomaly which would have been permanent. The University is not arguing about the need to attract persons into the administrative assistants jobs, but is merely arguing that to restructure the pay of the catering staff would involve a lot of work. As such, it is unlikely that there is an objectively justified reason for the difference in pay which affects the efficient carrying on of the University and the defence will fail.

Notes

Question 21

Although the coverage of the legislative provisions relating to equal pay for women increased with the introduction of the route of equal value, the impact of the law on wage levels of female workers was minimal due to inherent obstacles which existed within the Act. Recent amendments to the Equal Pay Act will do little to change things.

Consider the validity of the above statement.

Answer plan

This question is asking for a discussion of the procedures involved in an equal value claim and the defences available in s 1(3) of the EPA 1970. It is also asking the student to come to a conclusion after discussing all the points. It is important to note this. The question is asking for a judgment as to the effect on wage levels of women. This means that if the student has no proof (for example, current statistics) to show the case one way or the other, then the question cannot be answered fully.

Particular issues to be considered are:

- the procedures in an equal value claim in s 2A of the Act;
- criticisms of the procedure;
- whether changes to the procedure meet the criticisms;
- the defences in s 1(3);
- the limits on the defence in *Clay Cross (Quarry Services) v Fletcher* (1979);
- the widening of the defence in *Rainey v Greater Glasgow Health Board Eastern District* (1987);
- what constitutes a material difference;
- what constitutes an objectively justified reason under *Bilka-Kaufhaus GmbH v Weber von Hartz* (1987);
- the effect of *Enderby v Frenchay Health Authority and Secretary of State for Health* (1994);
- the impact of *Lawrence v Regent Office Care Ltd* (2002) and *Allonby v Accrington and Rossendale College* (2004);
- the consequences of *Evesham v North Hereford Health Authority* (2000).

Answer

In *Commission of the European Communities v United Kingdom* (1982), the ECJ ruled that the then EPA 1970 did not comply with the Equal Pay Directive as it did not allow a woman to claim equal pay for work of equal value. At the time, a woman who was not on like work could only claim equal pay if her employer had voluntarily undertaken a JES, and there was no legislative provision to compel an employer to conduct a JES if one was not in existence. As a result of the ruling, the government introduced the Equal Pay (Amendment) Regulations 1983 and introduced a third route to equal pay, that of equal value, by the addition of s 1(2)(c) into the Act, but at the same time introduced a separate and complex procedure for an equal value claim by the addition of s 2A. Smith and Wood (*Industrial Law*, 8th edn, 2003 London: LexisNexis Butterworths) have argued that the introduction of the route took tribunals away from matters which could be observed, such as whether the jobs were similar, into the realms of job evaluation. As a tribunal is inexperienced in this area, the procedure relies heavily on a report from an expert, although the tribunal does not have to appoint an expert and, if it does, it is not bound by the report (*Tennants Textile Colours Ltd v Todd* (1989)).

The procedure was altered in October 2004 by the Equal Pay Act 1970 (Amendment) Regulations 2004 and the Employment Tribunals (Constitution and Rules of Procedure)(Amendment) Regulations of the same year which insert a new Schedule 6 into the Employment Tribunals (Constitution and Rules of Procedure) Regulations 2004. The start of the procedure is conciliation by ACAS. If this is unsuccessful, then there is a stage 1 hearing to establish whether there is a potential claim. Prior to 2004, a tribunal could not appoint an independent expert if there were 'no reasonable grounds' for determining that the jobs were of equal value. This applied where a JES had given the jobs a different value unless the woman could show that the JES was discriminatory. Critcisms of the defence were that it led to tribunals striking out a lot of claims or, conversely, that it extended the time such claims took. As such, the defence has now been removed. If the employer has already undertaken a JES which has given different ratings to the jobs, by a new s 2A(2A)) this creates a presumption that the work is not of equal value, unless the tribunal has grounds for suspecting that the JES was discriminatory on the grounds of sex or is otherwise unsuitable to be relied upon. This amendment removes the burden on the applicant to show that the scheme is discriminatory. The Rules of Procedure set out standard orders for the stage 1 hearing. These are orders for the early exchange of factual information within stipulated time periods following the stage 1 hearing. For example, within 28 days of the stage 1 hearing the parties must provide each other with a written job description for the claimant and comparator and identify to each other in writing facts they consider relevant to the question. Within 56 days, the parties must present a joint statement to the tribunal, covering job descriptions and relevant facts and, at least 28 days before the hearing, the partles must submit a statement of facts on which they agree and facts on which they disagree, with reasons for the disagreement. If no independent expert is appointed, Rule 5(1)(c) says that a tribunal shall order, unless it considers it inappropriate to do so, the respondent to grant access to the claimant and her representative during a specified time period to enable the claimant to interview any comparator. If there is no independent expert appointed, once all of the above has been done (and the Schedule envisages 18 weeks), there is a full hearing. The total time period from presentation of the claim to hearing is envisaged to be 25 weeks. If an independent expert is appointed, a stage 2 hearing will take place. The aim of the stage 2 hearing is to resolve disputed facts to help the independent expert, who must prepare his report on the basis of agreed facts or facts determined by the tribunal. As with stage 1 hearings, there are standard orders laid down, including the date by which the expert must produce the report, by reference to the timetable in Schedule 6. The tribunal can remove the expert at any time and determine the case itself. The tribunal in this situation has the power to ask the expert for any documentation or make any other relevant request in order for it to make a decision. The independent expert's report is considered at the full hearing. The indicative timetable envisages 10 weeks between the stage 1 and 2 hearings, eight weeks for the expert report, four weeks for the parties to put written questions to the expert and eight weeks later the full hearing, making a total of 37 weeks.

Prior to the introduction of the new procedure, the average equal value case took approximately 20 months. In the ACAS Annual Report of 1992 and the Equal Opportunities Commission (EOC) Annual Report of 1991, there were severe criticisms of the length of time such cases were taking, suggesting that this deterred potential applicants and that this was responsible for the decline in the number of applications. In *Aldridge v British Telecommunications plc* (1990), the Employment Appeal Tribunal (EAT) stated that the procedures were in need of urgent review and the Justice Report on Employment Tribunals published in 1987 stated that, at the time, only 10 cases had completed the whole procedure in the first three years of its operation. The EOC published its own recommendations for reform and made representations to the government. As a result of these representations, the government introduced changes to the procedure in the Employment Tribunals (Constitution and Rules of Procedure) Regulations 1993, which came into effect in December of that year. These required that if an expert had been called upon to prepare a report, the expert had to give written notice of the date by which the report would be sent to the tribunal. This had be sent within 14 days of receiving the requirement to prepare the report. If the expert could not determine the exact date, he or she had to give reasons for the inability and give an estimated date. The tribunal could require progress reports from the expert and, if the tribunal felt that the original date for submission was longer than appropriate or the revised date created an unjustified delay, it could revoke the appointment of the expert and appoint a new one, after receiving representations from the parties. While these changes went some way to meet the criticisms raised in relation to the time it used to take for the expert to report, they fell a long way short of meeting all the criticisms levelled at the procedure. Changes introduced in 2004 are intended to alleviate the problems. However, it is suggested that this may not be the case. One of the problems with the old procedure was the length of time it took experts to produce a report. The EOC recommended in 1991 that experts should be full-time but this has never been adopted by the government. The old procedure envisaged the expert's report in six weeks but this proved to be impossible in reality, hence the changes introduced to allow the expert to give the tribunal a new date for receipt. The Government feels that with the introduction of a stage 2 hearing, the requirement on the respondent to give detailed information (including filling in an equal pay questionnaire) and the introduction of an indicative timetable should mean that the main deterrent to an equal value claimant – the time the claim takes – will be removed. Given that experts are still not full-time, it remains to be seen whether the changes introduced in 2004 will make equal value claims speedier. One change which may have a greater ipact in the future is that Rule 8(5) of the Rules of Procedure authorise the Presidents of employment tribunals to establish panels of chairpersons and members who are specialists in equal value claims. Such specialist panels should result in less reliance on independent experts and thus reduced time delays.

The changes also fail to take account of further criticisms. First, there is the cost of taking an action. An unofficial comment by a member of the EOC in 1991 put the cost of an equal value claim then at around £150,000. Given the lack of legal aid, this means that an applicant needs the support of either a trade union or the EOC to start a claim.

This is related to a further criticism, which applies to the EPA generally and not just equal value claims, which is that the tribunal is limited in the back pay it can award if the claim is successful (s 2(5)). While the Equal Pay Act 1970 (Amendment) Regulations 2003 increased this from two to six years, it still does not compare to claims under, for example, the Sex Discrimination Act (SDA) 1975 where compensation is unlimited. The cost of taking an equal value claim and the comparatively small sum which will be received in back pay still make such claims prohibitive.

A further criticism of the legislation is in relation to the defence available to the employer. The defence is found in s 1(3) of the Act and is, in relation to a like work or work rated equivalent claim, that there is a genuine material factor which is not the difference of sex and which is a material difference between the woman's case and that of the man. In relation to an equal value claim, the factor may be a genuine material difference between her case and his. The aim of this difference in the defence was to prevent the application of the decision of *Clay Cross (Quarry Services) v Fletcher* (1979) to equal value claims and so allow an employer to argue market forces. In the *Fletcher* case, the Court of Appeal held that the defence of genuine material difference was based on the personal equation between the man and the woman – that is, skill, experience or training – and that the employer could not use market forces arguments, such as the need to attract men to the post. The House of Lords in *Rainey v Greater Glasgow Health Board Eastern District* (1987), however, revised *Fletcher* to such an extent that it is debatable whether it is still good law. Their Lordships held that the need to attract entrants into the job to provide an expanded service justified the difference in pay and, that where there was no intention to discriminate, a difference connected with economic factors affecting the efficient carrying on of the employer's business could be a genuine material difference. In making this decision, the House of Lords was adopting the test for the justification of different pay rates under Art 141 stated by the ECJ in *Bilka-Kaufhaus GmbH v Weber von Hartz* (1987), where the Court said the measures had to correspond to a need on the part of the employer, they were appropriate to achieve the objectives pursued and were necessary to achieve that end. As such, the ECJ, on a reference in *Jenkins v Kingsgate Clothing Productions Ltd* (1981), ruled that a difference in pay rates between full- and part-time workers could be objectively justified on economic grounds if there was no intention to discriminate. This has now been followed in *Barry v Midland Bank plc* (1999). While it is clear from *Jenkins* and *Rainey* that objective justification is valid where different pay rates create indirect discrimination, it is still unclear how far the defence lies in a direct discrimination case. It can be argued that *Rainey*, in particular, has brought the defences in any equal pay claim together, so that there is in reality little difference between something that is a genuine material factor and something that is a genuine material difference.

Over the years, it has been decided that red circling is a genuine material difference (*Methven v Cow Industrial Polymers Ltd* (1980)) and different geographical location (*NAAFI v Varley* (1977)). Until recently, different bargaining structures which were not discriminatory were also a genuine material difference (*Reed Packaging Ltd v Boozer* (1988)). This, however, is now in doubt since the ECJ ruling in *Enderby v Frenchay Health Authority* (1994). The ECJ ruled that where a job had lower pay and was done predominantly by women compared with a job done predominantly by men, this established *prima facie* discrimination. The fact that those jobs had different pay bargaining structures was not an objectively justifiable reason for differences in pay, whether or not those bargaining structures were discriminatory. The court did add, however, that it was up to national courts to determine how far the need to attract applicants into a post justified pay differentials, so supporting the market forces defence which was successful in *Rainey*.

In the EOC Report of 1991, it was stated that the pay of full-time women workers in Britain was 77% of that of full-time male workers. In 1999, full-time women workers earned 81% of the male hourly rate and 74% of the male weekly rate for 91% of the hours. Research by Grimshaw and Rubery (*The Gender Pay Gap: a research review*, 2001) stated that the UK has the biggest pay gap in Europe. Given that the EPA has been in force since 1975, it is perhaps indicative that the Act has not created equal pay for men and women. It must be taken into account, however, that some areas of employment are female dominated and thus there are no valid comparators for an equal pay claim. While *Enderby* helps women where historically pay bargaining structures have created *de facto* discrimination and situations where an employer employs only women to do one kind of work and men another, it will not help in areas where no men are employed at all and the work is done solely by women and the Jenkins decision allows lower rates for part-time workers, a group which consists of more than 75% women. Female-only work has recently been identified as a factor in the pay gap in research done by Olsen and Walby (*Modelling Gender Pay Gaps*, 2004, Equal Opportunities Commission: www.eoc.org.uk/research) as has part-time work (*The Part Time Pay Penalty*, DTI, 2004). While the procedures and the opening up of the defences to admit market forces arguments does nothing to improve the pay position of the female workforce, the Act itself, by the definition of a male comparator in s 1(6), allows low paid women's jobs to continue without any form of legal redress.

There were indications that this limitation would change. In *Scullard v Knowles* (1996), the EAT stated that Art 141 gave a broader interpretation of male comparator than s 1(6) and applied this due to the principle of direct effect. However, in *Lawrence v Regent Office Care Ltd* (2002), Mrs Lawrence was transferred to Regent Office Care by North Yorkshire County Council. Her pay was reduced and she claimed equal pay with her former male council workers. The EAT held that workers employed by a former employer were not valid comparators. On reference to the ECJ, the Court upheld the EAT ruling saying that, although Art 141 did not require the same employer, in Lawrence there was no common employment because there was no single source from which the pay inequalities came and thus no one body responsible to restore equal treatment. In other words, there has to be a common collective agreement or similar from which the inequalities arise, even if there does not have to be the same employer. The Court of Appeal also referred the later case of *Allonby v Accrington and Rossendale College* (2004) to the ECJ, to determine whether a man employed by the college was in the same employment as a woman employed by a company which supplied services to the college. Again, the lack of a common source of pay inequalities meant the failure of her claim.

Even if a woman has a valid comparator, the case of *Evesham v North Hereford Health Authority* (2000) shows that the woman needs to choose him with care. In this case, a speech therapist successfully compared herself to a clinical psychologist. While the Court of Appeal held that she should be on the same pay scale as her comparator, she was only entitled to be on the same salary and not on a higher one, despite her longer service. This is because the Act only entitles the claimant to equal pay and not more pay. This shows that the Act fails to remedy injustice in that Mrs Evesham would have been on a higher salary than her comparator if her employer had not discriminated against her in the first place.

While changes made to the equal value procedure may remove some of the obstacles facing women who try to claim equal pay with their male counterparts, the wide nature of the defences, the restrictive nature of s 1(6) and the limitations of *Evesham* still lead to the conclusion that there is a long way to go in closing the gap between mens' and womens' wages.

Notes

Question 22

Vicky, Gail, Sally and Denise work for Coronation Products Ltd.

Vicky is a clerical assistant. Steve is also a clerical assistant, but is paid a higher hourly rate than Vicky. Coronation argues that this is because all the male clerical assistants have to work compulsory overtime and the collective agreement negotiated with the union in the workplace has negotiated higher hourly rates when some of the hours are overtime hours. The men do work the overtime. None of the women are members of the union because Coronation discourages female membership. Gail works in the printing shop. She feels that she is entitled to equal pay with the men who work in the paint shop. A recent JES gave Gail's job a lower rating than that of the paint shop workers. The reason for this is that although Gail's job has more responsibility, the paint shop is dirty and the work involves heavy lifting. As such, the job has been given a higher rating because of the working conditions and the amount of lifting that has to be done. None of the female staff has ever been allowed to work in the paint shop.

Sally and Denise job share. They both work a single machine, Sally working the machine from 8 am to midday and Denise taking over at 1 pm until 5 pm. Coronation pays them a lower hourly rate than the full-time machine operators. Coronation argues that this is because job sharing is less productive than full-time working.

Advise Vicky, Gail, Sally and Denise whether they will be successful in their equal pay claims against the company.

 ## Answer plan

This question mixes preliminary issues in relation to eligibility to claim with possible defences, and emphasises again that if students have a logical structure, all the points raised in a question should be covered. Thus, if the student first determines eligibility; secondly, determines the route and, lastly, looks at defences, that should leave no stone unturned.

Particular issues to be considered are therefore:

- the definition of the male comparator in s 1(6) of the EPA 1970;
- the definition of 'like work' in s 1(4);
- the defence of 'genuine material difference' in s 1(3);
- how far different bargaining structures can be a defence – particularly *Enderby v Frenchay Health Authority* (1994) and *British Road Services v Loughran* (1997);
- the definition of a JES in s 1(5) and *Eaton v Nuttall* (1977);
- the effect of a JES on an equal value claim;
- how far economic reasons can be a defence under *Jenkins v Kingsgate Clothing Productions* (1981).

 # ——————————— Answer ———————————

All four parties wish to claim equal pay against Coronation Products Ltd. To do so, they must establish that they have a route to claim equal pay under the EPA 1970, or that they have an action under Art 141 of the EC Treaty. None of the parties has the additional route under the Equal Pay Directive as Coronation Products Ltd is not an emanation of the state.

Vicky wishes to claim equal pay with Steve. She must first establish that Steve is a valid male comparator under s 1(6) and, should he be so, her choice of comparator determines her route to equal pay (*Pickstone v Freemans plc* (1988)). To be a valid male comparator under s 1(6), Steve must be employed by his employer or an associated employer and work at the same establishment, or at a different establishment where common terms and conditions are observed for that class of employee. Steve works for the same employer, and Coronation Products Ltd does not appear to operate on more than one site. Therefore, Steve is a valid male comparator within the definition in s 1(6).

As Vicky has chosen Steve, and as he is doing a job with the same title, it would appear that Vicky's route to equal pay is the like work route in s 1(4). The section defines like work as work which is the same or broadly similar and any differences between the things that the woman does and the things done by her comparator are not of practical importance. In *Capper Pass Ltd v Lawton* (1977), Phillips J said that the tribunal should take a broad view, looking to see if the work is generally similar, if there are differences and, if there are, if those differences are of practical importance. Thus, more responsibility (*Eaton v Nuttall* (1977)) will justify a difference in pay as long as this happens throughout the working year (*Redland Roof Tiles v Harper* (1977)). If there are differences between the woman's case and the man's, the tribunal must look at how frequently they occur in practice. In Vicky's case, Steve's work appears to be the same but Coronation will argue that there is a difference in that Steve works overtime and Vicky does not.

In *Dugdale v Kraft Foods Ltd* (1977), the men and women were doing the same work, but the men were paid at a higher basic rate because they worked night shifts and some Sundays. The EAT held that this was not a difference of practical importance, although it pointed out that an employer can pay a higher rate when the unsocial hours are worked, but not a higher basic rate. If Steve worked all of his hours at an unsocial time, therefore, this would render the work not broadly similar (*Thomas v NCB* (1987)), but, given that he appears to work at the same time as Vicky and in addition does overtime, he is doing like work within the definition in s 1(4).

Can Coronation raise a defence to defeat Vicky's claim? Steve's pay is union negotiated and therefore there are different pay bargaining structures within the establishment. By s 1(3)(a), the employer has a defence to an equal pay claim based on a like work comparison, if he can show that the variation in pay is due to a genuine material factor which is not the difference of sex and which is a genuine material difference between the woman's case and that of the man. In the case of Vicky and Steve, their pay is differently bargained. Can this be a genuine material difference? In *Reed Packaging Ltd v Boozer* (1988), it was held that the defence applied where the applicant and the male comparator were employed under different pay structures where those structures were not discriminatory. This decision, however, must now be subject to the ruling of the ECJ in *Enderby v Frenchay Health Authority* (1994). In that case, the ECJ ruled in relation to one of the questions referred to it by the Court of Appeal – that different non-discriminatory bargaining procedures did not necessarily amount to an objective justification for the different pay rates when the group affected was 'almost exclusively' women. While the case referred to was an equal value claim, it is submitted that given that the defence in an equal value claim is wider than that in a like work/work-rated equivalent claim, the decision in *Enderby* is relevant to Vicky's case and the fact that Steve's pay is union negotiated and hers is not will not be a genuine material difference within s 1(3).

If *Enderby* applies only in equal value claims, however, Vicky may be able to argue that the facts of her situation are different from those in *Reed Packaging*, in that here, there appears to be a discriminatory practice being committed by the employer in that women are not members of the union and therefore have no opportunity to take advantage of the collectively bargained terms. The reason for this appears to be that the employer discourages female union membership and therefore no women are union members. It could thus be argued that the pay structures are discriminatory in themselves; thus, Reed Packaging can be distinguished and Coronation has no defence to Vicky's claim.

Gail works in the printing shop and wishes to claim equal pay with the paint shop workers. Such workers will be valid male comparators under s 1(6). From *Pickstone*, above, her choice of male comparator will determine her route to equal pay, but should she choose the paint shop workers she, at first sight, has a problem. This is because a JES has been conducted. This means that her route to equal pay appears to be that of work rated equivalent in s 1(5) of the Act. However, the JES has given her job a lower value to that of the workers in the paint shop. While s 1(5) allows a woman to claim work rated equivalent under a JES if her work is given an equal value 'or would have been given an equal value but for the evaluation being made on a system setting different values for men and women on the same demand under any heading', thus allowing the tribunal to adjust the scheme, a tribunal cannot undertake its own JES under s 1(5) (*England v Bromley London Borough Council* (1978)). Should it be the case that the tribunal feels the scheme cannot be adjusted and dispose of it, Gail has no claim. Her better route would be to argue that her work is of equal value.

The new equal value procedures introduced by the Equal Pay Act 1970 (Amendment) Regulations 2004 and the Employment Tribunals (Constutution and Rules of Procedure) (Amendment) Regulations 2004 state that where a claimant lodges an equal value claim, there is a presumption (by s 2A(2A)) in favour of upholding any JES and therefore finding that the work is not of equal value, unless the tribunal has reasonable grounds for suspecting that the JES is sexually discriminatory or it is otherwise unsuitable to to relied upon. This removes the burden from the claimant in showing that a JES is discriminatory.

Section 1(5) of the Act states that a JES must be an evaluation of the jobs 'in terms of the demand made on a worker under various headings (for instance, effort, skill, decision)'. In *Eaton v Nuttall* (1977), the EAT stated that such a study should be 'thorough in analysis and capable of impartial application'. In *Bromley v H and J Quick Ltd* (1988), the Court of Appeal said that such a scheme should not be done on a job ranking basis and Art 1 of the Equal Pay Directive says that an evaluation study must be fair in that it is based on the same criteria for men and women and so exclude any sexual discrimination. In Gail's case, it appears that a predominantly male characteristic, strength, has been part of the evaluation. Likewise, the dirty conditions have been taken into account, despite the fact that women have not been asked to work in such conditions. It would therefore appear that the study is discriminatory in that a predominantly male characteristic appears to have been given a higher rating and the work conditions have been rated even though the women have no opportunity to work in those conditions. As such, it is open to the tribunal to rebut the presumption of upholding the JES at the stage 1 equal value hearing and allow Gail to continue her equal value claim.

Coronation Products may raise a defence under s 1(3) of a genuine material factor which is a difference between her case and that of her comparator. It would appear that women are not allowed to work in the paint shop. Therefore, should the employer argue that this is the reason for the disparity in pay, the policy of not allowing women to work there (and so earn higher wages) is discriminatory. While it is acceptable to pay extra for dirty working conditions, the company policy creates an impact on women and therefore is gender-biased. As such, a s 1(3) defence will not be successful (*Enderby*).

Sally and Denise job share. They are paid a lower hourly rate than the full-time workers. Their route to equal pay is like work as a man doing the same work full-time is a valid male comparator under s 1(6). The question again arises whether Coronation can raise the defence of genuine material difference in s 1(3)(a) of the Act. At one time, it was thought that the fact the woman worked part-time was a genuine material difference (*Handley v H Mono Ltd* (1979)). However, in *Jenkins v Kingsgate Clothing Productions* (1981), the ECJ held that the fact of being part-time can only be a genuine material difference if there is an economic objective that needs to be achieved and the lower rates achieve this objective. In other words, the concept of indirect discrimination was introduced into the area of equal pay with the effect that if the factor discriminates against women, it can only be a defence under s 1(3) if it can be objectively justified and there is no intention to discriminate; however, *Barry v Midland Bank plc* (1999) suggests that indirect discrimination cannot be established under Art 141 where there is no difference in treatment, even though there is a disparate impact. Jenkins was adopted by the House of Lords in *Rainey v Greater Glasgow Health Board Eastern District* (1987). *Jenkins* and *Rainey* have been widened by *Strathclyde Regional Council v Wallace* (1998). In that case, the House of Lords stated that where the applicant cannot show that the difference in pay is due to a practice which has a disparate impact on women, the employer merely has to show why the difference exists but does not have to justify it objectively. Therefore, in this case, the practice of paying less to staff who were acting as principal teachers as compared to permanent principal teachers affected 81 men and 53 women. The applicant could not therefore show a disparate impact on women and thus the employer did not have to justify the reason of financial constraints.

In the problem, Coronation argues that the full-timers are more productive, presumably because of the gap between midday and 1 pm when the machine lies idle. Such a claim must be investigated, however. If the full-timers have a lunch hour, during which the machines are turned off, and they work from 8 am to 5 pm, it is difficult to see what shortfall in production there can be in relation to Sally's and Denise's machine. It could be that Coronation could argue that administrative costs are such that they need to encourage full-time working rather than part-time working, but they have not argued this point. As such, if, in reality, there is little difference between the output of the machines, and production is the only argument raised by the employer, it is difficult to see that the employer has the defence of economic necessity under *Jenkins* and s 1(3) and Sally and Denise will be entitled to the full-time hourly rate.

On the other hand, *Wallace* may have an impact. Sally and Denise will have to show that the practice of paying job sharers less has a disparate impact on women. Clearly, under *Barry*, there is a difference in treatment, in that the question states that job shares are paid a lower rate and thus any men job sharing will get paid the same as the claimants. However, if this equally affects men (that is, there are a number of men who job share in the factory), then the employer can simply point to why the difference exists without objectively justifying it (*Wallace*). If, on the other hand, only women are in reality affected by this practice, then Coronation Products must objectively justify the practice, presumably, given their arguments, on the basis of reduced production, which, as stated above, they will have to prove. Should this argument be unsuccessful, Sally and Denise will be entitled to the full-time hourly rate.

Notes

_____

_____

_____

_____

_____

_____

_____

_____

_____

_____

_____

Question 23

Dick, Mary and Kath work for Mutley Ltd, a company which manufactures aeroplane parts for the Ministry of Defence.

Dick has recently been made redundant. He is 57. Under the company redundancy scheme, men cannot claim a pension until they are 60; women, however, can claim a pension if they are made redundant at 55. The normal retirement provisions for the company enable both sexes to retire at 60.

Mary designs some of the parts manufactured by the company. Due to an increase in orders, the company has brought in designers from outside on a temporary basis who are all men. The company has agreed to pay these designers £5,000 a year more than the existing designers.

Kath works part-time. Her job is identical to Fred's (who is full-time), but he is paid a higher hourly rate. Fred does compulsory weekend working which Kath does not. Fred has been at the company for 10 years and covers for the departmental supervisor for three months of the year, when he is away on holiday or on courses. Kath has worked for the company for two years.

Advise Dick, Mary and Kath whether they may successfully claim equal pay with their relevant counterparts.

Answer plan

The first thing to note about this question is that the employer is a private employer and not an emanation of the state. Just because a company does work for the government does not make them an organ of government, therefore, students should make sure that they read questions carefully. The first part of this question brings in the right to sue under Art 141 of the EC Treaty and therefore requires a discussion of the meaning of pay. The other two parts are again looking at the defences available to an employer and the widening of the defence of genuine material difference.

Specific issues to be considered are therefore:

• the independent right to pursue an equal pay claim under Art 141;
• the definition of pay within Art 141;
• the impact of *Barber v Guardian Royal Exchange Assurance Group* (1990);
• the concept of like work under s 1(4) of the EPA 1970;
• the defence of genuine material difference under s 1(3)(a);
• the impact of *Rainey v Greater Glasgow Health Board Eastern District* (1987); *Barry v Midland Bank plc* (1999); *Strathclyde Regional Council v Wallace* (1998);
• the 'personal equation' defence under *Clay Cross (Quarry Services) v Fletcher* (1979);
• how far the whole of the difference in pay has to be covered by s 1(3)(a).

——————— Answer ———————

All the parties in the question are seeking advice in relation to claiming equal pay. There are three routes to equal pay under the EPA 1970 and one or two routes under European law, depending on the nature of the employment. All individuals in Member States have the right to sue under Art 141 of the EC Treaty (*Defrenne v SABENA* (1976)) and that right can be pursued in the national courts (*Barber v Guardian Royal Exchange Assurance Group* (1990)). In addition, those employees employed by an emanation of the state may sue under the Equal Pay Directive because, as it is the fault of the state that the Directive has been misimplemented, the state should be liable if its employees suffer as a result (*Marshall v Southampton and South West Hampshire Area Health Authority* (1986)). Those employed by a private employer, however, cannot sue under the Directive.

In the problem, the first party to require advice is Dick. Although the normal applicant in an equal pay claim is a woman, the EPA 1970 applies equally to men (s 1(13)). Likewise, Art 141 is broad in its requirement to ensure equality between the sexes and therefore also applies to both men and women. Dick can therefore pursue a claim under both national law and under the Article if national law does not provide him with a remedy. He cannot pursue a claim under the Directive as Mutley Ltd is not an emanation of the state, but merely does work for such an emanation (*Doughty v Rolls Royce plc* (1992)).

Dick may have a comparator within s 1(6) of the EPA 1970, but, on the facts, he appears unable to claim under national law. In *Marshall* (1986), it was held that different compulsory retirement ages were contrary to the Equal Treatment Directive and the argument that such retirement ages in the private sector merely reflected the state retirement ages was untenable, as state retirement ages were covered by different Directives – that is, Social Security Directives. As Mrs Marshall was employed by an emanation of the state, the Equal Treatment Directive was directly effective. The effect of the decision was to create an anomaly, in that employees employed in the public sector had the right to equal retirement ages whereas those in the private sector did not. As such, s 2 of the Sex Discrimination (Amendment) Act 1986 amends both the SDA 1975 and the EPA 1970 so that it is unlawful to discriminate in the provisions relating to retirement in the area of promotion, transfer, training, demotion or dismissal. This itself creates another anomaly, however, in that on the wording, although it is unlawful to discriminate in relation to retirement ages, it is not unlawful to discriminate in relation to pension ages. In Dick's case, the retirement ages are the same, but he is at a disadvantage in relation to his pension. As such, the provisions operated by Mutley Ltd comply with national law and Dick will not have a claim under the EPA 1970.

Dick still has the right to sue under Art 141. In *Barber v Guardian Royal Exchange* (1990), the facts were similar to those of Dick's case. Barber sued under Art 141 (then Art 119) because he did not have an action under national law. The ECJ, in a landmark decision, ruled that benefits paid out under a contracted-out private pension scheme fell within the definition of pay within Art 141, which defines pay as 'the ordinary, basic or minimum wage or salary and any other consideration, whether in cash or in kind, which the worker receives, directly or indirectly, in respect of his employment from his employer'. Given that the ECJ had already ruled that concessionary travel benefits paid to retired employees were pay for the purposes of the Article (*Garland v British Rail Engineering Ltd* (1982)), it was not surprising that in *Barber* the definition was also held to apply to pensions. For some time, this created an anomaly between state and private pension schemes in that the effect of *Barber* is that private pension ages must be equal but that, until the implementation of the Social Security Directive, it was not unlawful to have different state pension ages. Due to the lack of clarity as to whether Barber was retrospective, and if so how far, the government delayed the equalisation of pension ages until clarification came from a later ECJ ruling. This clarification occurred in *Tjen Oever v Stichting Bedriefspensioonfonds voor het Glazenwassers* (1993). Thus, although Dick has no claim under the EPA 1970, given that the rights under Art 141 are directly effective and can be pursued in the national courts, Dick may use the Article to equalise the pension rights and claim his pension from the date of his redundancy. Member States enforce Art 141 by applying the relevant national law (here, the EPA 1970) and disallowing conflicting provisions (*Biggs v Somerset County Council* (1996)).

Dick should be aware, however, that the ECJ in Barber agreed to block retrospective reliance on it and thus, in Dick's case, equalisation of pension rights will only be based on service after the date of *Barber* (17 May 1990). This is seen by *Quirk v Burton Hospitals NHS Trust and Secretary of State for Health* (2002). In that case, until *Barber*, the rules of the health service allowed women to retire at 55, but men could not retire until 60. After Barber, the ages were aligned but women who retired before 60 were entitled to receive benefits calculated by reference to all of their pensionable service, whereas men retiring before 60 were entitled only to benefits by reference to service after 17 May 1990. The EAT held that this was a correct interpretation of *Barber*, but has given leave to appeal to the Court of Appeal. As such, although Dick is entitled to his pension from the date of his redundancy, he will not be entitled to benefits calculated on service before 17 May 1990 even if the women who retire early are entitled to benefits calculated on service before and after that date. The limitations on *Barber*, confirmed by *Quirk*, establish this.

Mary is employed as a designer and wishes to claim equal pay with the designers brought in temporarily to deal with the increase in work. Mary can use one of the temporary designers as a valid male comparator as these men fall within the definition of a valid comparator within s 1(6) of the EPA 1970, in that they are employed by her employer at the same establishment. Her route to equal pay will be under s 1(2)(a) in that she is employed on like work within the definition of s 1(4). The question which must be raised, however, is whether Mutley has the defence of genuine material difference in s 1(3).

The original case which interpreted the defence was *Clay Cross (Quarry Services) v Fletcher* (1979), where the Court of Appeal said that this meant a difference in the 'personal equation' of the man as opposed to the woman. The later case of *Rainey v Greater Glasgow Health Board Eastern District* (1987), however, felt that the definition of the defence in Fletcher was unduly restrictive and widened the defence to include any objectively justifiable reasons for the difference in pay, so adopting the test under Art 141 as expounded by the ECJ in *Bilka-Kaufhaus GmbH v Weber von Hartz* (1987) – that is, the employer had to show that the measures adopted corresponded to a real need on the part of the undertaking and the measures were appropriate and necessary to meet that need. In *Rainey*, there was a need to expand the prosthetist service within a reasonable length of time and the measures adopted by the employer (that is, offering a higher rate of pay for those coming in from private practice) were appropriate and necessary to achieve that aim. The fact that the private practitioners were men was an accident. While it has been suggested that the decision was influenced by policy considerations, the decision and the widening of the s 1(3) defence is highly relevant to Mary. It can be seen from the facts that the additional designers have been brought in on a temporary basis to meet an increase in orders. As such, the situation is similar to *Rainey* in that the employer has a need, that is, to increase production, and the way of meeting that need is to offer higher salaries to entice people into the firm quickly. There appears to be no intention to discriminate and the fact that the temporary designers are men appears to be an accident rather than deliberate. In addition, *Barry v Midland Bank plc* (1999) suggests that equal treatment does not establish indirect discrimination under Art 141, even if it creates disparate treatment; thus, if the company intend to pay all the new designers a higher rate, whether male or female, and it is coincidence that they are all male, again Mary may find her claim rejected. Furthermore, the effect of market forces on pay levels and how far such forces can be used as objective justification, appears to be a matter for national courts to decide according to the ECJ in *Enderby v Frenchay Health Authority* (1994). On the authority of *Rainey* and *Barry*, therefore, it would appear that Mutley can raise the defence of genuine material difference in s 1(3) and Mary will be unsuccessful in her claim.

Kath works part-time but is paid a lower rate than Fred who is full-time. Again, Fred is a valid comparator within s 1(6) and Kath's route to equal pay will be like work under s 1(2)(a). The fact that Fred works compulsory weekends and deputises for the supervisor does not make the work different and therefore the jobs do not fall outside the definition under s 1(4) (*Dugdale v Kraft Foods* (1977) and *Redland Roof Tiles v Harper* (1977)). Again, however, it is necessary to see if Mutley have the defence of genuine material difference in s 1(3)(a). While *Fletcher* can no longer be regarded as good law since

Rainey, the concept of the 'personal equation' between the man and the woman will still be recognised as a genuine material difference. When comparing Fred's case to Kath's, it can be seen that Fred has worked much longer for the company and presumably, therefore, has a great deal more experience. In addition, when working at weekends, it may be that he is unsupervised or carries more responsibility. Such differences have always been recognised as genuine material differences within s 1(3) (*National Vulcan Engineering Insurance Group Ltd v Wade* (1978)) which justify the difference in pay. On the other hand, if, despite her short time working for the company, Kath has equal experience from elsewhere and Fred does not work unsupervised at weekends and only has extra responsibility when he covers for the supervisor, there is no justification for paying a higher basic rate but Mutley can pay him extra when he takes on additional responsibilities (*Redland Roof Tiles*).

Notes

7 Employment Protection

Introduction

Employment protection rights are often mentioned in employment law courses, but very few go through them in a large amount of detail. In the context of this book, employment protection rights are taken to mean those rights which are derived from statute: originally the Employment Protection Act 1975, now the Employment Rights Act (ERA) 1996 and the Trade Union and Labour Relations (Consolidation) Act (TULR(C)A) 1992, both as amended by the Employment Relations Act 1999, and the Employment Acts 2002 and 2004, which create a set of basic minimum rights which the employer cannot contract out of. Some courses deal with these rights at appropriate points in the course, for example, the right to an itemised pay statement being dealt with when looking at the implied duty to pay the employee. However, it is useful for the purposes of this text to separate the rights out and look at them in isolation, as long as students are aware that such rights may permeate throughout other examination questions. In this particular chapter, we will look at rights owed by the employer to the employee, excluding dismissal rights which are dealt with in Chapter 9, below. Once these rights are extracted, general rights which the student needs to understand are:

- notice rights;
- rights in relation to payment;
- maternity, adoption and parental rights;
- rights not to suffer a detriment in certain cases;
- time off provisions.

It has already been mentioned that often these rights are dealt with in other areas of an employment law course and therefore may come up in a problem in almost any other area. The questions in this chapter, therefore, aim to ensure that students fully understand the rights.

In particular, students should be familiar with:

- the minimum notice provisions in s 86 of the ERA 1996;
- rights in relation to itemised pay statements;
- guaranteed weeks;
- pay during lay-offs and short-time working;
- medical suspension pay;
- maternity rights, in particular, time off for ante-natal appointments, maternity leave, the right to return, suspension on maternity grounds and statutory maternity pay;

- parental rights, in particular, parental leave, paternity leave, adoption leave, paternity pay, adoption pay;
- what constitutes a detriment on health and safety grounds – because the employee is an employee representative, a trustee of an occupational pension fund or refusing Sunday working; because the employee took parental leave, time off to deal with an emergency involving a dependant; the employee made a protected disclosure; the employee exercised rights to be accompanied at a disciplinary or grievance hearing or took action in respect of recognition or derecognition of a trade union; or the employee requested flexible working;
- the rights to time off for trade union duties, public duties, trade union activities, health and safety duties, trustees of occupational pension funds, employee representatives, time off to look for work if under notice of redundancy, time off to deal with an emergency involving a dependant and time off for union learning representatives.

Finally, a knowledge of all the above rights can impact particularly on the area of dismissal, as a refusal on the part of the employer to allow the employee to exercise these rights may lead to a finding of constructive dismissal.

Checklist

Students should be familiar with the following specific areas:

- the minimum notice the employee must give and receive;
- details within the itemised pay statement and remedies for breach of the provisions;
- what constitutes a guaranteed week;
- what constitutes a lay-off or short-time working;
- what are the rights in relation to medical suspension;
- the implementation of the Pregnant Workers Directive (92/85/EC);
- parental rights, paternity rights, adoption rights and rights to request flexible working;
- the protection from suffering a detriment;
- what constitutes reasonable time off and, in particular, the ACAS Code of Practice, *Time Off for Trade Union Duties and Activities* (revised 2003) and the new Code on Union Learning Representatives.

 —————————— **Question 24** ——————————

Martin, Ronnie and Phil work as teachers for Middlewich School. The recognised union in the school is the National Union of Teachers (NUT).

Martin has been a member of the governing body of the local university for the past four years. During that time, he has had, on average, 14 days off to attend meetings during term time. Due to a recent scandal involving the university vice chancellor, the governing body has met frequently in the past three months and Martin has had 21 days off to date. The chair of the governing body has just informed him that he will be required to attend meetings for at least another 15 days during the rest of this academic year.

Martin's headmaster has refused to allow him any more time off, saying it is unfair to other colleagues who cover his classes. Martin has never been paid for his time off.

Ronnie is the union health and safety representative at the school. Given that the school has just opened a chemistry department, Ronnie has had three weeks off over the past six months to attend training courses in the handling of chemicals. He now requires a further seven days off to train the chemistry teachers. The headmaster has refused to allow Ronnie the time to train the teachers and has said that Ronnie must train them during the vacation. In addition, Ronnie's class size has doubled recently and he has been given extra classes to teach, to make up for the time he has been out of the school.

Phil is a member of the NUT. The union has held regional meetings in the past to discuss action against the national curriculum. These meetings are normally held at lunchtime or in the evenings and Phil has always attended them. He has just been informed that the next two regional meetings will be held on two separate mornings when classes are on and that the union wish him to be a member of a party which is being sent down to London for a week, during term time, to lobby Parliament. The headmaster has refused to allow Phil to attend the regional meetings or to join the lobby.

Advise Martin, Ronnie and Phil.

Answer plan

This question is dealing with time off rights in relation to all of the parties. In each case, the reason for the time off is different and students should be careful to distinguish whether the issues raised are in relation to time off for duties or activities.

Particular issues to be considered are:

- whether Martin's appointment to the governing body is a public duty within s 50(2) of the ERA 1996;
- the balance between the employee's rights and the employer's needs;
- the right to time off for health and safety duties under the Safety Representatives and Safety Committees Regulations 1977 and the Code of Practice issued by the Health and Safety Commission;
- the right to time off for trade union activities;
- what is a trade union activity;
- what constitutes reasonable time off;
- the provisions relating to time off for trade union activities in the ACAS Code of Practice.

Answer

The Employment Protection Act 1975 created a series of basic time off rights for employees. These rights are now contained in the ERA 1996. Some of the rights allow paid time off and some allow unpaid time off. In addition, both ACAS and the Health and

Safety Commission have issued Codes of Practice in this area to provide guidance for employers and tribunals and the courts.

Martin has been a member of the governing body of a local university for the past four years. In the past, he has averaged only 14 days off in the performance of these duties, but to date he has had 21 days and will be required for a further 15, totalling 36 in all. By s 50(2) and (9) of the ERA 1996, membership of the governing body of a higher education corporation such as a university is deemed to be a public duty and the sub-section requires the employer to allow an employee time off during working hours to perform those duties. Section 50(4), however, states that the amount of time off an employee is permitted to take and any conditions attached to the time off must be reasonable in all the circumstances, and a tribunal must have regard to how much time off is required to perform the duties, how much time off the employee has already received under s 50, the circumstances of the employer's business and the effect of the employee's absence on that business. In the case of a dispute, the tribunal cannot substitute a figure if it considers that reasonable time off has not been allowed (*Corner v Buckinghamshire County Council* (1978)). It can merely make a declaration that the complaint by the employee is well founded and in a suitable case make an award of compensation. In *Corner*, however, Slynn J suggested *obiter* that a failure to pay during the time off could be construed as a failure to pay. As such, Martin may have two lines of argument: the refusal to allow any more time off and the fact that the time off already taken has been unpaid.

In relation to the refusal to give more time off, the tribunal is required to consider the time off Martin has already had and the effect of his absence on the employer's business. In *Borders Regional Council v Maule* (1992), the EAT stressed that the tribunal had to achieve a balance between the needs of the employer and the rights of the employee. On the facts of the case, the fact that the employer had allowed the employee time off to perform her duties as a member of a social security tribunal, did not mean that the employer was acting unreasonably in refusing her time to attend a training session in relation to such membership, and there was a duty on the employee to moderate the activities to fit in with the employer's business needs. Safety considerations may, for example, mean that it is dangerous for the employee to have time off because of dangerous manning levels (*Walters v British Steel Corp*). On the other hand, the time off must be allowed. In *Ratcliffe v Dorset County Council* (1978), it was held that re-arranging a lecturer's classes so that they did not conflict with his public duties was not allowing him time off.

In Martin's case, there has been no problem until this year when a problem at the university necessitated a great many more meetings. To date, he has had more time off this year than in the past and, if he attends all the future meetings, he will have nearly tripled the time he has had off in the past. What effect is this having on the employer's business, however? It appears that his classes have been covered by colleagues and there is nothing in the facts to suggest that they are now complaining, merely that the employer does not think it is fair. In addition, the time off for this year has only occurred because of a problem at the university and there is nothing to suggest that this will be repeated in future years. There appears to be no safety risk attached to Martin's absence and nothing to suggest that it causes problems for the employer. In *Corner v Buckinghamshire County Council*, the employer allowed the employee 15 days off but refused to allow any more. Despite the fact that the tribunal was overruled on a jurisdictional point, it felt that 19 days was not unreasonable. In *Emmerson v Inland Revenue Commissioners* (1977), it was held that 30 days' absence was not unreasonable, given that the employee was prepared to use 12 days' holiday as part of his time off. On the other hand, 36 days during term time is just over seven weeks and this is a considerable proportion of time in relation to an academic year. Taken in context, therefore, it may be that the tribunal feels that the employer's refusal is not unreasonable. If, on the other hand, the tribunal in Martin's case picks up on the obiter by Slynn J in Corner in relation to unpaid leave, it could be that it makes the necessary declaration in Martin's favour on the basis that he has been refused time off full stop. This is unlikely, however, as s 48 does not require that such time off be paid.

Ronnie is the union health and safety representative and the NUT is the recognised union. The Safety Representative and Safety Committees Regulations 1977 were made under the authority of s 2(4) of the Health and Safety at Work, etc Act 1974. These provide in reg 4(2) that an employer shall allow paid time off for representatives appointed by recognised trade unions to perform functions listed in reg 4(1) and to undergo training in relation to those functions. In addition, the Health and Safety Commission has issued a Code of Practice entitled *Time Off for Training Safety Representatives* (1978). The functions listed in reg 4(1) include representation of employees in consultations with the employer and the enforcement authorities and the investigation of complaints. The Regulations do not include time off to train other employees, although the employer is under a duty under reg 11 of the Management of Health and Safety at Work Regulations 1992 to ensure that employees are periodically trained with regard to to health and safety matters. In relation to the employer's refusal to allow Ronnie time off to train the employees, however, such time off does not appear to fall within the 1977 Regulations and therefore the tribunal has no jurisdiction.

Ronnie, however, may have another action he may pursue against the employer. In *Ratcliffe v Dorset County Council*, it was held that a reorganisation of a lecturer's classes amounted to a refusal of time off. If it could be argued that, in essence, the employer is obtaining the same amount of work from Ronnie, there is a possibility under *Ratcliffe* that the tribunal will grant the declaration. Could the employer's action, however, be construed as subjecting Ronnie to a detriment?

Section 44 of the ERA 1996 creates the right not to suffer a detriment by the employer on the basis that the employee was a designated health and safety representative and the detriment was suffered because the representative was carrying out activities in connection with preventing or reducing risks to the health and safety of employees at work (s 44(1)(a)). The employee must present a claim to an employment tribunal which can award such compensation it considers just and equitable should it find the complaint well founded. The onus is on the employer to show the ground on which the act was done (s 48(2)). In Ronnie's case, he has had additional pupils in his classes and additional classes to teach. If there is no economic reason for this, the inference appears to be that the employer is imposing the extra work on Ronnie because he has taken time off in relation to his health and safety duties. The provision is closely modelled on the provisions protecting trade union members from having action short of dismissal taken against them because of their trade union membership or activities. In *Carlson v Post Office* (1981), the EAT held that the equivalent section encompassed any action which subjected the employee to a disadvantage and refusing the employee a parking space was held to be sufficient to create liability. On the basis of this decision, it would appear that Ronnie has suffered a detriment and can sue for compensation.

Phil is a member of the NUT and has, in the past, attended union meetings outside working hours. The employer has now refused to allow him time off to attend two meetings within working hours and a week off to participate in the lobby of Parliament. By s 170 of the TULR(C)A 1992, an employer must allow an employee, who is a member of an independent recognised trade union, unpaid time off during working hours to take part in trade union activities or any activities in relation to which the employee is acting as a representative of the union. The ACAS Code of Practice on *Time Off for Trade Union Duties and Activities* (revised 2003) gives examples in paras 21 and 22 of those activities for which time off should be given, and they include workplace and regional meetings. Such time off should be reasonable in all the circumstances (s 170(4) of the TULR(C)A 1992). Paragraph 39 of the ACAS Code stresses, however, that time off does not have to be permitted for activities which consist of industrial action. While the regional meetings Phil wishes to attend fall within the activities listed in the Code, it is debatable whether the lobby would do so. In *Luce v Bexley London Borough Council* (1990), the EAT held that a parliamentary lobby was not a trade union activity within the meaning of the Act and, therefore, the employer had not refused time off for trade union activities. Following this, it would appear that Phil may get a declaration in respect of the refusal to allow him time off to attend the regional meetings but not in respect of the refusal to allow him time off to participate in the parliamentary lobby.

Think point

1 Students should note that action short of dismissal because of trade union membership is often part of an unfair dismissal question.

Notes

_____

_____

_____

_____

_____

_____

_____

_____

_____

_____

Question 25

Brookside Ltd is a company which produces widgets for the aircraft industry.

Terry is employed as a quality controller. Due to the loss of a major order, the company temporarily sold from stock which had accumulated rather than produce any new widgets. Terry and other employees were laid off for a period of six weeks as a result. For the first two weeks, the union held a protest and pickets prevented entry to the works. The lay-off ended two weeks ago. During the lay-off Terry received no pay. Terry has now heard that there may be another lay-off in two weeks' time.

Barry works in the shop which sprays the widgets. The paint used contains lead. He was suspended in November due to the high levels of lead in his blood stream. He was paid his full salary until Christmas. In January, he was ill with shingles but got over the illness by the end of January. In February, Brookside offered him work loading vans, which Barry refused. He returned to work on 1 March, having received no pay since Christmas.

Jimmy has worked for Brookside for six months; before that he was unemployed. Three weeks after starting the job, Jimmy was ill. He returned to work last week. During his illness, he received no pay. Three weeks into his illness he was examined by the company doctor but Brookside refused him access to the doctor's report.

Advise Terry, Barry and Jimmy in respect of their statutory employment protection rights.

Answer plan

In this question, the student is asked to advise the parties in respect of statutory employment protection rights only. In relation to all three parties, the main issues to discuss are statutory rights in relation to pay in certain circumstances.

Particular points to discuss are:

- the right to a guarantee payment under ss 28 to 32 of the ERA 1996;
- the exclusions which operate in relation to such a right;
- the right to claim redundancy in certain periods of lay-off under s 148;
- the right to pay during medical suspension under s 64;
- when the right to pay during medical suspension does not arise;
- loss of entitlement to medical suspension pay;
- the employee's rights to access to his medical records;
- the right to statutory sick pay under the Social Security Contributions and Benefits Act 1992.

Answer

The question requires advice as to the statutory rights of the parties involved. In all cases, it will be assumed that the contract is silent as to pay in the situations given and that the employees' only rights to pay will come from statute.

Terry has been laid off temporarily for six weeks due to the loss of an order. Under ss 28 and 29 of the ERA 1996, an employee who has been continuously employed for at least one month and who is not on a fixed-term contract of three months or less is entitled to a guarantee payment in respect of a whole day when he is not provided with work because there is a diminution in the requirements of the employer's business for work of the kind the employee is required to do or any other occurrence affecting the normal working of the employer's business (s 28(1)). The section is designed to protect employees in relation to occurrences outside the employer's control; thus, in *North v Pavleigh Ltd* (1977), it did not cover the days when the owner of the factory closed because of Jewish holidays. In Terry's case, it appears that the workless days are due to an 'occurrence' which is outside the employer's control and therefore, on the face of it, he is entitled to a guarantee payment. There are exclusions to the right, however, contained in s 29. By s 29(3), an employee is not entitled to a guarantee payment in respect of a workless day if the failure to provide work occurs in consequence of any industrial action.

In *Garvey v Maybank (Oldham) Ltd* (1979), there was a national lorry drivers strike and pickets at the factory refused to allow lorries to enter or leave. The employer ordered his lorry drivers to cross the picket lines but they refused. As a result, there were insufficient supplies entering the factory and Garvey was laid-off. It was held that he was not entitled to a guarantee payment as the lay-off was a consequence of the picket outside the factory.

In Terry's case, the union has objected to the lay-off and consequently has picketed the factory for the first two weeks. On the facts, it appears that the trade dispute was a consequence of the lay-off rather than the other way round. On the wording of s 29(3), therefore, Terry has not been laid-off as the result of a trade dispute but because of the loss of an order. As such, Terry is entitled to a guarantee payment under s 28(1) and does not fall within the excluded classes of employees.

Having said that, the amount of payment is not large. By s 31(3), Terry is entitled to five one-day payments in any three-month period. Any contractual entitlement to remuneration in relation to a day when no work is provided is set off against the statutory payment and any contractual payment per day counts as payment in the statutory calculation of the five days (*Cartwright v G Clancey Ltd* (1983)). In the problem, Terry was laid off for six weeks. He is therefore entitled to five one-day payments and will not be entitled to any further payments for another six weeks. Should another lay-off occur before that time, Terry will not be entitled to further statutory payments until the three months have elapsed.

Terry has not received any pay. He can ask Brookside for his statutory entitlement and, should Brookside refuse to make the guarantee payments, Terry can complain to an employment tribunal within three months of the failure to pay. Terry may have an additional remedy, however. If the contract provides a right on the part of the employer to lay-off, such a lay-off is not a breach of contract. If such a right does not exist, however, the employer is in repudiatory breach, which will justify the employee in resigning and claiming constructive dismissal. This prejudices the employee when there is a contractual right to lay-off, because should he leave because he has no pay, he has resigned and will have no protection. To provide such protection, s 148 of the Act ERA 1996 provides that if an employee is laid off for four consecutive weeks or six weeks in any 13, he may claim a redundancy payment. Lay-off means that he receives no remuneration under his contract. He must give written notice to Brookside that he intends to claim a redundancy payment within four weeks of the end of the lay-off and must terminate his contract by giving the contractual notice (s 148(1) and (2)). Brookside may challenge the claim of redundancy by giving a written counter-notice within seven days of the receipt of Terry's notice, giving evidence that within four weeks of the receipt of the employee's notice Terry will be employed for 13 consecutive weeks without lay-off or short-time working (less than half a week's pay being earned). The question is decided by the tribunal, but if, after the hearing, the tribunal discovers that in the four weeks after the employee's notice the employee was laid off or on short time, this conclusively decides the case against the employer (s 152(2)).

Barry was suspended from work when the lead content in his blood stream became too high. The lead appears to come from the paint he uses to spray the widgets and, thus, Barry has been suspended on medical grounds under s 64. Sections 64 and 65 provide that an employee who has been continuously employed for more than one month and who is not on a fixed-term contact of three months or less is entitled to remuneration if he is suspended from work in consequence of a requirement imposed by certain statutory provisions or a recommendation made under a Code of Practice issued or approved under s 16 of the Health and Safety at Work, etc Act 1974. The statutory regulations are contained in s 59(3) and include provisions relating to lead (the Control of Lead at Work Regulations 1980). The employee is entitled to be paid for a period of up to six months from the day the suspension begins.

Exclusions to payment are contained in s 65. These include periods when the employee was incapable of work due to disease (s 65(3)) or periods when the employee was offered suitable alternative employment by his employer, whether or not it was work which the employee is required to do under his contract, and the employee unreasonably refused to perform that work (s 65(4)).

Barry was suspended in November and received pay until Christmas. During January, he had shingles and was therefore unable to work, but this appears to be due to the shingles as well as to the lead content in his blood stream. Medical suspension pay is only payable if the employee is fit to work but is unable to do so because of the suspension. In *Stallite Batteries Co Ltd v Appleton* (1988), the applicant became ill after falling into a skip containing lead paste. No medical suspension certificate was issued by the company doctor, although his own doctor considered him unfit to work. It was held that he was not entitled to medical suspension pay as he was unavailable for work due to sickness and was therefore excluded by s 65(3). Similarly, it would appear that, in Barry's case, during the whole of January he was unable to work because he had shingles. He will therefore fall within the provisions of s 65(3) and is not entitled to medical suspension pay for the period of his illness.

In February, Brookside offered Barry alternative work loading lorries, which he refused. Section 65(4) excludes the employee from payment if he refuses suitable alternative work, whether such work is what he is required to do under his contract or not.

Clearly, Barry is not employed to load lorries but, by virtue of s 65(4), this does not mean that the employer has not offered suitable alternative work. Whether the work is suitable is a question of fact for the tribunal, taking into account the employee's skill and aptitude. Similarly, the reasonableness of the employee's refusal is also a question of fact for the tribunal, which will look at the circumstances of Barry's case. Barry must present his claim to the tribunal within three months of the failure to pay, although the tribunal can extend the three-month period if it feels that it was not reasonably practicable for the applicant to present his claim in time. While Barry will not be able to claim payment for January, he may have a claim for February.

Jimmy was unemployed until he began working for Brookside six months ago. He worked for three weeks and then fell ill and returned to work last week. This indicates that the period of his illness was five months. During his illness, he received no remuneration. The question which needs to be asked is whether Jimmy should have received statutory sick pay (SSP) from his employer. The scheme was introduced by the Social Security and Housing Benefits Act 1982 (now the Social Security Contributions and Benefits Act 1992) and is designed to put the administrative burden of sickness benefit on the employer who can, at present, reclaim some or all payments from the state. There is a statutory obligation on all employers to pay SSP in respect of their qualifying employees (s 151). In order to qualify, the employee must claim in respect of a day which is part of the period of incapacity for work (that is, a period of four consecutive days or more); the day must fall within a period of entitlement (that is, the end of the illness or the expiry of 28 weeks); and the day claimed for must be a qualifying day (that is, a day on which the employee would normally work). Certain employees are disqualified from receipt of SSP (Sched 2, para 2). One of these exclusions is where the employee's first date of sickness is within 57 days of a claim in receipt of other state benefits, such as incapacity benefit or jobseeker's allowance if there has been a previous entitlement to invalidity benefit. Jimmy was unemployed before starting work for Brookside and presumably in receipt of jobseeker's allowance. His illness began within 57 days of his starting the job, but this will not disentitle him to SSP unless there was a previous entitlement to incapacity benefit. Unless this is the case, Jimmy is entitled to SSP for the whole of his period of illness and, because of Brookside's failure to pay, he may refer their failure to the local insurance officer and any decision made in his favour may be enforced in the county court.

In addition to his lack of payment, Jimmy is also concerned that he has not been allowed to see the company doctor's medical report. The Access to Medical Reports Act 1988 gives the employee the right to refuse permission to his employer who is seeking to examine his medical records, or the right to see the report beforehand and refuse to give consent to allow it to be sent to the employer, or request that the doctor amend the report before transmission to the employer. A medical report is defined in s 2(1) as 'a report ... prepared by a medical practitioner who is or who has been responsible for the clinical care of the individual'. As such, these rights apply only to reports written by the employee's own doctor and, as such, Jimmy has no legal right to see the report written by the company doctor or prevent its transmission to Brookside.

_____

_____

_____

_____

_____

_____

_____

_____

_____

_____

_____

_____

_____

_____

——————————— Question 26 ———————————

Bet, Vicky and Emily work for Street Ltd. All of them recently became pregnant.

Bet has worked for the company for six years as a stock controller. She took maternity leave 20 weeks ago and, until recently, had no intention of returning to work. Her partner is now unemployed, however, and Bet wants to return at the end of her maternity leave. She has raised the matter with Street Ltd, who has told her that she cannot return to work because the job of stock controller has now been amalgamated with that of stock organiser and the existing stock organiser (who has been at the company for 18 months) now performs both jobs.

Vicky had been employed for eight months when she became pregnant. She works on the factory floor where a great many of the workers smoke. Vicky is asthmatic and her asthma has worsened since her pregnancy and is now causing a risk to the baby. As a result, Vicky has been off work for 10 weeks and is now three weeks from her expected date of confinement. Street Ltd has refused to pay her anything apart from SSP for the first two weeks of her illness and has told her she must return to work within one week of the birth.

Emily also works on the factory floor and has been employed by Street Ltd for one year. Her maternity leave period finished three weeks ago. She is, however, breast feeding the baby and, due to her obsessive concern about the smoky atmosphere in which she works and the effect on her baby, she had a doctor's certificate stating that she was incapable of work for four weeks after the end of her maternity leave. Today, the employer terminated her contract.

Advise Bet, Vicky and Emily of their statutory maternity rights against Street Ltd.

Answer plan

It is obvious from the problem that this deals exclusively with the maternity rights which are available to women. It is important to note the length of employment of the individual parties because this will determine exactly what their rights are.

Specific points to discuss are:

- the right to return to work under s 73(4)(c) of the ERA 1996;
- any notice requirements in relation to the exercise of the right;
- the provisions in relation to redundancy before the right to return is exercised;
- the right to 26 weeks' ordinary maternity leave;
- the right to additional maternity leave;
- when ordinary maternity leave begins in relation to sickness during pregnancy;
- suspension from work on maternity grounds;
- dismissal on maternity grounds after ordinary maternity leave.

Answer

All the parties in the question require advice in relation to their maternity rights. These rights vary depending upon the length of employment and have been extended by the Employment Relations Act 1999 and the Maternity and Parental Leave Regulations 1999 (as amended by the MPL (Amendment) Regulations 2002). The original rights were brought in to give effect to the Pregnant Workers Directive. The basic rights are now governed by ss 71 to 75 of the ERA 1996.

Bet has been employed for six years. By s 73 of the ERA 1996 and reg 18(1) of the 1999 Regulations, a woman, irrespective of hours of work or length of service, is entitled to 26 weeks' ordinary maternity leave and has a right to all the benefits under her contract (excluding pay) and a right to return to the job in which she was employed before her absence. In addition, as she has been employed for more than 26 weeks at the beginning of the 14th week before her expected week of childbirth (EWC), she is entitled to additional maternity leave of a further 26 weeks. This period is called 'additional maternity leave' to distinguish it from the shorter ordinary maternity leave period of 26 weeks. Bet therefore appears to have the right to 52 weeks' maternity leave.

Should she wish to return at the end of her ordinary maternity leave, no notice is required unless she wishes to return early. In that situation, she must give 28 days' notice to her employer (reg 11). After ordinary maternity leave, she has a right to return to the job in which she was employed before her absence (reg 18(1)). However, by reg 10, if a redundancy has arisen during her ordinary maternity leave, which makes it impracticable for the employer to continue to employ her under her original contract of employment, she is entitled to be offered alternative employment. Failure to offer such employment renders the dismissal automatically unfair (reg 20(1)(b)). She may only exercise her rights (and thus gain protection) if she has satisfied the notice requirements. She must have informed her employer at least 28 days before her ordinary maternity leave starts (i) that she was pregnant, (ii) the EWC and (iii) the date she intended to start her leave. If she gave birth before she had notified a date or before the notified date, she should have informed her employer of the actual date (in writing if requested) as soon as reasonably practicable. On receipt, the employer must have informed her of the date on which both her ordinary and additional maternity leave would end. As long as she has complied with the notice provisions for ordinary maternity leave, she is entitled to take additional maternity leave because of her continuity of service. There is no longer a requirement that she must give her employer notice of her date of return unless, as in the case of ordinary maternity leave, she wishes to return early in which case she must give 28 days notice (reg 11(1)).

The facts are unclear whether Bet wishes to return after her ordinary maternity leave or whether she intends to take a further period of additional maternity leave. Whereas if she returns after ordinary maternity leave she has a right to return to her old job, as seen above, her right to return after additional maternity leave is to a job defined as 'the nature of the work which she is employed to do in accordance with her contract and the capacity and place in which she is so employed' (reg 2). This shows that she is not entitled to return to the same job in the same department. Although Bet is entitled to return on terms and conditions which are no less favourable than those before she left, if the terms are less favourable then the employer is refusing her her right to return (*McFadden v Greater Glasgow Passenger Transport Executive* (1977)). Her continuity is preserved for statutory purposes.

The reason for Street's refusal to allow Bet to return appears to be that she is redundant in that Street no longer require a stock controller. If the redundancy occurs before she returns, she has the right to be offered a suitable vacancy if one is available (reg 10). If suitable work is available and she is not offered it, she is treated as unfairly dismissed. In *Community Task Force v Rimmer* (1986), the EAT ruled that a redundancy dismissal was unfair even though the only vacancy could be filled only by an unemployed person under the rules of the Manpower Services Commission funding.

In Bet's case, there appears to be a redundancy situation, but the employer has chosen to keep on a person with much less continuity than Bet. If Bet can establish that the reason for her redundancy was her pregnancy or taking of maternity leave, or any other reason in reg 20(3), her selection for redundancy will be automatically unfair (s 99 and *Brown v Stockton-on-Tees Borough Council* (1988)). Regulation 20 does not apply if Street Ltd employs less than five employees.

Vicky has eight months' continuity and thus her rights are restricted. Since April 2003, all women, regardless of length of service or hours of work, are entitled to 26 weeks' ordinary maternity leave. By s 71(4) of the ERA 1996 (as amended), she is entitled to all the benefits of her contract, excluding pay. To some extent, a woman may choose when her ordinary maternity leave starts, but she cannot choose a date earlier than the beginning of the 11th week before the EWC (reg 4(2)(b)). Her ordinary maternity leave will automatically be triggered, however, by any day she is absent wholly or partly because of pregnancy or childbirth after the beginning of the fourth week before the EWC (reg 6(1)(b)). As with Bet, Vicky must have complied with the notification requirements in relation to her leave. She has the right to return to her job (s 71(4)).

Vicky has now been off for 10 weeks and it is three weeks to her EWC. Given that her illness is related to her pregnancy, her ordinary maternity leave will have started at the beginning of the fourth week before the EWC – that is, one week ago – unless she informed Street of an earlier date. If one week ago is the start of her ordinary maternity leave, she has a further 25 weeks to go: that is, she can take 21 weeks after the birth and not the one week that Street is insisting upon.

Vicky has only received sick pay during her time off. In order to qualify for statutory maternity pay (SMP), she must be earning more than the lower rate for making national insurance contributions, she must give her employer medical evidence of the EWC; give him at least 28 days' notice of the date on which she expects his liability to pay SMP will begin; she must have been employed by her employer for at least 26 weeks ending with the qualifying week (that is, the 14th week before the EWC) and she must have reached the 11th week before the EWC (or recently have given birth) and she must have stopped work. If she satisfies these conditions, she will be entitled to six weeks at the higher rate of pay (nine-tenths of her week's pay) and the further 20 weeks at the lower rate, which is fixed by regulations.

If Vicky is earning less than the lower rate for making NI contributions, she will not fit into the conditions for SSP. Street has only paid her SSP for two weeks. By s 153 of the Social Security Contributions and Benefits Act 1992, SSP is not payable to a pregnant woman during the disqualifying period – that is, for 26 weeks beginning with the 11th week before the EWC. As such, Street is not obliged to pay her SSP and, unless there is a provision in her contract, she will be unable to sue, although she may be entitled to the state maternity allowance.

Emily has given birth. Although her ordinary maternity leave has ended, she has a medical certificate covering the period afterwards. Her contract has now been terminated. Section 99 of the ERA 1996 and reg 20 of the 1999 Regulations provide that a dismissal is automatically unfair if the principal reason for her dismissal is, amongst other reasons, a maternity reason. No continuity period is required to enter a complaint of unfair dismissal on these grounds. Emily appears to have been signed off because of her obsession about the effect of the atmosphere in which she works on her breast milk. Regulation 20(3) states that a dismissal is unfair if the reason for the dismissal is connected with the pregnancy of the employee or the fact that the employee has given birth. Her obsession appears to be due to her pregnancy and the birth of her child and, if the dismissal is due to her extra time off, this could be due to her having recently given birth. If this interpretation is correct, Emily has therefore been unfairly dismissed and can pursue a claim in the employment tribunal.

Notes

_____

_____

_____

_____

_____

_____

_____

_____

_____

_____

_____

_____

_____

_____

Question 27

The present government, in the 1998 White Paper, *Fairness at Work*, stated that its proposals were intended to create a framework for the future. One of the elements of this framework was to introduce provisions which enhanced family life. Critically assess whether changes introduced since 1998 are, in reality, family friendly.

Answer plan

This question is asking the student to look at rights introduced through a number of statutory provisions and assess whether the rights *in toto* are family friendly and lead to an enhancement of family life. The question requires the student to discuss a number of rights from a number of different sources and missing some out will not answer the question or allow the student to engage in an adequate assessment to answer the question. As such, it is a question to answer only if the student knows all of the sources.

Issues to be considered include:

- the Part-Time Workers (Prevention of Less Favourable Treatment) Regulations 2000;
- parental leave and the protection of the right;

- the right to time off for dependants and protection of the right;
- the new maternity leave and maternity pay provisions;
- the new rights for paternity leave, paternity pay, adoption leave and adoption pay;
- the Fixed-Term Employees Regulations 2002;
- the right to request flexible working in the Employment Act 2002.

Answer

Since 1998, there have been a number of provisions which could be described as 'family friendly'. It could be argued that the Working Time Regulations 1998 and the National Minimum Wage Act of the same year started this policy, in that the former restricted the number of hours a week an employer could require his employees to work and the latter introduced the right to three (now four) weeks' paid holiday. However, it is the protection of workers who do not work full-time, the introduction of a number of rights to time off for family reasons, increased maternity rights and the new right to flexible working which, when looked at together, could be said to create family friendly policies.

The start of family friendly policies came with the Employment Relations Act 1999 and regulations made thereunder. This extended the right to ordinary maternity leave to all pregnant employees, irrespective of length of service, and increased the period of leave from 14 to 18 weeks to bring the leave period in line with SMP. In April 2003, the leave period was further increased to 26 weeks. The right is accompanied with a right to return to her old job unless this is not reasonably practicable, and is protected by the right not to be unfairly dismissed or selected for redundancy on the grounds that leave was taken. The Act also introduced additional maternity leave. While this did not, in reality, create new rights for women, the importance of the Act was that it made clear, by s 73, that the contract of employment continued during the period of additional maternity leave, an issue which had been unclear under the previous law. Again, the right is protected by unfair dismissal and redundancy provisions. In April 2003, the additional maternity leave period was increased to 26 weeks and became available to women with a minimum of 26 weeks service at the beginning of the 14th week before the EWC. In addition, the new rights simplify the notification and notice provisions. This now means that the total maternity leave entitlement for those women who qualify is 52 weeks compared to 40. Additional maternity leave will be available to more women with the reduction of the service requirement from originally two years down to 26 weeks. In addition, the removal of the service requirement for ordinary maternity leave means that more women now have this right.

The Employment Relations Act 1999 also implemented the Parental Leave Directive. This created two new rights. First, it introduced a right to take parental leave, now found in the Maternity and Parental Leave Regulations 1999 (as amended). This allows an employee who has or expects to have parental responsibility for a child and who has one year's continuity of service the right to up to 13 weeks' unpaid leave to care for that child. This right lasts until the child's fifth birthday and applies to every child, so that if an employee has two children under five, that employee is entitled to a maximum of 26 weeks' parental leave. The employee taking such leave has the right to return to his old job and there is the usual protection from unfair dismissal and redundancy, in addition to the right not to suffer a detriment because parental leave has been taken.

The second right introduced by the Employment Relations Act 1999 was the right to time off for dependants. The Act inserted a new s 57A into the ERA 1996 and gave employees the right to reasonable time off to cope with a family emergency, such as a dependant falling ill or childcare arrangements falling through. Again, this right is protected by the right not to suffer a detriment because the right has been exercised, and protection against unfair dismissal and redundancy for the reason that the right has been exercised.

While these rights, without doubt, help those employees with children, the government has gone further. Many women work part-time, often because of childcare or other responsibilities. While legislation such as the Sex Discrimination Act (SDA) 1975 provided some protection against less favourable treatment of part-time workers, litigation under this Act is expensive and can take a long time. As such, in 2000, the government introduced the Part-Time Workers (Prevention of Less Favourable Treatment) Regulations implementing the Part-Time Worker Directive 97/81/EC. These provide a remedy where a part-time worker is treated less favourably than a full-time worker employed by her employer engaged in the same or broadly similar work, unless the employer can objectively justify the less favourable treatment. While the regulations operate on a *pro rata* basis, they prevent an employer paying reduced hourly wages to part-timers (the majority of whom are women) and provide an environment whereby women who wish to can work part-time without suffering a disadvantage.

The Paternity and Adoption Leave Regulations 2002 introduced the right to paternity and adoption leave. Paternity leave is the right to two weeks' paid leave, at a flat rate. In order to qualify, the father must have been continuously employed for 26 weeks at the 15th week before the EWC, be either the child's biological father or the mother's husband or partner and have responsibility for the child's upbringing (reg 4). The employee must inform his employer (in writing if requested) of his intention to take leave by the 15th week before the EWC and tell the employer the week of the child's birth, amount of leave he wishes to take and the date on which he wants his leave to start (reg 6). Similar provisions exist when a child is adopted, although the adoptive father must give notice to the employer no later than seven days after notification of being matched with a child and the notice must state the date of notification and the date on which the child is expected to be placed (reg 10). Employees must take the leave within 56 days of either the birth or date of placement. Employees are only able to take leave in blocks of one or two weeks. In addition, in respect of an adopted child, the Regulations introduce the concept of adoption leave which is based on maternity leave provisions. Either adoptive parent can take the leave (reg 2(1)), the other being entitled to paternity leave. While similar to maternity leave in notification provisions, unlike maternity leave, an employee must be employed for 26 weeks by the time of notification of being matched with a child, for both ordinary and additional adoption leave. Statutory Adoption Pay is available for the same length of time as SMP and at the same rate. As with maternity leave, there is protection against dismissal or detriment for exercising rights to paternity or adoption leave.

While these rights will allow new parents the right to time off (some paid) to be with their new offspring, perhaps the most important new right is the right to request flexible working, introduced by the Employment Act 2002 by the insertion of s 80F into the ERA 1996. This allows qualifying employees the right to apply to his or her employer for a change in the terms and conditions of employment in order to care for a child for whom the employee is responsible. Examples of such changes can be to hours of work, times of work or place of work to enable them to care for a child. To qualify, the employee must have 26 weeks' continuous service at the date of application. The changes must be requested before the 14th day before the child reaches the age of six, or, if the child is disabled, 14 days before the child reaches 18. The employer may reject the request on specified grounds, *inter alia*, a detrimental effect on the ability to meet customer demands and the burden of additional costs. There is protection against detriment and unfair dismissal.

It is submitted that this right to request flexible working is perhaps the most important, coupled with protection against less favourable treatment now given to part-time workers, and shows a clear commitment by the government to promote family friendly policies. The extension of maternity leave and the introduction of paternity leave and adoption leave all help parents at the start of a child's life, but the right to request flexible working will allow more employees to spend time at home discharging domestic responsibilities. The question which must be asked, however, is do the provisions go far enough?

While on the face of it, the government seem committed to family friendly policies, the reality may be different. The original parental leave provisions applied only to parents of children born after 15 December 1999, and it was only after a challenge by the TUC (*R v Secretary of State for Trade and Industry ex p TUC* (2001)) that the government extended the right to the parents of all children who were under the age of five on that date. The parental leave provisions, the provisions giving leave for dependants and the part-time worker protection were all introduced because of a requirement to implement EC Directives and it may be questioned whether the government would have introduced these measures without that compulsion. Furthermore, the right to request flexible working is just that. There is no right to work flexibly, merely a right to request to do so. Further, such a right was introduced as an amendment to the Employment Act 2002 very late in the day and was not part of the original proposals. All of this may lead a person to question whether the government does truly see family friendly policies as central to its employment legislation.

It may also be questioned whether all of these new rights will allow the flexibility of working needed to balance work and family life. For many employees, flexible working will mean working fewer hours. This means the protection afforded to part-time workers is crucial. However, in order to prove less favourable treatment, the part-time worker must have a full-time comparator on the same or broadly similar work. A full-time worker on different work is not a valid comparator for the purposes of the Regulations. It is submitted that this is a major loophole in the Regulations, a loophole which was in the original EPA 1970, which severely restricted the number of women who could claim equal pay and which took some 11 years to remove.

Furthermore, it must be questioned how many employees can afford to exercise the rights above. Parental leave is unpaid and many workers simply will not be able to take it. In addition, while many workers may wish to work more flexibly, the cost of childcare while working may make this option prohibitive. While the rights may be in place, without adequate state-funded childcare, such as is available in other EC countries, it may mean that the victory for those who wish to see a balance between home and working life is a hollow one.

Notes

8 Termination at Common Law

Introduction

The common law rules on termination of an employment contract are important in that they apply to all employees but, more importantly, they are the only form of protection for an employee who does not have the right to sue for an unfair dismissal.

Termination is a large area on its own, but is wider than dismissal because it covers not only termination by the employer but also termination by operation of law and employee termination. In addition, questions relating to common law can arise in the context of statutory rights, particularly in relation to unfair dismissal and redundancy, as we shall see in Chapters 9 and 10. As such, the principles relating to common law termination really need to be understood when answering the type of questions seen in those two chapters.

For questions specifically on this area, general issues which the student needs to understand include:

- the concept of termination by operation of law;
- termination by agreement;
- repudiation;
- resignation;
- common law dismissal;
- reasons for dismissal;
- procedure for dismissal;
- remedies.

As will be seen from the questions in this chapter, issues often raised are what type of termination has occurred and what are the available remedies.

In particular, therefore, students should be familiar with:

- the consequences of finding that there is termination by operation of law or agreement;
- the automatic and elective theories in relation to repudiation;
- what constitutes a resignation or dismissal;
- the types of common law dismissal;
- contractual and public law procedures and remedies.

Finally, as stated above, issues raised in this area need to be understood in relation to unfair dismissal and redundancy. Obviously, an employee cannot sue for unfair dismissal or a redundancy payment unless it can be shown that there is a dismissal. In some questions, therefore, the examiner may be looking for the relationship between common law and statutory termination.

Checklist

Students should be familiar with the following areas:

- the doctrine of frustration in relation to employment contracts;
- the reality of termination by agreement – in particular, cases such as *Birch and Humber v University of Liverpool* (1985); *Caledonian Mining Co Ltd v Bassett* (1987); *Igbo v Johnson Matthey Chemicals Ltd* (1986);
- repudiation – in particular, cases such as *Marshall (Thomas) (Exports) Ltd v Guinle* (1978); *Gunton v Richmond upon Thames London Borough Council* (1980); *London Transport Executive v Clarke* (1981); *Rigby v Ferodo Ltd* (1988);
- the reality of resignation;
- the concepts of summary dismissal and dismissal with notice;
- the differences between common law and statute in relation to reasons and procedure for dismissal;
- the difference between a breach of contractual procedures and natural justice, and the resultant remedies.

Question 28

These complications arise, and only arise, if there is grafted on to the old common law rule that a repudiated contract is only terminated by acceptance, an exception in cases of contracts of employment. In my view, any such exception is contrary to principle, unsupported by authority binding on this court and undesirable in practice. (Templeman LJ in *London Transport Executive v Clarke* (1981)

Consider whether any such exception exists and the advantages of applying the orthodox elective approach to contracts of employment.

Answer plan

This question falls into two separate parts: whether there are any cases when the automatic approach has been applied in cases of repudiation of an employment contract and the advantages of applying the elective approach.

Particular points to discuss are:

- the normal common law doctrine (*Howard v Pickford Tool Co* (1951));

- cases where the automatic theory has applied (particularly the judgment of Shaw LJ in *Gunton v Richmond upon Thames London Borough Council* (1980) and the House of Lords in *Rigby v Ferodo Ltd* (1988));
- the reinforcement of the common law position by statute;
- the advantages in adopting the elective approach, particularly in relation to continuity and statutory rights.

———————— Answer ————————

A repudiatory breach is a breach going to the root of the contract. Such a breach, however, may have a variety of consequences. It may be a rejection of the original contract and bring into operation new terms, for example, a reduction in pay. In this situation, the innocent party has two options. First, he can treat the breach as terminating the contract and leave. In an employment context, where the innocent party is the employee, then in this situation, if he does not have the protection of statute, he has resigned and can only sue for damages if the change was introduced without the necessary notice being given. Secondly, he can treat the breach as a variation in his terms and agree to continue the contract working under the new terms. In this situation, there is a variation and, as such, no termination. In both of the above situations, it is the innocent party who makes the choice and the contract will not terminate until he accepts this as a consequence of the breach.

Such is the normal situation under contractual principles. Asquith LJ in *Howard v Pickford Tool Co* (1951) said: 'An unaccepted repudiation is a thing writ in water and of no value to anybody; it affords no legal rights of any sort or kind.' The problem in the field of employment contracts, however, is that in some cases there is no real choice on the part of the innocent party. If an employer wrongfully dismisses his employee, for example, in practical terms the employee has no real choice as to whether to work or not. In addition, at common law, the courts will not force parties to continue with a contract for personal services (a position adopted by s 236 of the Trade Union and Labour Relations (Consolidation) Act (TULR(C)A) 1992). As such, it would appear that a repudiatory breach, such as a wrongful dismissal, terminates the contract immediately as acceptance by the employee is irrelevant.

Such an interpretation goes against established contractual principles and can have unfortunate consequences for the employee. For some time, however, the idea of automatic termination was accepted by the courts and contracts of employment were seen as the exception to the normal contractual rule. This view was expressed by Viscount Kilmuir LC in *Vine v National Dock Labour Board* (1957) and, in *Sanders v Ernest Neale Ltd* (1974), Sir John Donaldson P stated that repudiation of a contract of employment 'terminates the contract without the necessity for acceptance by the injured party'.

Later cases have challenged the theory of automatic termination. Megarry VC, in *Marshall (Thomas) (Exports) Ltd v Guinle* (1978), argued that the automatic theory would give the guilty party the right to decide when the contract came to an end and so allow him to benefit from his wrongdoing (for example, an employer could wrongfully dismiss an employee to avoid him acquiring continuity to claim unfair dismissal). In *Gunton v Richmond-upon-Thames London Borough Council* (1980), the majority of the Court of Appeal favoured the elective theory, but stressed that, in reality, there may be little difference between the two theories, as often the employee has no option, in reality, but to accept the repudiation and that the rule of practice that contracts of employment should not be specifically enforced means that the employee is merely left with an action in damages, as he would be on an automatic termination. Shaw LJ, in *Gunton*, tried to find a middle ground by arguing that, in some situations, the nature of the repudiatory act was such that it automatically destroyed the contract and acceptance would be unnecessary. This appears to leave the way clear to say that in other situations, where the contract has not been destroyed, acceptance would be necessary before the breach brought the contract to an end. The House of Lords, in *Rigby v Ferodo Ltd* (1988), limited cases to where an automatic termination could occur to a wrongful dismissal by the employer or a walk-out by the employee who fails to return, although their Lordships declined to consider whether or not acceptance was required in other cases. In *Smith v Phil's TV Service* (1991), an employee walked out after a dispute with the employer. When he failed to show up for work the next day, the employer assumed he had resigned and wrote a letter accepting the resignation. The Employment Appeal Tribunal (EAT) held that a repudiatory breach by the employee would only terminate the contract when the employer had accepted it as such. The employer had accepted the termination of the contract by his letter and therefore there was a dismissal as this ended the relationship.

It will appear, therefore, that whether the automatic or elective theory applies to an employment contract is still undecided. It is, however, vitally important for the employee in relation to his statutory rights. First, if the elective theory applies, then the employee may be able to increase his continuity and so bring himself within the requirements to claim unfair dismissal or redundancy. While this may be beneficial, it can cause problems in determining the effective date of termination for the purposes of ensuring a claim is presented to a tribunal in time, in that it can create uncertainty for both sides as to the date the relationship ended. On the other hand, if the automatic theory applies, this supports the idea of a constructive resignation; in other words, the employee behaves so badly that his contract terminates automatically because of his conduct. Such an interpretation would appear to go against statute for two reasons. In *London Transport Executive v Clarke* (1981), the Court of Appeal refused to accept that an employee's failure to return to work on a set date constituted a constructive resignation or self-dismissal. The argument of the court was that statute, by s 95(1)(c) of the Employment Rights Act (ERA) 1996, created the concept of a constructive dismissal (where the employee resigns due to a repudiatory breach by the employer) but had not created the corollary. Furthermore, by that section, it is only when the employee resigns (that is, accepts the breach as terminating the contract) that a constructive dismissal takes place, so supporting the elective theory.

In addition, ss 238 and 238A of the TULR(C)A 1992 give certain protection from unfair dismissal for strikers. Such protection would not be available if the strike (repudiatory conduct by the employee) automatically terminated the contract. Adopting an elective theory gives further advantage in that it allows the party in breach to withdraw the breach before it is accepted and restore the status quo. This may be favourable to either party. The employee who resigns in a temper can withdraw his resignation before it is accepted by the employer. Likewise, an employer can withdraw a fundamental change in terms before it is accepted by the employee, as in *Norwest Holst Group Administration Ltd v Harrison* (1985), and the employee will retain his job with no change in terms.

It would appear, therefore, that the elective theory has a number of advantages for the employee. This still leaves concern, however, as to the uncertainty it can cause in relation to the date of the dismissal and the limitation period on presenting a claim. While Clarke favoured the elective theory to avoid the concept of self-dismissal, the EAT, in *Brown v Southall and Knight* (1980) and *Robert Cort and Sons Ltd v Charman* (1981), refused to use the elective theory when determining the effective date of termination because of the wording of the (then) Employment Protection (Consolidation) Act 1978 and the need for certainty in this area. McMullen (A Synthesis of the Mode of Termination of Contracts of Employment [1982] CLJ 110) suggests that this different approach, depending on the issue before the court, is the most logical. It would appear, therefore, that there are exceptions to the general rule that a repudiatory breach must be accepted as such by the innocent party before the contract will terminate. On the whole, however, the courts prefer the elective approach and, as seen above, this can act to the advantage of the innocent party.

Notes

Question 29

The following has recently occurred at Mucktown Secondary School:

Mr Logan, the PE teacher, was recently convicted of theft and sentenced to two years' imprisonment. During the time of the police investigation, Mr Logan was off sick for three months prior to his trial. At an appeal against sentence held one month later, his sentence was reduced to six months' imprisonment. His post had not been filled at the time of his release from prison and he is claiming a redundancy payment. The school argues that Mr Logan is no longer on the books.

Mr Francis, a caretaker at the school, was recently found to have borrowed money from the school's petty cash box, although he returned the money the very next day. On one previous occasion, when he had done a similar thing, he was spared from disciplinary action on the signing of a statement which read 'I understand that should I borrow or take money from my employers on any future occasion that my contract of employment will automatically terminate'. The school contends that by this recent act of borrowing from the school, Mr Francis has terminated his contract by agreement. Mr Francis is now claiming unfair dismissal.

Advise Mr Logan and Mr Francis only on the issue of whether they have been dismissed.

Answer plan

The main thing to note about this question is that, while one party is claiming a redundancy payment and the other is claiming unfair dismissal, the question is not asking for a detailed analysis of either of those areas, and to go off at a tangent will gain the student no marks. The question is very specific and concentrates on the issue of whether there has been a dismissal, that is, an employer termination. This question shows the importance of reading the question properly before attempting to answer it.

As the question is only looking at different forms of termination, topics that will need to be considered are:

- frustration and how the doctrine is applied to an employment contract;
- the judicial discussion on self-induced frustration and imprisonment;
- termination by agreement;
- s 203 of the ERA 1996.

Answer

The question asks us to advise the two parties in relation to whether the situations in which they find themselves can be deemed to be a dismissal and so allow Mr Logan to claim a redundancy payment and Mr Francis to claim an unfair dismissal. In situations of both redundancy and unfair dismissal, the employee must show he has been dismissed before he can enter a claim in an employment tribunal. The fact that there has been a dismissal does not necessarily mean that the employee is entitled to a redundancy payment or that the dismissal is unfair; establishing a dismissal merely opens up the tribunal jurisdiction.

Mr Logan was ill for three months and imprisoned for six months. The school argues that Mr Logan is no longer on the books and appears to be arguing that because of his illness, imprisonment or both, the contract has now been frustrated. Frustration occurs when, in the words of Streatfield J in *Morgan v Manser* (1948):

> ... there is an event or change of circumstances which is so fundamental as to be regarded by the law as striking to the root of the contract as a whole, and as going beyond what was contemplated by the parties ...

Should an employment contract be frustrated, the contract terminates immediately on the happening of the frustrating event, with no liability on either party, as the law regards that neither party is at fault. The employee is not entitled to any pay after the frustrating event has occurred and, as frustration ends the contract automatically, the employee is not dismissed nor has he resigned. Two major events which may occur and frustrate the contract are illness and, potentially, imprisonment. The test to establish whether illness has led to a frustration was formulated by Donaldson P in *Marshall v Harland and Wolff Ltd* (1972) when he said that tribunals had to ask 'whether the nature of the employee's incapacity was such that further performance of his obligations was impossible or radically different from that originally intended when he entered the contract'. He then gave a list of factors tribunals should consider when looking to see if frustration had occurred. These factors were added to in the later case of *Egg Stores Ltd v Leibovici* (1977) and have now been summarised and approved by the EAT in the case of *Williams v Watsons Luxury Coaches Ltd* (1990):

- the court must be careful not to use the doctrine too easily;
- the date the frustration occurred;
- there are a number of factors which should be considered, which include the length of employment prior to the frustrating event and the length of future foreseeable employment; the nature of the job and the terms of employment; the nature, length and effect of illness and the prospect for recovery; the employer's need for a replacement; the risk of the employer incurring statutory liability to a replacement; the conduct of the employer; whether wages or sick pay have been paid and whether in all the circumstances a reasonable employer would have waited longer;
- the frustrating event has not been caused by the party seeking to rely on it.

In *Hart v AR Marshall and Sons (Bulwell) Ltd* (1977), the employee was a key worker, who was ill for 20 months and was replaced during his illness. The EAT held that his contract had been frustrated. By contrast, in *Hebden v Forsey and Sons* (1973), an employee was off for two years with the employer's agreement. There was insufficient work for him to do while he was sick and it was held that the contract had not been frustrated.

Applying the above to Mr Logan, while there are no facts as to how long he had been employed, there is no evidence that he intended to leave in the near future. He was not replaced and presumably sick pay would have been paid. Taking these factors into account, it is unlikely that the court would argue that his contract had been frustrated because of his three-month illness. In relation to his imprisonment, the court's attitude towards this has changed over the years. The problem which used to arise was whether imprisonment could be classed as self-induced frustration and therefore no frustration at all. In *Hare v Murphy Bros* (1974), Lord Denning said that where an employee had been imprisoned for 12 months, the contract was clearly frustrated and that it was not self-induced as the frustrating event was the imposition of the sentence and not the criminal behaviour. Later EATs, however, were in disagreement and, in *Norris v Southampton City Council* (1982), the EAT decided that, as the imprisonment had been caused by the employee's own misconduct, there could be no frustration and that the employee was guilty of repudiatory conduct which, if accepted by the employer as ending the contract, would lead to an employer termination and therefore a dismissal. The Court of Appeal resolved the issue in *Shepherd (FC) v Jerrom* (1986) when it decided that a six-month prison sentence could frustrate a four-year contract of apprenticeship. Balcombe LJ accepted Denning's argument in *Hare* that it was the imposition of the sentence which was the frustrating event; Lawton LJ and Mustill LJ argued that a self-induced frustration only had no effect on the contract when a party was seeking to rely on his own misconduct. Given that it was the employer in *Shepherd* arguing that there had been a frustration, this could not be self-induced.

Where does this leave Mr Logan? While *Shepherd* establishes that imprisonment can be a frustration, it may be possible to distinguish Mr Logan's situation. In *Shepherd*, a six-month prison sentence frustrated a four-year contract, but we have no evidence that Mr Logan was on a fixed-term contract. In *Shepherd*, the sentence was one-eighth of the employment period, but Mr Logan may have been employed for some years before his misdeeds and intended to stay for some time afterward. It is also important to know when Mr Logan was imprisoned. If this was during the summer vacation, given that he would probably not have served the full six months, then the imprisonment may have had little or no effect on the performance of his duties. It is suggested, therefore, that *Shepherd* can be distinguished and that this particular imprisonment will not frustrate the contract.

This leads to one final question. Could the illness and imprisonment together frustrate the contract? Mr Logan was ill for three months and then served his sentence. If he served the whole of his sentence, he would have been away from work for nine months. In *Chakki v United Yeast Co Ltd* (1982), it was held that an 11-month prison sentence could frustrate a contract (although not proved on the facts). It is submitted that if Mr Logan was off for nine months and this affected the performance of his work, the attitude and actions of the employer must be examined. If the employer had no intention of allowing him to return and did not maintain contact with him, it is possible to distinguish *Hebden*, although no replacement was appointed. Such a question would be for the tribunal to decide.

In respect of Mr Francis, Muckton is arguing that there is a termination by agreement. While the courts are prepared to recognise such terminations, Donaldson P in *McAlwane v Broughton Estates Ltd* (1973) said that tribunals should be careful when finding an agreement to terminate and ensure that the employee was aware of the financial implications of doing so. In cases where the employee has received some financial consideration, the courts are more prepared to find that there is a genuine agreement. For example, in *Birch and Humber v University of Liverpool* (1985), two employees who volunteered for early retirement and acquired certain financial advantages were deemed to have mutually agreed to terminate their contracts and they had not been dismissed for redundancy even though their posts were not filled. A similar conclusion was reached in *Scott v Coalite Fuels and Chemicals Ltd* (1988). On the other hand, an employee who resigned because he was told by his employer that he would be made redundant was held to be dismissed because his employer's conduct made it clear that he would be dismissed in the near future (*Caledonian Mining Co Ltd v Bassett* (1987)).

The problem in Mr Francis' case is that before he borrowed the money, he appeared to sign a document agreeing that his employment would end should there be a repetition of his previous conduct. In the early case of *British Leyland (UK) Ltd v Ashraf* (1978), an employee signed a similar document when he was given five weeks' unpaid leave to visit his family in Pakistan. He agreed that should he fail to return on the due date, his contract would terminate automatically. The EAT held that there had been an agreement to terminate. Later cases tried to distinguish *Ashraf*, but the challenge came in the Court of Appeal in *Igbo v Johnson Matthey Chemicals Ltd* (1986). The court held that a document similar to that in *Ashraf* was contrary to s 203 of the ERA 1996 and was therefore void. On the basis of *Igbo*, therefore, it would appear on the face of it that the agreement Mr Francis signed is contrary to s 203 and, as such, Muckton has terminated his contract and so dismissed him.

Muckton may try and argue on the basis of *Logan Salton v Durham County Council* (1989). In this case, the employee had been redeployed as a result of disciplinary proceedings. Further disciplinary proceedings were to be initiated, with a recommendation that the employee be dismissed. Prior to this, the union representative negotiated with the employer that the employment be terminated and a car loan waived out. After the agreement, the employee sued for unfair dismissal on the basis that the agreement was contrary to s 203. The EAT distinguished *Igbo* on the basis that there was a separate agreement to terminate which did not depend on the happening of some future event, which was supported by consideration. The parties had therefore mutually terminated their contract. On the facts of Mr Francis' case, the agreement did depend on the happening of some future event, but there was consideration in that he was spared from disciplinary action on the first occasion. While in *Logan*, there was financial consideration in wiping out the car loan, the employee was also spared disciplinary action and dismissal and it could be that the tribunal will hold that Mr Francis' case can be distinguished from Igbo and that the agreement is not void. If this is the conclusion, Mr Francis will have agreed to terminate his contract and has not therefore been dismissed. His only possibility is to rely on the comments of Donaldson P in *McAlwane* and argue that the agreement was entered into under pressure and that he was not aware of the financial consequences of signing the agreement. This may sway the tribunal to find that Mr Francis signed the agreement because of the fear of the consequences (that is, potential dismissal) and, as such, there is no real agreement at all.

Notes

_____

_____

_____

_____

_____

_____

_____

_____

_____

_____

_____

_____

_____

_____

_____

Question 30

Remedies for wrongful dismissal are limited by the restricted measure of damages recoverable in many cases. There are, however, a number of exceptions which mitigate this harsh general rule and thus the common law provides sufficient protection for those employees unprotected by unfair dismissal provisions.

Critically evaluate this statement.

Answer plan

This type of question can be dangerous if not read properly because it is the sort of question where students use the 'shovel' approach – that is, write all they know about the exceptions with no critical analysis. The question is asking for a discussion of the exceptions to the general rule that damges are restricted in a wrongful dismissal claim and asks the student to evaluate the statement that therefore the common law provides adequate protection for employees. To merely list the exceptions is insufficient

Issues which need to be considered are therefore:

• the definition of a wrongful dismissal;

• the restrictions on the award of damages in respect of a wrongful dismissal claim;

- the exceptions to the general rule;
- an evaluation of whether the exceptions give employees sufficient protection.

Answer

A wrongful dismissal is a dismissal which is in breach of contract, in that either no notice has been given or short notice has been given in circumstances where the employer has no right to ignore the employee's notice rights. Until the employee has the continuity to claim unfair dismissal (normally one year), his only rights are in contract and therefore should that contract be broken, he has the right to sue for damages for his loss. His loss, however, is restricted by the notice he is entitled to receive under his contract. If an employee is entitled to three weeks' notice and is dismissed with one week's notice, his loss is two weeks' net pay, because his employer at common law has the right to terminate the contract with three weeks' notice and his breach has only caused the employee to lose two of those weeks. As such, the employee's damges are restricted to his actual loss.

In some cases, the courts have argued that the employee's actual loss is greater than his notice period. Therefore if, for example, the employee has a contractual disciplinary procedure which has not been observed, his damages may reflect his wages for the length of time it would have taken the employer to observe the procedure in addition to his notice period (*Boyo v Lambeth LBC* (1995)). How far this will be an argument in wrongful dismissal claims since the introduction, in 2004, of statutory dismissal and disciplinary procedures has yet to be seen, although the government, in introducing those procedures, did not avail itself of the opportunity to make the statutory procedures contractual, arguably because of the fear of breach of contract claims. In addition, where the employee has also been deprived of a benefit for which he would have qualified had he been given the correct notice, he may also be compensated for that loss. For example, in *Silvey v Pendragon plc* (2001), if the employee had been given the correct notice he would have reached 55, which had an effect on his pension and his damages reflected this loss. Until recently, this principle did not extend to loss of discretionary benefits, (*Laverack v Woods of Colchester Ltd* (1967)); however Laverack has since been departed from. In *Clarke v BET plc* (1997), Clarke was a chief executive on a fixed-term contract. His salary was subject to discretionary pay rises and bonuses. He was wrongfully dismissed and the question for the EAT was whether the discretionary pay rises and bonuses should form part of the award for damages. On the basis of Laverack, the answer should have been in the negative; however, the EAT said that given that such payments had been made in the past, damages should be calculated on what he would have been paid if the employers had continued to exercise their discretion in good faith. Similarly, in *Clarke v Nomura International plc* [2000] IRLR 766, a highly successful trader, who received large discretionary bonuses based on his trading, was dismissed and received no bonus for his final year, even though he had continued to be successful. Burton J held that the bonus should be part of his award of damages (despite the fact that the dismissal was lawful). However, unlike the court in *Clarke v BET plc*, he did not base his argument on the duty of trust and confidence but on the principle of perversity, arguing that no reasonable employer would have failed to exercise their discretion and not pay the bonus. This argument was adopted by the Court of Appeal in *Mallone v BPB Industries plc* (2002), where an executive, who was lawfully dismissed, had his rights to share options cancelled by the company (a right the company had under the terms of the contract). The Court of Appeal granted damages for the loss of the share options on the basis that the company had acted irrationally in cancelling them, particularly as it could provide no evidence of the basis on which the decision had been made.

The introduction of perverse or irrational conduct on the part of the employer almost seems akin to the requirement of reasonableness in an unfair dismissal claim. Whereas traditionally an employer in a common law dismissal situation merely has to give the required notice (or wages in lieu), this importation of looking at the employer's conduct appears to restrict the previous unfettered actions by the employer. It is submitted that there is a vast difference between perverse and unreasonable actions, but the Court of Appeal in *Mallone* made two important points which could be developed further. First, the court found the employer's action to be irrational, not perverse. It is submitted that this is a lower standard than that in *Clarke v BET plc* and is arguably more akin to the requirement of reasonableness. The court also made the point that it had reached this decision because of the lack of evidence showing how the employer's decision had been reached. If these two strands are developed, it could mean that case law in the area of unfair dismissal, which creates requirements for the employer to show evidence to support his decision to dismiss and to treat the employee reasonably in terms of a hearing, may be transposed into the common law. Arguably, this may already be the case given the introduction of the statutory procedures, despite the fact that the government declined to make them contractual.

In addition to the discussion above, there are other situations where the employee may get damages in excess of notice provisions. On the basis of *Silvey* above, where the employer's breach of contract prevents the employee from gaining sufficient continuity for statutory protection, continuity he would have acquired if the contract had not been broken, his damages should reflect this loss. After a number of cases questionning whether this should be the case, the EAT in *Raspin v United News Shops Ltd* (1999) allowed an award representing the loss of his potential claim for unfair dismissal. While this is in line with previous cases, such as *Silvey*, it will apply only in two situations. First, where if the employer had given the correct notice, the employee would have acquired the correct continuity and, secondly, where a contractual disciplinary procedure has not been observed and such observance would have meant that the employee would have the required continuity at the time of his dismissal. As stated above, the impact of the statutory procedures on such claims has yet to be seen. It should also be noted that such a claim cannot lie where the employer has a contractual right to pay wages in lieu as he is not in breach but exercising a contractual right.

There are two other potential exceptions to the rule that an employee is entitled only to damages to represent his lack of notice. If the employee is on a fixed-term contract, where there is no express contractual notice clause, it is likely that the courts would hold that the intention of the parties was that the contract should run its full term and not imply into the contract the statutory minimum notice period under s 86 of the Employment Rights Act (ERA) 1996. In that case, the employee's loss is the full term of the contract and his damages would reflect this.

A further potential exception lies where damages may be awarded in respect of the manner of the dismissal. The House of Lords, in *Addis v Gramophone Co Ltd* (1909), held that an employee was not entitled to damages for injury to feelings nor for the fact that the manner of his dimissal had damaged his reputation and made it difficult for him to find another job. However, in *Malik v BCCI* (1997), the BCCI bank collapsed owing $6 billion. It had been having problems for some time, but these problems had been hidden by the fraudulent dealings of the senior officers of the bank. These facts became public knowledge. As a result of the collapse, all 1,400 employees lost their jobs and two sued claiming damages for injury to their reputation and their employment prospects as a result of their association with a dishonest and corrupt employer. The House of Lords upheld their potential claim on the basis that the conduct of the employer was a breach of the duty of trust. This was despite the fact that the employees did not know of the breach until after the employment ended. *Addis* was distinguished on two grounds. First, it was a claim relating to the manner of dismissal, whereas *Malik* was a claim for future loss, and, secondly, *Addis* was decided before the development of the duty of trust and confidence.

Malik appeared to be opening up the way for additional claims in wrongful dismissal cases – that of so called 'stigma' damages – in that the manner of dismissal breached the duty of trust and confidence. (The claim, in fact, eventually failed on the basis of causation: *BCCI SA (in liquidation) v Ali* (2002).) This, however, was stopped by the later House of Lords decision in *Johnson v Unisys Ltd* (2001). In this case, an ex-employee sued for damages in respect of a nervous breakdown and consequent inability to work, caused by the manner of his dismissal. The House of Lords said that such damages were not available for two reasons. First, the decision in *Malik*, that there had been a breach of the duty of trust and confidence, related to breaches which had occurred during the employment but such a duty did not survive the termination of the contract and therefore the manner of dismissal could not be a breach. The second reason was that the law should not circumvent the statutory rights of unfair dismissal for which there are compensation limits. Unfair dismissal, according to Lord Hoffman, is the proper action in which to claim compensation for the manner of dismissal.

While Johnson raises issues of when the contract actually terminates, the present law is demonstrated by the Court of Appeal in *McCabe v Cornwall County Council* (2004). There the court said that the issue is to see if there is any damage flowing from the breach of the duty which is separate from the damage flowing from the manner of the dismissal. The latter cannot be compensated for.

So do the exceptions to the general rule provide adequate protection at common law? While Raspin provides some protection, it will apply only in limited circumstances and the same can be said for many of the other exceptions. The developments seen in the *Clarke* and *Mallone* cases show that the equivalent of statutory principles may be imported into the common law, but, it is suggested that these cases are based on unusual facts and the principles may be limited to such facts and unlikely to aid the average employee. *Malik* opened up potential claims for damages but *Johnson* clearly stemmed the flow. As such, the average employee, suing for wrongful dismissal, will still only get the wages owed under his notice and, as such, the common law does not provide sufficient protection.

—*Notes*

— Question 31 —

Robert, Tom and David work for Prior Products Ltd, a company specialising in garden furniture. Recently, the following events took place.

Robert, who has worked for Prior Products for six months, was given two days' notice of dismissal and was told that he was being sacked for incapability. He was never warned that he was incapable of doing the job. During his notice period, Robert sabotaged some machinery, a fact not discovered by Prior Products until three weeks after he had left.

Tom, who worked for the company for nine months, has always been a practical joker. Last week, he had an argument with his manager, during which the manager said 'I can't stand you joking around any longer and neither can the bosses, just clear off.' Tom replied 'If you think I'm staying where I'm not wanted, you've got another think coming.' With that, Tom left. The next day, Tom received his P45 with a note from the company accepting his resignation. The works rules state that all resignations must be in writing.

David has been employed for 11 months. His contract entitles him to four weeks' notice and contains a disciplinary procedure, entitling him to a hearing and an appeal. He was given two weeks' notice of dismissal last week. The reason given for his dismissal is bad time-keeping. He feels that this is unjustified and has asked to exercise his right of appeal contained in the contractual disciplinary procedures, but this has been refused.

Advise Robert, Tom and David.

Answer plan ──────────────────────────────────

The first thing to note about this question is the time all the employees have been employed. All of them have been employed for less than one year and so the question relates to the common law and not the statutory provisions. The question also raises the issue of remedies, particularly in relation to David.

Issues which the student should consider are:

- statutory notice provisions in s 86 of the ERA 1996;
- the effect at common law of misconduct during notice;
- what action by the employer constitutes a dismissal;
- what action by the employee constitutes a resignation;
- the effect at common law of a breach of contractual disciplinary procedures;
- remedies, particularly the availability of an injunction.

────────────────── # Answer ──────────────────

None of the employees at present have the necessary one year continuity of employment to claim an unfair dismissal, so all of their rights will arise under common law. At first glance, it would appear that all the employees will wish to sue for damages for wrongful dismissal. A more detailed examination of the individual cases is necessary, however, to determine whether claims for wrongful dismissal lie.

Robert has been employed for six months. There is no evidence in the problem that there is a notice provision in his contract and therefore the statutory minimum notice provided by s 86 of the ERA 1996 applies. Section 86(1)(a) provides that for a person employed for more than four weeks, but less than two years, the statutory minimum notice period is one week. If Robert's contract gives a longer notice period, then the contractual notice applies. If the contractual notice is shorter than the statutory notice, the statutory notice applies and the contractual provision is void. This means that, whatever may or may not be in Robert's contract, by giving him two days' notice, Prior Products is in breach of the relevant notice provision and, on the face of it, it would appear that Robert has been wrongfully dismissed. Robert, however, sabotaged some machinery during his two-day notice period.

At common law, the employer does not have to have a reason to dismiss, but merely has to give the correct amount of notice. In certain situations, however, the employer does not have to give notice and this is where the employee is guilty of gross misconduct or gross neglect. Furthermore, whereas under unfair dismissal provisions, the employer must have a reason which justifies the dismissal at the time he dismissed, the same is not true at common law and an original wrongful dismissal can be retrospectively made lawful if the employer discovers a reason after dismissal which would justify him dismissing instantly.

In the old case of *Ridgway v Hungerford Market* (1835), an employee, while under notice of dismissal, committed an act of gross misconduct. It was held that while the original dismissal had been wrongful because insufficient notice had been given, his misconduct justified instant dismissal and therefore rendered the original wrongful dismissal lawful. In a similar case, *Boston Deep Sea Fishing and Ice Co v Ansell* (1888), the misconduct was not discovered until some time after the dismissal had taken effect but again the original wrongful dismissal was retrospectively rendered lawful. Applying these cases to Robert's situation, without doubt, his act of sabotage is gross misconduct and, therefore, while originally his dismissal was wrongful because of insufficient notice, his actions have now made his dismissal lawful and he will be unable to sue for damages.

The question in Tom's case is, first, whether the words of the manager constitute a dismissal. The problem here is that the manager has not used normal words to signify a dismissal, but told Tom that he and the bosses are fed up and that he should clear off. In situations like these, the tribunal will look at the intention behind the words. Cases such as *Futty v Brekkes Ltd* (1974) and *Davy v Collins Builders Ltd* (1974) show that swear words used in the heat of an argument do not necessarily constitute a dismissal when the intention of the employer is looked at, together with the situation in which they are spoken and the working environment the employee comes from. In *Tanner v Kean* (1978), the employer lost his temper with an employee and said: 'That's it, you're finished with me.' The EAT decided that these words were spoken in anger and not intended to be a dismissal. Likewise, in *Martin v Yeoman Aggregates Ltd* (1983), an employer told the employee to leave after he refused to obey an order, but within five minutes, he recanted his words and suspended the employee instead. The employee insisted on treating himself as dismissed. Kilner Brown J said that it was a matter of common sense, vital to good industrial relations that either party should be able to retract words spoken in the heat of the moment. On the basis of the above, therefore, it is unlikely that the tribunal would interpret the words 'clear off' as a dismissal, particularly as they appear to have been spoken in anger and Tom left without giving the manager time to withdraw them.

This leads to the second question. Do Tom's words and actions constitute a resignation? The works rules state that resignations must be in writing and therefore it would appear that a verbal resignation will be insufficient, although the employer can always waive the right to a written resignation if he wishes. In Tom's situation, he appears to have reacted in the heat of the moment and it is debatable whether he intended to resign. As such, it could be argued, at best, that his words were ambiguous. In such situations, the tribunals again apply a common sense approach. In *Kwik Fit (GB) Ltd v Lineham* (1992), the employee, Mr Lineham, a manager, used the depot toilet on the way home from the pub one night. This was not contrary to any rules and he reactivated the alarm. The security staff reported him and a director gave him a written warning in front of a junior colleague. Lineham threw down his keys, walked out and did not return to work the next day, so the employer sent him a letter confirming termination of the employment. In a subsequent unfair dismissal claim, the employer argued that Lineham had resigned. The tribunal found that there was an ambiguous resignation and the burden therefore fell to the employer to establish the intention of the employee. The EAT held that the employer was not under such a heavy burden unless there were special circumstances but where these existed, the employer should wait a reasonable time before accepting the resignation at face value. In *Lineham's* case, special circumstances existed and therefore the employee had not resigned, the contract had been terminated by the employer.

In Tom's case, the words are not specific. He did not say, for example, 'I am resigning', but merely appeared to react angrily to the words spoken by the manager. As such, on the basis of *Lineham*, it could be argued that the words were spoken in anger and that there were special circumstances. The employer should have waited a reasonable time to establish Tom's intention. In Tom's case, the employer sent his P45 the next day (as in *Lineham*). It is submitted that this is not a reasonable time and that the sending of the P45 constituted an employer termination and thus a dismissal. As with Robert, Tom is entitled to at least one week's notice, unless his conduct in joking around can be construed as gross misconduct. If he is not guilty of gross misconduct during his employment and the court feels that his reaction to the manager's words is not gross misconduct, then Tom is entitled to one week's pay as damages.

David, by the time his notice expires, will be two weeks short of continuity for unfair dismissal. In his case, there are two potential breaches of contract on the part of his employer: the short notice which he has been given and the refusal to allow him to pursue a contractual disciplinary procedure. In David's case, unlike Robert and Tom, the contract gives better notice rights than s 86 of the ERA 1996 and therefore the contract will prevail. On the assumption that David's conduct during his employment does not amount to gross misconduct, David is entitled to four weeks' notice and therefore can sue for two weeks' pay. This leads to the second breach. David is entitled to pursue an appeal against dismissal by his contract and the employer has refused to let him exercise his contractual right. If he had been given the correct amount of notice, he would have the continuity to claim unfair dismissal. Likewise, if he had been given a hearing and allowed to pursue his contractual right of appeal, it could be that the process would not have been completed before David had been employed for 12 months, although if the appeal confirmed his dismissal then the date of termination would be the original date of dismissal and not the date of the appeal (*Sainsbury (J) Ltd v Savage* (1981)).

If there is no evidence to support the employer's argument that David is a bad time keeper, this could affect the remedies he can claim. In *Jones v Lee and Guilding* (1980), the employee was dismissed without being allowed to exercise his contractual right to a hearing. The Court of Appeal granted him an injunction restraining the employers from purporting to dismiss the employee until the hearing had been granted. In contrast, in *Gunton v Richmond upon Thames London Borough Council* (1980), the employee was dismissed with one month's notice although his contractual disciplinary procedure had not been fully implemented. The Court of Appeal held that his loss included a reasonable period in which it would have taken his employer to implement the disciplinary procedures fully and, in *Robert Cort and Sons Ltd v Charman* (1981), it was stated obiter that damages may include a sum to cover the loss of unfair dismissal compensation if the nature of the dismissal was such that the employee had been excluded such protection. The later case of *Raspin v United News Shops Ltd* (1999) confirms that this is the case.

In David's case, it would appear that he has had no hearing whatsoever, despite the right in his contract. The court may therefore adopt the approach taken in *Jones v Lee and Guilding* and issue an injunction to prevent the employers from dismissing him until he has been granted a hearing, provided that the criteria necessary for an injunction exist – that is, damages are an inadequate remedy and there is no loss of trust and confidence in the employee (*Wadcock v London Borough of Brent* (1990)). Alternatively, the court may award damages in excess of two weeks' pay either on the basis that it would take longer than two weeks to instigate the procedures (*Gunton*) or to compensate for the loss of unfair dismissal protection (*Raspin*).

Notes

9 Unfair Dismissal

Introduction

There can be few employment law examination papers which do not contain at least one question on unfair dismissal. Sometimes, essay type questions are set in this area, but more often than not the questions are problems. There is a very simple way to break down unfair dismissal problems which leads the student through the question logically and should help to identify which particular area the problem concentrates upon.

Thus, students should ask themselves the following questions:

- Has the employee the required continuity?
- Is the employee excluded from the statute?
- Has the employee been dismissed?
- Has the employer got a statutory fair reason to dismiss?
- Has the employer acted reasonably?

If students work through the above questions in relation to each party, there should not be too many problems. Questions in this area can concentrate on any of the issues above.

Therefore, students should understand:

- issues relating to continuity;
- the effective date of termination;
- exclusions under the statute;
- the definition of dismissal in s 95 of the Employment Rights Act (ERA) 1996;
- the statutory fair reasons for dismissal;
- the automatically unfair reasons for dismissal;
- the concept of reasonableness;
- the impact of the Employment Act 2002 (Dispute Resolution) Regulations 2004;
- remedies.

It should be noted that, when considering the question of dismissal, the common law concepts dealt with in Chapter 8 are just as applicable in this area. An employee can hardly claim unfair dismissal if he has not been dismissed. It is necessary, therefore, to understand the different forms of termination before tackling an unfair dismissal question.

Checklist

Students should be familiar with the following areas:

- weeks which do/do not break continuity;
- the effect of a change of employer on continuity;
- classes of excluded employees, particularly cases relating to normal retirement age;
- the meaning of dismissal, including constructive dismissal;
- the five statutory fair reasons: capability and qualifications; conduct; redundancy; statutory restriction and some other substantial reason;
- the concept of a fair decision and procedural fairness;
- automatically unfair dismissals;
- the remedies of reinstatement, re-engagement and financial compensation.

Question 32

Marvo and Ricardo are both employed by Big Top Circuses Ltd, Marvo as a clown, Ricardo as general manager.

Marvo was first employed three years ago 'for the circus season'. The season is 11 months and Marvo was employed on a series of 11 month contracts, each of which expired on 1 January and each of which were renewed one month later on 1 February. Each contract contained a clause whereby Marvo waived his rights to unfair dismissal and redundancy protection and a further clause which stated that the contract could be terminated earlier by either party giving notice. This year, Marvo's contract was not renewed.

Ricardo was employed for 52 weeks, on a contract which required three months' notice on either side. His employment was continuous, apart from a period of one week when he took part in industrial action. Ricardo was instantly dismissed two and a half months ago, when he refused to submit to a body search. The employers had introduced body searches, without consultation with the employees, because of an increase in theft. A recent appeal endorsed the dismissal.

Advise Marvo and Ricardo about their eligibility to claim unfair dismissal.

 Answer plan

This is a long problem but close analysis reveals that, in relation to each of the parties, the question is whether they have the required continuity and additionally, in Marvo's case, whether he is excluded from unfair dismissal protection. The question is specifically asking about eligibility and that is all that is required. There is no necessity to go into issues of fairness.

Particular issues which need to be considered are:

- the definition of a fixed-term contract;

- weeks counting in the computing period;
- the validity of waiver clauses;
- the effect of a refusal to obey an order;
- the time limit to present an unfair dismissal claim.

————————— Answer —————————

The question to be asked in relation to both the parties in the problem is whether they are eligible to claim unfair dismissal. Not all employees are protected by unfair dismissal provisions.

Normally, an employee must have one year's continuous service and not be excluded from the legislation before he or she can present a claim. Thus, the questions to ask in relation to Marvo and Ricardo are whether they have the correct continuity and whether they are excluded by the statute from presenting a claim.

Marvo has been employed at Big Top Circuses Ltd for three years. He has been employed, however, on a series of 11-month contracts. His contract has not been renewed when it expired recently. Failing to renew a fixed-term contract can constitute a dismissal by s 95(1) of the ERA 1996. Fixed-term contracts, however, raise a variety of issues. First, are the three contracts Marvo enters into fixed-term contracts within the meaning of the legislation? The fact that the contracts allow either party to terminate earlier by giving notice does not prevent them being fixed-term contracts (*BBC v Dixon* (1979)). To constitute a fixed-term contract within the meaning of the statute, the contract must expire on a definite date and not on the happening of some particular event (*Wiltshire County Council v NATFHE* (1980)). If, therefore, Marvo's contract for the 'circus season' terminates on a specific date, even if this is not mentioned in the contract but is easily ascertainable, then it does constitute a fixed-term contract. If no such date is ascertainable, it will be a contract for an indefinite period. It is submitted that, in Marvo's case, all his contracts were for a fixed-term because they all ended on 1 January. Thus, Marvo was employed on three fixed-term contracts. The second question to raise in relation to Marvo is does he have 11 months' continuity (the length of time of his last contract) or can all his contracts be lumped together to give him 33 months' continuity? Section 212 of the ERA 1996 provides for situations where an employee is not at work although his continuity continues. Weeks of absence which fall within these paragraphs do not break the continuity period and count in the final computation of continuous employment. Section 212(3)(b) covers the situation when the employee is absent due to a temporary cessation of work. Temporary cessation envisages situations when there is no work available for the employee (*Fitzgerald v Hall, Russell and Co Ltd* (1970)). This raises the question, however, of how long is temporary? In *Bentley Engineering Co Ltd v Crown* (1976), an absence of two years was held to be temporary as it was a relatively short period in the context of the employment relationship as a whole. Thus, the decision as to whether the absence is temporary takes place at the end of the break when all factors are taken into account.

A case akin to Marvo's situation is *Ford v Warwickshire County Council* (1983). The employee in this case was a teacher employed on a sessional basis. Her contracts ended in July and were renewed in September. She was employed for eight years. The House of Lords stated that the holidays were a temporary cessation of work, given the length of the employment and the length of the holidays. Temporary means transient. While the Employment Appeal Tribunal (EAT) has stated that a strict mathematical approach is wrong, in *Berwick Salmon Fisheries Co Ltd v Rutherford* (1991), the same tribunal held that it would not be possible to call a cessation temporary when the periods of lay-off were longer than the periods of working.

Applying the cases to Marvo's situation, his case is similar to *Ford* above. He has worked for three years with two one-month breaks. Given the length of employment and the length of the breaks, it is likely that the tribunal will conclude that he has three years' continuity and therefore has the necessary continuity to claim.

Marvo has a waiver provision in each of the contracts by which he has waived his rights to claim unfair dismissal. Until recently, it was possible to insert a waiver provision in a fixed-term contract of one year or more and the employee would thereby exclude himself from unfair dismissal protection (s 197 of the ERA 1996). The provision in Marvo's contract is invalid for two reasons. First, his contracts have only been for 11 months and thus would not fall within s 197. Secondly, s 18 of the 1999 Employment Relations Act repealed the sub-sections of s 197 which relate to exclusion of unfair dismissal protection. Therefore, even if Marvo's contracts were one-year fixed-term contracts, the waiver provision would be void in so far as it purports to exclude protection from unfair dismissal, and Marvo will be able to take action.

Ricardo, on the face of it, looks as if he has the necessary continuity of 52 weeks to claim unfair dismissal. Section 216, however, states that certain weeks do not break the continuity period but do not count in the final calculation.

Section 216(1) states that any week when the employee takes part in a strike shall not count towards continuity. In the problem, it states that Ricardo took part in industrial action for one week during the year of his employment. If this industrial action was a strike, Ricardo cannot count that week in the calculation of his continuity and therefore will have only 51 weeks' continuous service, one week short of the necessary one-year period. If the action was not a strike, for example, an overtime ban or a work-to-rule, given the specific wording of s 216, he will not lose that week and will have the necessary continuity to claim. Should this not be the case, the court may be sympathetic and grant an injunction to give him the necessary length of employment.

Ricardo has been instantly dismissed for failing to comply with a body search. The search was introduced without any consultation with employees, which suggests that it is a unilateral imposition by the employer and therefore not part of the employee's obligations under the contract of employment. Even if it is not part of his contractual obligations, Ricardo may still be contractually obliged to submit to such a search under the implied duty on all employees to obey lawful reasonable orders issued by his employer, but the question must be raised as to whether an order to subject oneself to a body search which has been unilaterally imposed is a reasonable order, whatever the problems of the employer. If such an order is not reasonable, Ricardo was under no contractual obligation to obey it. As such, he has been wrongfully dismissed and is entitled to three months' net pay as damages. Ricardo's dismissal, however, should he have 51 weeks' continuity instead of 52, has led to his exclusion from unfair dismissal protection. By s 97(1)(b), where a contract is terminated without notice, the effective date of termination of the contract is the day the termination takes place. If a later appeal confirms the dismissal, the date of termination is the original dismissal date and not the date of the appeal (s 97(1)(b)). Thus, as Ricardo's wrongful dismissal has excluded him from statutory protection, would the courts grant an injunction to prevent the termination taking effect until the date of the appeal?

Injunctions are rarely granted to force parties to continue a contract for personal services. Section 236 of the Trade Union and Labour Relations Consolidation Act (TULR(c)A) 1992 provides that no court shall compel an employee to do any work or attend a place for the doing of work. However, in rare cases, the courts have issued interim injunctions to prevent the employer from treating the employee as dismissed until the happening of a certain event, for example, the completion of disciplinary procedures (*Jones v Lee and Guilding* (1980)) or the injunction has extended the employee's notice period (*Hill v CA Parsons and Co Ltd* (1972)). The court, however, will not grant an injunction unless damages are an inadequate remedy, there has been a breach of contract by the employer and there is no loss of confidence between the parties.

In this case, Ricardo is the general manager of a company which has been suffering from thefts.While it has been argued that the employee is in breach, given that he refused to submit to a body search, it could be argued that the employer had lost all trust and confidence in him. In addition, the damages which he would receive for wrongful dismissal are likely to be three months' salary (given his contractual notice period). If the employer argues that he has lost trust and confidence in the employee, in an unfair dismissal claim, it is unlikely that the tribunal would award reinstatement or re-engagement and would merely grant financial compensation. On his length of service, this is not likely to be much greater than damages at common law. As such, it is unlikely that the court would grant an injunction.

There is one further problem with Ricardo. Should it be decided that he has in fact 52 weeks' continuity, given that by s 97(1)(b) the effective date of termination of his contract was the date of actual termination, he now has only two weeks in which to present his claim to the tribunal. An unfair dismissal claim must be presented within three months of the effective date of termination (s 111(2)(a) of the ERA 1996).

Notes

Question 33

Bill worked until recently as a lorry driver for Jock's Haulage, a company in Hull. At the date of his dismissal, Bill was 61. He worked for the company for five years. His contract stipulated that the retirement age for lorry drivers working for the company was 60, but in practice, many drivers work until they are 65. Two months ago, shortly before Bill's dismissal, the company issued a statement reiterating that the retirement age was 60. Bill has never seen a copy of the statement.

One year ago, Bill received a cash bonus at the end of the year in substitution for his final week's pay. This was a deliberate attempt by Jock's Haulage to evade tax, although the bonus was the same as his salary.

Two weeks ago, Bill was paid three months' wages in lieu of notice. The reason given for his dismissal was that his age now made it dangerous to do his job.

Advise Bill on his eligibility to pursue a claim for unfair dismissal.

Answer plan

This is another question on the area of eligibility, although it concentrates more on the exclusion provisions with only one point on continuity. Again, it concentrates on eligibility only and does not require discussion of whether the dismissal is fair or unfair.

Particular issues to be considered are:

- the normal retirement age for the job, particularly, judicial discussion in cases such as *Nothman v London Borough of Barnet* (1979); *Waite v GCHQ* (1983); *Brooks v British Telecommunications plc* (1991);
- the effect of the tax-free bonus on continuity;
- the effect of the payment of wages in lieu.

Answer

While Bill appears to have been employed for five years and, on the face of it, meets the necessary continuity requirements, certain employees are excluded from claiming unfair dismissal. One of these exclusions is an employee who has reached the normal retirement age for the job (s 109(1)(a) of the ERA 1996). In addition, the tax-free bonus Bill received may have stopped his continuity and could raise issues as to whether he has the necessary one year's continuous employment which he needs to make a claim.

Dealing with the first point, Bill has been dismissed at 61. The contract states that the retirement age is 60, although, in practice, employees have worked up to 65. Section 109(1) creates two ages – either the normal retirement age for the job within the employer's undertaking or 65. On the original interpretation of the wording, it was thought that attainment of 65 excluded the contractual retirement age, so that entitlement to claim unfair dismissal ceased at 65 whatever the normal retirement age in the contract. However, the House of Lords in *Nothman v London Borough of Barnet* (1979) decided that the statutory age of 65 applies only if there is no normal retirement age. Thus, if the normal retirement age is 70, this is the age at which the employee becomes excluded. If this case is applied to Bill's situation, the contractual retirement age in his case is 60. The employer could thus argue that this is the normal retirement age and, therefore, Bill is excluded from statutory protection. However, the age stated in the contract may not be the normal retirement age if in practice, employees can work beyond that age. In *Waite v GCHQ* (1983), there was a discrepancy between the contractual retirement age and the age at which employees actually retired. Lord Fraser stated that the normal retirement age was the age at which the employees could reasonably expect to retire. The starting point is the contractual retirement age and this will be the normal retirement age, but this can be displaced if it is regularly departed from in practice. If there is an age at which employees normally retire, this will become the normal retirement age. If employees retire at a variety of different ages, then there is no normal retirement age and the statutory age of 65 applies. In Bill's case, many drivers work until they are 65 and, on the basis of *Waite*, it could be argued that this is the normal retirement age for the job.

The problem which arises, however, is that Lord Fraser talked about the age at which employees could reasonably expect to retire. In *Hughes v DHSS* (1985), the Civil Service conditions of employment specified a retirement age of 60, but the practice was to allow employees to work until 65. However, there was a well publicised change in departmental policy to reintroduce 60 as the retirement age. The employees had worked past 60 and were compulsorily retired and claimed unfair dismissal. The House of Lords held that by the time of their dismissals, their expectation must have been to retire at 60 because the change in policy had been well publicised. Thus, they were excluded from unfair dismissal protection.

So, too, in *Brooks v British Telecommunications plc* (1991), where the employer, who had a contractual retirement age of 60 but in practice allowed employees to work beyond that age, issued a notice to all staff reiterating the contractual retirement age and stating retention beyond that age was unlikely. The court held that Brooks could reasonably expect to retire at 60 and that that was the normal retirement age for the job. *Barclays Bank plc v O'Brien* (1994) further states that if the employer has laid down a clear policy, he has established a clear retirement age even if there are limited exceptions. In Bill's case, the employer issued a statement reiterating that the retirement age was 60. Bill did not receive that statement. Looking at Lord Fraser's judgment in *Waite* and later judgments in *Hughes* and *Brooks*, although the employer has laid down a clear policy, it seems difficult to argue that 60 was the age at which Bill could reasonably expect to retire as, at the date of his dismissal, he had no idea that the contractual retirement age had been confirmed and would still feel that employees could work until 65. As such, it is possible to distinguish *Hughes* and *Brooks* and argue that Bill is not excluded because of his age and that the normal retirement age in Bill's case is 65.

Although Bill is not an excluded employee, he may not have the continuity period to claim unfair dismissal. The problem states that he was employed for five years but one year ago he received a tax-free payment from his employer. In *Hyland v JH Barker (North West) Ltd* (1985), a lorry driver had been employed for 16 years when he received a tax-free lodging allowance for one month in the 12 months prior to his dismissal. It was held that he did not have the continuity to claim unfair dismissal as the illegality of performance meant neither party could rely on rights arising from the contract until the illegal performance ceased. Thus, the employee had wiped out all his acquired continuity and a new continuity period began once the illegality ceased. However, in this area, normal contractual doctrine applies and innocence can be pleaded as a defence (*Tomlinson v Dick Evans 'U' Drive Ltd* (1978)). Furthermore, it is actual knowledge which is important and not whether the employee ought to have known what was happening (*Corby v Morrison* (1980)). To some extent, however, the actual knowledge of the employee may still allow him to claim his rights. In *Hewcastle Catering Ltd v Ahmed* (1992), Beldam LJ stated that the modern law is that the doctrine of illegality only applies if, in all the circumstances, it would be an affront to the public conscience to allow the claim to proceed. Furthermore, the employer should not be allowed to raise the defence of illegality if the employer's conduct was more reprehensible than that of the employee and it would be wrong for the employer to benefit from it.

Applying the above to Bill's case, if Bill was unaware of the tax-free payment, as it was the same as his salary, *Hyland* can be distinguished and the one-off payment will not stop his continuity running. If, on the other hand, he realised what was happening, despite the judgment of Beldam LJ, it is possible that *Hyland* will be applied and

Hewcastle can be distinguished as in that case the employees knew of the employer's VAT fraud but did not benefit from it, although it could be argued that, as Bill received the same amount as his normal salary, there was no benefit to him.

If the illegality means that Bill's continuity started from the end of the tax-free payment, it depends on whether one year has elapsed on the date he was paid wages in lieu of notice. Payment in lieu terminates the contract on the date the payment is made and not at the end of the notice period (*Stapp v Shaftesbury Society* (1982). Thus, by s 97(1), his contract terminates on the day of payment and not three months later. As such, Bill may not have the requisite one year's continuity.

Notes

_____

_____

_____

_____

_____

_____

_____

_____

_____

_____

_____

_____

Question 34

Rita and Mavis both worked for Alec Machine Tools Ltd.

Rita was the machine shop floor supervisor. She was dismissed when she missed a shift because she was visiting her sick mother in hospital. After an internal appeal, she was reinstated at a lower grade, with a consequent reduction in salary, after consideration had been given to the fact that:

(a) she had worked there for 15 years;

(b) she had an exemplary work record; and

(c) she had arranged for another supervisor to cover her shift and no disruption to the business occurred.

Rita resigned after the appeal.

Mavis worked on the shop floor for five years. Due to foreign imports, Alec had been striving to produce more products in less time and the workers were ignoring safety procedures – such as fencing machinery – to meet targets Alec had set. Mavis refused to remove the fence on her machine and therefore could not work as quickly as the others. Alec warned her that if she could not meet her targets, he would reduce her wages. Because of the stress placed upon her, she resigned.

Ignoring the issue of fairness under s 98(4) of the ERA 1996, advise Rita and Mavis whether they may claim unfair dismissal.

Answer plan

This is a question that needs to be read carefully. Too many students do not read the question properly and go into issues which do not need to be addressed. The question says to ignore the issue of fairness. Going through the questions posed at the beginning of the chapter when faced with an unfair dismissal problem, we know that the persons are employees, we know that they have the requisite continuity and that there is nothing to suggest that either of them is excluded from unfair dismissal protection. The question therefore concentrates on the issue of dismissal and asks whether the parties have been dismissed at law or whether one or both have resigned. Given that, on the face of it, both the parties have terminated their own contracts, we can see that the question is more focused and requires a discussion of one type of dismissal (constructive dismissal).

Issues which need to be discussed are therefore:

- the definition of constructive dismissal in s 95(1)(c) of the ERA 1996;
- the test in *Western Excavating (ECC) Ltd v Sharp* (1978);
- whether the imposition of a lesser sanction than dismissal can be a breach of contract;
- whether insisting on breaches of health and safety procedures can be a breach of contract;
- whether threatening a potential breach of contract can set up a constructive dismissal claim;
- whether causing an employee stress is a breach of contract.

Answer

The question asks us to advise the two parties as to whether they can claim unfair dismissal. In both the situations, the parties have terminated their own contracts, but this does not mean that there has not been a dismissal in law. By s 95(1)(c) of the ERA 1996, once an employee is protected by unfair dismissal provisions, a dismissal can occur where the employee terminates the contract 'with or without notice, in circumstances such that he is entitled to terminate it without notice by reason of the employer's conduct'.

A resignation in these circumstances is known as a constructive dismissal. From the definition in s 95(1)(c), however, it can be seen that not all conduct on the part of the employer entitles the employee to resign. In *Western Excavating (ECC) Ltd v Sharp* (1978), Denning MR said that, for the employer's conduct to amount to a constructive dismissal the conduct had to be 'a significant breach going to the root of the contract of employment, or which shows that the employer no longer intends to be bound by one or more of the essential terms of the contract', thus indicating that the essence of a constructive dismissal is a fundamental or repudiatory breach by the employer. Unreasonable conduct per se on the part of the employer will normally not establish a constructive dismissal claim. In all the cases in the problem, therefore, it is necessary to establish whether the employees have terminated their contracts due to a fundamental breach of contract by Alec.

Rita resigned after an appeal reinstated her after her original dismissal, but at a lower grade and on a reduced salary. As previously stated, given that Rita resigned, her resignation will only be a constructive dismissal for the purposes of the ERA 1996 if Alec was in fundamental breach of the employment contract. The first question which must be asked is: did Alec have a right to demote Rita as part of his disciplinary procedures and were such procedures part of Rita's contract? Disciplinary procedures may become contractual, particularly if they are given to the employee at the same time as the contract and the contract refers to them. Many employers make such procedures contractual because if one of the sanctions within the procedures is a reduction in wages, for example, by a demotion, then the employer must have contractual authority to reduce the wages (or the employee's authority to reduce his pay) to prevent being in breach of contract. If Alec has no contractual authority to demote Rita, then he has unilaterally altered her contract. Such an alteration will involve a change in her job duties and in her term relating to pay.

Whereas, in some cases, it has been held that a failure to pay wages or a pay reduction was not a repudiatory breach (*Adams v Charles Zub Associates Ltd* (1978)), generally, a reduction in pay will be a repudiation by the employer. In addition, in *Millbrook Furnishing Industries Ltd v McIntosh* (1981), the transfer of highly skilled sewing machinists to unskilled work was held to be a breach, for it was to last until work picked up in their normal area and the time this would take could not be predicted. In *Adams*, there was no breach by the employer because there was a temporary cash flow problem and the employee would be paid in the near future. In Rita's case, it does not appear that either the demotion or the reduction in pay is of a temporary nature and, as such, it is possible to distinguish *Adams* on the issue of her pay reduction and to follow *McIntosh* in relation to the demotion. Thus, if Alec has no contractual authority to demote as a disciplinary sanction, he has committed a repudiatory breach of contract within the terms of s 95(1)(c) of the ERA 1996 and Rita has been constructively dismissed.

This then leads to the following question: what if Alec has the contractual right to demote in disciplinary situations? On the face of it, there appears to be no breach of contract as Alec is merely exercising his contractual rights. Such an approach is subject, however, to the decision in *Cawley v South Wales Electricity Board* (1985). In that case, Cawley was seen urinating out of the back door of a company vehicle. He was originally dismissed, but a subsequent appeal reinstated him but at a new site and with a reduction in salary of £1,400 a year. Cawley resigned. An employment tribunal held that the action by the employer was disproportionate to the employee's conduct and therefore there had been a breach of contract and a constructive dismissal. The tribunal held, however, that the dismissal was fair. Cawley appealed, arguing that the tribunal was using two different standards of reasonableness. By stating that the action by the employer was so unreasonable in the circumstances that there was a breach of contract, it must therefore follow that the dismissal must also be unreasonable and, as such, unfair. The EAT agreed with Cawley and ruled that he had been unfairly dismissed. This means that even if the employer has the contractual right to demote or reduce salary, he is subject to the proportionality principle: in other words, the sanction imposed must not be out of proportion to the conduct of the employee. If the sanction is excessive, following *Cawley*, its very excessiveness is a breach of contract because it is a breach of the implied duty of mutual trust and confidence and the ensuing constructive dismissal is unfair.

If we apply this to Rita's case, she did not work one shift because she was visiting her sick mother. Her absence did not disrupt the business as she had arranged for a replacement and she had never been disciplined before in 15 years of employment. Given these facts, it would appear that a demotion and a reduction in salary is a harsh sanction to impose for a first disciplinary offence, particularly one which did not affect the business. Following *Cawley*, it can be argued that the employer's sanction was disproportionate and unreasonable and that this unreasonable action constituted a repudiatory breach because it was a breach of the implied duty of mutual trust and confidence. This means that Rita has been constructively dismissed and, further, that her dismissal must be unfair.

Mavis has resigned due to pressure put upon her to meet targets set by Alec. The only way she can meet these targets appears to be by ignoring safety procedures in relation to the fencing of machinery. While Alec has not actually appeared to have told her to break safety procedures, given that the other workers were removing the fences to meet targets suggests that this is the only way that the targets can be met.

Mavis resigned when Alec threatened to reduce her wages if she failed to meet the targets. As yet, at the time of her resignation, Alec had not told her to remove the fence or reduced her wages. Allowing the use of machinery without a fence when one is required by law is a breach of the common law implied duty of safety that an employer owes to all his employees, in particular, the requirement to provide a safe system of work. In addition, lack of fencing is contrary to s 14(1) of the Factories Act 1961 unless the lack of a fence does not make the machinery unsafe.

Furthermore, under s 7 of the Health and Safety at Work, etc Act 1974, Mavis is under a statutory duty to take reasonable care for the health and safety of herself and others who may be injured by her acts and omissions at work and as regards any duty or requirement imposed under any statutory provision. In short, Mavis will be in breach of her statutory duty if by law the machinery should be fenced and Alec is in breach of both common law and statutory duties by allowing the workers to operate the machinery without the fences on. If the implication of Alec's warning is that Mavis must remove the fence, he is giving an unlawful order. While an employee must obey all lawful, reasonable orders issued by the employer, there is no duty to obey any order which is unlawful (*Morrish v Henlys (Folkestone) Ltd* (1973)) or unreasonable (*Ottoman Bank Ltd v Chakarian* (1930)). Thus, if in essence this is what Alec requires Mavis to do, she can refuse, and her refusal will not be a breach of contract. If, however, it is possible to meet the targets complying with safety procedures and Mavis is merely slower than the rest, Alec is not in breach of contract by trying to get her to work to target.

Alec threatened to reduce Mavis' wages if she could not make the target set. At the time Mavis resigned, this remained as a threat which had yet to be carried out. This will not necessarily defeat Mavis claiming dismissal, as it is possible to have an anticipatory breach (*Norwest Holst Group Administration Ltd v Harrison* (1985)). The question which arises, however, is whether a reduction in wages is within Alec's contractual rights as part of a disciplinary procedure for not meeting targets. The discussion above on Rita, and the contractual status of disciplinary procedures, is pertinent here. Even if Alec was acting within his contractual rights, if the targets can only be made by removing the fences, imposing a sanction for refusing to act contrary to statute is unreasonable and, on the basis of *Cawley v South Wales Electricity Board*, Alec is in anticipatory breach of contract and as such Mavis can claim constructive dismissal. If, on the other hand, the targets can be met legally and there is a contractual right to reduce wages in these circumstances, unless it could be argued that threatening the sanction without training or giving an opportunity to improve falls within the ambit of the decision in *Cawley* (which is doubtful), there is no breach of contract on the part of the employer.

A final issue in relation to Mavis is whether Alec is in breach of the duty of mutual trust and confidence by putting so much pressure upon her that stress causes her to resign. The duty is a fairly recent innovation from the courts and has still to be fully developed. Cases such as *Bliss v South East Thames Regional Health Authority* (1987) show that the employer must not act in such a way as to destroy the trust and confidence necessary to make the relationship work. If Alec's conduct can be construed as destroying that trust and confidence, particularly as Mavis has resigned because of stress, then this would be a repudiatory breach and, as such, again Mavis could claim constructive dismissal.

Notes

Question 35

The test for determining whether a termination of a contract of employment by an employer amounts to a constructive dismissal is not a reasonableness but a contractual test. Courts and tribunals deny the existence of a duty upon employers to act reasonably towards their employees. Nevertheless, in practice, the difference between the two tests is minimal if not illusory.

How far do you consider this statement to be an accurate reflection of the law?

Answer plan

The question is asking for a discussion of the definition of a constructive dismissal and the interpretation of that definition by the courts. It is easy to think that this is all the question demands, but it also requires a discussion of cases where tribunals have refused to imply a term that the employer shall act reasonably and cases where in reality the contractual and reasonableness tests seem to have been used interchangeably. The question therefore calls for a detailed knowledge of a number of cases and the student to come to his or her own conclusion on the accuracy of the statement.

Issues which need to be considered are therefore:

- the contractual test in *Western Excavating (ECC) Ltd v Sharp* (1978);
- the reasonableness test in *United Bank Ltd v Akhtar* (1989) and *Cawley v South Wales Electricity Board* (1985);
- limits on the reasonableness test in cases such as *White v Reflecting Roadstuds Ltd* (1991) and *Courtaulds Northern Spinning Ltd v Sibson* (1988);
- the effect of the development of the duty of mutual trust and confidence in this area;
- areas where a strict contractual approach is used.

Answer

The definition of a constructive dismissal is found in s 95(1)(c) of the ERA 1996. This section provides that an employee is to be treated as dismissed by his employer if the employee terminates the contract 'with or without notice, in circumstances such that he is entitled to terminate it without notice by reason of the employer's conduct'. The key word in the statutory definition, however, is 'entitled'. What conduct on the part of the employer entitles an employee to resign and claim he has been dismissed?

In early cases, courts and tribunals took the view that unreasonable conduct by the employer justified the employee in resigning and claiming constructive dismissal (*George Wimpey Ltd v Cooper* (1977)). This reasonableness test was rejected for a narrower contractual test by the Court of Appeal in *Western Excavating (ECC) Ltd v Sharp* (1978).

Lord Denning MR said:

> If the employer is guilty of conduct which is a significant breach going to the root of the contract of employment, or which shows that the employer no longer intends to be bound by one or more of the essential terms of the contract, then the employee is entitled to treat himself as discharged from further performance.

In the case, an employee was suspended without pay for taking unauthorised time off. Due to the fact that he had no money, he asked the employer for his holiday pay to date or alternatively for a loan. The employer refused both requests and the employee resigned and claimed constructive dismissal on the basis that the employer's conduct was so unreasonable that he was entitled to resign. The employment tribunal upheld his complaint, but the employer's appeal was allowed in the Court of Appeal, which stated that the true test under s 95(1)(c) was whether the employer had broken a fundamental term of the contract. In that case, the employer was not contractually obliged to pay accrued holiday pay or grant the employee a loan. As such, there was no breach of contract by the employer and therefore no constructive dismissal.

The court gave three main reasons for adopting the contractual approach. First, the statute distinguished between dismissal and unfairness and therefore the same test of reasonableness could not apply to both. This may now be in doubt since the decision of *Cawley v South Wales Electricity Board* (1985). Secondly, the words in the section were 'entitled to terminate' and these had a legal and therefore contractual connotation. Thirdly, unreasonableness as a test was too indefinite and imprecise. While Lord Denning enunciated that the test was contractual, however, Lawton LJ obviously envisaged a flexible approach. He said:

> Sensible people have no difficulty in recognising such conduct (needed to entitle the employee to terminate the contract) when they hear it ... what is required for an application of this provision is a large measure of common sense.

It would therefore seem that at least one judge in the *Western Excavating* case intended a much more flexible approach.

While the Court of Appeal has since reiterated the contractual test in cases such as *Courtaulds Northern Spinning Ltd v Sibson* (1988), it is arguable that the reasonableness test in reality is being applied in recent cases. There are two reasons why this is suggested. First, in recent years, the EAT, in particular, has developed what has become known as the duty of mutual trust and confidence as an implied term in the contract of employment. To some extent, this can be seen as the corollary of the employee's duty of faithful service. In *British Telecom plc v Ticehurst* (1992), the Court of Appeal appeared to resurrect *Secretary of State for Employment v ASLEF* (1972) and allowed an employer to refuse to permit an employee to work if she was not prepared to sign a document saying that she would work normally and take no further industrial action. In other words, the employer could prevent an employee from working if he no longer had trust in that employee because he feared she would work to rule. Likewise, it appears that if the employer is guilty of conduct which destroys the trust the employee has in the relationship, the employer is in breach of contract (see, for example, the judgment of Browne-Wilkinson P in *Woods v WM Car Services (Peterborough) Ltd* (1981)).

While this would at first sight merely support the contractual test, its importance lies in the fact that the duty can be seen as what Smith and Wood (*Industrial Law*, 8th edn, 2003, London: LexisNexis Butterworths) describe as an 'overriding term' which can override the express terms of the contract. The essence of the term means that the employer must exercise his contractual rights reasonably. This was first propounded by the EAT in *United Bank Ltd v Akhtar* (1989). In *Akhtar*, there was an express mobility clause in the contract allowing the employer to move the employee anywhere in the UK. The employer ordered the employee to move from Leeds to Birmingham, giving him six days' notice, and refused the employee's request for more time because of personal circumstances. The employee resigned and the EAT held that he had been constructively dismissed. This was despite a previous decision by the same tribunal (*Rank Xerox v Churchill* (1988)) which held that the courts will not imply an element of reasonableness where the term is clear and unambiguous. The essence of the judgment in *Akhtar* is seen from the quote from Knox J. He said:

> ... there may well be conduct which is either calculated or likely to destroy or seriously damage the relationship of trust and respect between employer and employee which a literal interpretation of the written words of the contract might appear to justify, and it is in this sense that we consider that in the field of employment law it is proper to imply an overriding obligation which is independent of, and in addition to, the literal interpretation of the actions which are permitted to the employer under the terms of the contract.

The later EAT decision of *White v Reflecting Roadstuds Ltd* (1991) may appear to go against Akhtar and so refute the reasonableness test, but in reality, this is not the case. In White, an employee resigned after he had been transferred to a lower paid job at another site, a move for which the employer had contractual authority. Wood P said that *Akhtar* did not establish such a sweeping principle that an employer must always exercise his contractual rights reasonably. *Akhtar* lays down the principle that an employer, when exercising his rights under a mobility clause, should not exercise them in such a way as to render it impossible for the employee to do his job. In *Akhtar*, the employee could not commute from Leeds to Birmingham. In *White*, the site was within easy travelling distance of the employee's home. Furthermore, Wood P in *White* stated that a capricious decision to move an employee would not be within the ambit of an express mobility clause and that, as a result of *Woods*, there is an overriding implied term of mutual trust and confidence.

As mutual trust and confidence is now a term of the contract, breach of such can establish a constructive dismissal within the decision of *Western Excavating*. The importance of this term, however, lies in its overriding nature. From both *Akhtar* and *White*, it would appear that the term means that the employer must not act capriciously – that is, he must act reasonably, otherwise he is in breach of contract. The reality therefore appears to be that by imposing the term of trust and confidence on the employer, there is little difference between acting reasonably and treating the employee in such a way that it does not destroy the trust and confidence the employee has in the relationship..

The second reason for stating that the reasonableness test is, in reality, one of the tests applied is the decision in *Cawley v South Wales Electricity Board* (1985) in which an appeal against dismissal reinstated the employee but at a lower salary and at another site. The reduction in salary was £1,400 per annum. The EAT held that the demotion was an excessive sanction in the light of the employee's conduct and, as such, the employee's resignation was a constructive dismissal which was unfair. The reasoning behind the decision was that there was an implied term in the contractual disciplinary procedures that the employer would impose a sanction proportionate to the conduct. If the sanction was out of proportion, the employer's conduct was unreasonable and the employee was entitled to resign. If the employer's conduct was so unreasonable that it was a breach of contract, it followed that the constructive dismissal must be unfair as there could not be different standards of reasonableness in relation to dismissal and fairness. This interpretation goes against the reasons given by Lord Denning MR for his decision in Western Excavating and the Court of Appeal decision in *Savoia v Chiltern Herb Farms Ltd* (1982). What is important, however, is that, yet again, the EAT has introduced a concept of reasonableness into the way the employer exercises his rights, albeit it is arguable that *Cawley* is merely another demonstration of the duty of mutual trust and confidence.

It would appear, therefore, from the above discussion, that there is little difference in reality between the reasonableness test and the contractual test and that the differences are minimal and illusory. It is arguable, however, that there are two important situations in the area of constructive dismissal where the contractual test prevails and where a reasonableness test would give a different result. The first of these is where there is an anticipatory breach. Following the strict contractual approach, in *Norwest Holst Group Administration Ltd v Harrison* (1985), it was held that where the employer is in anticipatory breach of contract, he can rectify the breach before the employee accepts it as repudiatory and any later resignation by the employee after the breach has been withdrawn is not a dismissal. This requires the employee to make a decision before he is certain that the breach will occur or lose his rights to claim unfair dismissal. The second situation is where there is a dispute as to the terms of the contract. In *Frank Wright and Co (Holdings) Ltd v Punch* (1980), the employee resigned when he was not paid cost of living expenses. His contract issued in 1973 said that he was so entitled, but a statement issued in 1978 was silent as to the expenses. The employer genuinely believed that the expenses were not payable. The EAT said that the conduct of the employer in carrying out the contract in accordance with his own erroneous interpretation of its terms was not repudiatory. This shows that there must be an intention to commit a repudiatory breach and, while the decision is in line with normal contractual principles, it can work harshly against an employee who can only claim dismissal if he can show that the employer's belief is not genuine.

From the discussion above, it can be seen that in a great many situations where constructive dismissal is alleged, the test used by courts and tribunals can arguably be called a reasonableness test and that there is little difference between this test and the contractual test in reality. In the two areas, however, of anticipatory breach and disputed terms, the strict contractual test is used, showing the vast difference in these two areas between the two tests – a difference which often works against the employee.

Notes

_____

_____

_____

_____

_____

_____

_____

_____

_____

_____

_____

_____

_____

Question 36

Brahms and Liszt work for the Legless Brewery Company. Brahms took a week off work without permission and without telling his manager the reasons for his absence. (In fact, Brahm's wife had left him.) He has worked for the firm for 20 years but of late has shown little interest in his job. The manager told him yesterday that, because of his attitude, he was being taken off his job as supervisor and put back to working the machinery. Brahms told his manager to 'stuff' his job and left saying 'See you in court.'

Liszt was employed as a sales representative for 10 years. He was employed under a contract which required him to work 35 hours a week. Two weeks ago, on 1 April, the company announced that it will require all sales representatives to work up to five hours a week compulsory overtime from 1 May. Staff were not consulted about this change. Although most of the sales representatives have accepted this change, Liszt has refused to do so and has resigned with effect from 30 April. Legless has introduced the change because of an anticipated increase in competition.

Advise Brahms and Liszt whether they may sue for unfair dismissal.

Answer plan

This is a fairly common type of unfair dismissal problem and demonstrates that employment law cannot be separated into neat little boxes. This problem raises questions about the employee's duty to obey lawful, reasonable orders which was discussed in Chapter 4. It also raises issues in relation to the establishment of a reason and procedures in relation to a conduct/ capability dismissal.

Issues which need to be considered are:

- what constitutes a constructive dismissal under s 95(1)(c) ERA 1996;
- the relevance of the knowledge of the employer at the time of the dismissal and *British Home Stores v Burchell* (1978);
- the procedure in a conduct/capability dismissal;
- what constitutes a lawful, reasonable order;
- some other substantial reason as a potential fair reason for dismissal.

Answer

In both of the cases in the problem, the parties have the necessary continuity to claim unfair dismissal. Both parties appear to have resigned, Brahms by his walking out and Liszt has resigned because of the imposition of overtime. It is necessary in both cases to see if the resignations can be treated as constructive dismissals under s 95 (1)(c) of the ERA 1996.

The problem states that Brahms walked out when his manager told him he would be demoted. The manager's reason for the demotion was Brahms' attitude. In order for Brahms to be able to claim unfair dismissal, by s 95(1)(c) he must establish that he has resigned and that resignation was prompted by the employer's conduct. Since *Western Excavating (ECC) Ltd v Sharp* (1978), the conduct which entitles Brahms to resign and claim constructive dismissal must be a breach of contract by the employer.

Does Brahms walking out constitute a resignation? The court will look at Brahms' intention. It may be that he walked out in the heat of the moment and intended to go back when he had calmed down. If, on the other hand, he intended to permanently leave, he will have terminated his contract – that is, he has resigned. It is obvious from the facts that the reason for his resignation is the fact that the manager told him he had been demoted. If there is no contractual right to demote, then the employer is in breach and Brahms has been constructively dismissed (*Western Excavating (ECC) Ltd v Sharp*). If there is a contractual right to demote, it may still mean that the employer is in breach of contract. In *Cawley v South Wales Electricity Board* (1985), an employee was initially dismissed after a member of the public complained that he had been seen urinating out of a company van. After an appeal, the dismissal was substituted for a demotion, resulting in a reduction in his salary of £1,400. He resigned and the EAT upheld his claim of unfair dismissal on the basis that the employer had imposed too harsh a sanction in respect of his misconduct and that in itself was a breach of the duty of mutual trust and confidence. If the action by the manager, therefore, is seen as too harsh a sanction, on the basis of *Cawley* the employer is in breach and Brahms is entitled to resign and claim constructive dismissal. In addition, given that the manager has acted unreasonably and hence breached the duty, such a dismissal must be unfair as the employer will be unable to satisfy the reasonableness test. Given that Brahms has worked for the company for 20 years and it is only of late his work has been poor, a tribunal may well hold that demotion is too harsh a sanction.

The problem states that the reason for the employer's actions was Brahms' attitude. The problem also states that his absence was because his wife had left him. By *British Home Stores v Burchell* (1978), if the employer wishes to dismiss under s 98(2)(b) of the ERA 1996, the employer must have a genuine belief, based on reasonable grounds after a reasonable investigation, that the employee is 'guilty'. To conduct an investigation, the employer must gather all the evidence so he can make a reasoned and fair decision (*Scottish Daily Record and Sunday Mail (1986) Ltd v Laird* (1996)). Here it appears that no investigation has been conducted; indeed, if it had it may have revealed that the reason for Brahms' conduct was his problems at home As such, given that the employer has not really investigated why Brahms has changed, a tribunal may find that the employer has not established conduct as a reason. The same reasoning will apply if the employer raises capability (s 98(2)(a)) as a reason for dismissal.

If an employer establishes to the satisfaction of the tribunal that a reason under s 98(2) existed, s 98(4) requires the tribunal to consider whether the employer acted reasonably in treating the reason as sufficient to dismiss. Reasonableness falls into two categories: fairness of the decision and procedural fairness.

In relation to fairness of the decision, a tribunal will look for consistency, taking past work record into account and whether the employer has considered alternative employment in respect of a redundancy or incapability dismissal. In relation to consistency, the employer has to treat truly identical cases the same; therefore, the decision can only be challenged on the ground of consistency if, in the past, an employee with the same length of service and with a similar performance problem was not demoted. It is not inconsistent to treat employees with different work records differently (*Sherrier v Ford Motor Co* (1976)). In relation to his past work record, there is nothing in the problem to suggest that until recently there has been any problem in the 20 years of his employment and tribunals expect employers to treat long-serving good employees more leniently than those of shorter lengths of service or blemished work records (*Johnson Matthey Metals Ltd v Harding* (1978)). As such, demoting someone with Brahms' work record may be unreasonable and thus an unfair dismissal. The employer has offered alternative employment, but, it is suggested, it is some way removed from his job as supervisor. In *Hall v Lodge* (1977), a manager who had been overpromoted was demoted to sales assistant in another branch. Given her incapability to do the manager's job, and the fact that she had been removed from the branch where she had been manager, the constructive dismissal was held to be fair. In Brahms' case, however, there is no suggestion that he is permanently incapable of doing the job, merely that his personal problems have affected him temporarily; as such, the offer may in itself be unreasonable.

In relation to procedural fairness in respect of conduct, first of all, the Employment Act 2002 (Dispute Resolution) Regulations 2004 require the employer to go through a statutory procedure before dismissing. The standard procedure would apply in Brahms' case, which reqires the employer to inform the employee of the reason for considering dismissal or other disciplinary action and invite the employee to a meeting (with a representative, if the employee wishes). After such a meeting, the employer must inform the employee of his decision and offer the employee an appeal. If the employee wishes to appeal, the employer must set up a further meeting and afterwards inform the employee of the decision. The ACAS *Code of Practice on Dismissal and Disciplinary Procedures* (2004) suggests also that an employer should investigate before making the decision to start disciplinary action. Although the Code is not legally enforceable, tribunals are required to take its provisions into account (s 207 of the Trade Union and Labour Relations (Consolidation) Act (TULR(C)A) 1992). Here there has been no such investigation. The Code also recommends that dismissal should not be a sanction for a first disciplinary offence and that a warning (albeit a final warning in this case, warning of the consequences of the continued conduct) is more appropriate As such, the employer has not complied with the statutory procedures nor the Code. Failing to comply with the statutory procedures renders the dismissal automatically unfair and compensation can be increased by between 10% and 50%.

Should the employer argue capability as the reason for dismissal, the same statutory procedures apply. In addition, the Code states that the employer should investigate the reason for the incapability, tell the employee the standard to be achieved, give him a reaonable opportunity to improve and tell him the consequences of a failure to improve (ACAS Code, paras 22-25). None of this seems to have happened in Brahms' case, further enforcing the decision that this is an unfair dismissal.

Liszt has been told that the employer is unilaterally altering his contract to include compulsory overtime As a result, Liszt has resigned. By *Western Excavating (ECC) Ltd v Sharp*, this will be a constructive dismissal only if the employer is in breach of contract. Here the employer appears to have unilaterally altered the terms and is therefore in breach and, as such, Liszt has been constructively dismissed.

The employer may try to argue one of two reasons for the dismissal. He may first try to argue that, given the anticipated increase in competition, the order to work compulsory overtime is reasonable and Liszt is in breach of the duty to obey lawful reasonable orders and as such is guilty of misconduct. Given that the change in terms is a breach by the employer in that it is a permanent unilateral variation in the terms of the contract, it is submitted that a tribunal would not regard this as a reasonable order and this reason would fail. It is more likely that the employer would argue some other substantial reason under s 98(2) (e) of the ERA 1996. Changing business needs has been recognised as falling under this head, in particular, a need to change hours (*Johnson v Nottinghamshire Combined Police Authority* (1974)) and, as such, it is likely that the employer has a fair reason to dismiss.

The tribunal, however, also has to decide whether the employer has acted reasonably. In situations such as this the tribunal will first ask itself if the changes were necessary. Originally, the test appeared to be that without them the business would be brought to a standstill (*Ellis v Brighton Co-operative Society Ltd* (1976)). But the test is not so stringent today and all a tribunal should ask is whether there is a sound business reason behind the changes (*Hollister v National Farmers' Union* (1979)). *Chubb Fire Security Ltd v Harper* (1983) states that, in seeing whether the employer acted reasonably, a tribunal might consider the advantages to the employer and weigh them against the disadvantages to the employee. Other factors are whether other employees have accepted the change and the attitude of the union, if there is one (*Caramaran Cruisers*

Ltd v Williams (1994), *Bowater Containers Ltd v McCormack* (1980)). Given that most of the other sales representatives have accepted the change, a tribunal may hold that the needs of the employer may still be met without insisting that Liszt change his hours (*Martin v Automobile Proprietary Ltd* (1979)), although in *Robinson v Flitwick Frames Ltd* (1975), the fact that all the other employees had agreed to the change made the dismissal fair. Trivial changes are likely to result in a fair dismissal for refusal (*Baverstock v Horsley Smith and Co*, unreported date), although it is submitted that in Liszt's case the change is not trivial. In addition, a reaonable employer consults with his employees before making the changes, although lack of consultation has not in the past always been fatal to an employer's claim (*Hollister*). It is suggested that if Liszt is the only one who refuses to accept the change, the employer's needs will still be achieved and thus the employer's insistence is unreasonable.

In addition to introducing new statutory disciplinary procedures, the Employment Act 2002 (Dispute Resolution) Regulations 2004 introduced statutory grievance procedures. These will apply to Liszt. Failure to go through the grievance procedure will automatically prevent him from pursuing an unfair dismissal claim. He must inform the employer of his grievance and ask for a meeting. If he has done so and one has not been set up, he cannot lodge a complaint in the tribunal until 28 days have elapsed.

Notes

Question 37

Hissan is a Japanese car company with two plants, one in Leicester and one in Birmingham. The company recently dismissed three employees.

Bill was the spokesman for a group of workers at the Leicester plant who had a grievance with the company. He was a member of an independent trade union and had worked for the company for six months at the date of his dismissal. He had arranged meetings and organised a petition in support of the grievance which had been vetted by the union. It was these activities, all conducted during working hours, which resulted in his dismissal.

Wally was one of a group of workers at Leicester who took strike action recently in respect of a pay rise. The union supported the strike. He worked for the company for 10 years. The strike began on 1 October and, on 7 October, Hissan wrote to all of those employees not at work saying that, if they did not return on 10 October, they would be dismissed. Some workers did return, but Wally was one of 20 who remained out on 10 October. All 20 employees were sent letters of dismissal on 12 October.

Dick worked at the Birmingham plant. He worked for the company for three years. During the time of unrest at Leicester, the workers at Birmingham organised a work-to-rule to put pressure on the employer to grant the pay rise. The union also supported this action. On 1 October, the company locked them out. On 7 October, the company sent letters to all the Birmingham workers stating that the factory would open on 10 October and that they should return to work on that date. Some workers did return but Dick did not. The next day he was sent a letter of dismissal.

Advise Bill, Wally and Dick whether a tribunal has the jurisdiction to hear their claims for unfair dismissal.

Answer plan

This problem is looking at dismissal for trade union activities, for which no continuity period is required, and the exclusion of tribunal jurisdiction in situations of dismissals during lock outs. Quite detailed knowledge is therefore needed of the statutory provisions and the case law in this area. The problem looks quite complicated because it covers two sites and a variety of dates. However, you will see that the dates of the strike and the lock out are the same and this should make things easier.

Issues which need to be considered are:

- the continuity period for dismissal for taking part in trade union activities;
- the meaning of 'at the appropriate time' in s 152(1) of the TULR(C)A 1992;
- definition of strike and lock out in s 235(4), (5) of the ERA 1996;
- the protection under s 238A of the TULR(C)A 1992 as amended by the Employment Relations Act 2004;
- definition of relevant employees – exclusion of tribunal jurisdiction by s 238 of the TULR(C)A 1992.

Answer

By s 152(1) of the TULR(C)A 1992, a dismissal is automatically unfair if the principal reason for the dismissal was membership or non-membership of a trade union, or because the employee 'had taken, or proposed to take, part in the activities of an independent trade union at an appropriate time'. By s 154 of the same Act, dismissal for this reason does not need the normal one-year continuity period before the employee is protected by unfair dismissal provisions. If, therefore, Bill can show that the reason for his dismissal fell within s 152(1), it is irrelevant that he had only been employed for six months at the time of his dismissal.

To fall within s 152, Bill must show that he was taking part in the activities of an independent trade union at the appropriate time. The problem states that his trade union is independent but that leaves two questions to be answered. What are trade union activities for the purpose of the statute and what constitutes an appropriate time?

Trade union activities appear, from the cases, to be given their ordinary meaning. The statute therefore covers union meetings, recruitment, elections, etc. In Bill's case, he had become the spokesman for a group of employees and had organised a meeting and a petition supporting the employees' grievance. While such activities may be legitimate trade union activities, the question must be asked whether Bill was acting on behalf of the union. In *Chant v Aquaboats* (1978), the employee was dismissed for organising a petition about an unsafe machine. Although he was a union member, he was not an official nor was he organising the petition on behalf of the union. It was held that his dismissal was not for trade union activities. The EAT stated that:

> ... the mere fact that one or two employees making representations happen to be trade unionists and the mere fact that the spokesman happens to be a trade unionist does not make such representations a trade union activity.

Furthermore, in *Stokes and Roberts v Wheeler Green* (1979), it was held that the fact that trade union officers felt that the course of conduct was in the interests of their members did not make the conduct trade union activity. On the basis of these cases, it would appear that even though the union vetted the petition organised by Bill, as he is not an official and the union has not asked him to organise the meeting or the petition, these activities are unlikely to be seen as trade union activities.

Should this not be the case, Bill will still only be protected if he is taking part in the activities 'at an appropriate time'. Section 152(2) defines 'appropriate time' as 'outside working hours or within working hours which, in accordance with arrangements agreed with, or consent given by his employer, it is permissible for him to take part in the activities'. In *Zucker v Astrid Jewels Ltd* (1978), an employee who, while she was working, tried to persuade other employees to join the union was held to be taking part in activities at the appropriate time. On the other hand, in *Marley Tile Co Ltd v Shaw* (1980), a union meeting held where the employer had not given his consent but merely remained silent when informed it was taking place was not held with the employer's consent and, in *Robb v Leon Motor Services Ltd* (1978), it was held that, despite a term in the employee's contract that he would be allowed to take part in trade union activities at the appropriate time, there was no agreement on the part of the employer because the term in the contract was too vague and did not define which times were appropriate. In Bill's case, it appears that there has been no express or implied consent or agreement on the part of his employer that the meeting be held or the petition signed. It would appear from cases such as *Marley Tile Co* and *Robb* that even if Bill was engaged in trade union activities, he was not so doing at an appropriate time and therefore does not have the protection of s 152. As such, he cannot put in a complaint of unfair dismissal as he does not have the requisite continuity of one year.

In respect of the claims of Wally and Dick, it is assumed that because the union supported both the strike and the work to rule, both actions are official. A tribunal has no jurisdiction to hear a complaint of unfair dismissal, whatever the circumstances, where there are dismissals during unofficial action (s 237 of the TULR(C)A 1992). Where the action is official action, Wally may be protected by s 238A of the TULR(C)A 1992. In Dick's case, however, by s 238 of the 1992 Act, the tribunal has no jurisdiction to hear an unfair dismissal complaint where the employer was conducting a lock out 'unless one or more of the relevant employees of the same employer have not been dismissed' (s 238(2)).

In Wally's case, he has been dismissed for taking part in a strike. The definition of a strike is found in s 235(5) of the ERA 1996, which states that it is:

> ... a cessation of work by a body of persons acting in combination, or a concerted refusal ... to continue to work for an employer in consequence of a dispute, done as a means of compelling their employer ... to accept or not accept terms and conditions of or affecting employment.

While the definition in the ERA 1996 applies only to that Act, it is useful as a starting point for the discussion here. By s 238A of the TULR(C)A 1992, which was introduced by the Employment Relations Act 1999 and amended by the Employment Relations Act 2004, any employee who takes part in protected industrial action (that is, endorsed by the union and protected from tortious liability by s 219) who is dismissed within a period of 12 weeks beginning with the day on which the employee started the protected action, is regarded as unfairly dismissed. Thus, Wally can sue and the dismissal will be held to be unfair if the reason for the dismissal is the fact that he took protected action, which appears to be the case on the facts.

In relation to Dick, s 238 applies. This means that Dick may only claim if one or more of the relevant employees have not been dismissed. 'Relevant employees' in these circumstances means those employees directly interested in the dispute (s 238(3)(a)). This has been interpreted to mean any employees who have been locked out at any time during the dispute. In *Campey and Sons v Bellwood* (1987), the company, because of the threat of industrial action, closed the factory on 18 October. On 22 October, the employer sent notices to the employees telling them to return on 24 October. Some did not return and were eventually dismissed. It was held that the relevant employees for the purpose of the statute were those employees locked out on 18 October. As some of those employees had not been dismissed, there had been selective dismissals and the tribunal had the jurisdiction to see if those who had been dismissed had been dismissed unfairly. In Dick's case, some of the employees who had been locked out on 1 October had returned to work and only those who refused to return on 10 October were dismissed. As such, on the authority of *Campey*, some of the relevant employees were not dismissed and the tribunal has the jurisdiction to hear Dick's claim.

Notes

_____

_____

_____

_____

_____

_____

_____

_____

_____

_____

_____

_____

Question 38

Pinch, Nick and Swipe are all employed by Triggerhappy Ltd. Pinch and Nick have been employed for 10 years and Swipe has been employed for two years. During their periods of employment, only Swipe has any disciplinary sanctions against him. This is a warning issued six months ago for bad timekeeping.

Last bank holiday, only Pinch, Nick, Swipe and another employee, Sneak, were at work. During that working day, Sneak had a radio-cassette player stolen while at work. The company was of the opinion that one of the three other employees was responsible for the theft. In fact, Sneak has repeatedly told the company that he has severe reservations about Swipe's honesty, but the company has failed to investigate his complaints.

All three employees were dismissed. Their dismissal notices contained the following statement: 'You are aware, of course, that you are obliged to report instances of theft by fellow employees to the management promptly.'

All the employees had a contractual right to an appeal. All the employees appealed against their dismissals. The appeals consisted of a review of the evidence. The dismissals of Nick and Swipe were confirmed for theft, that of Pinch for failing to report theft by a fellow employee. Nick and Swipe had threatened Pinch that if he reported what had really happened, he would be hurt, but the company are unaware of this because in all the disciplinary hearings, the employees were merely allowed to answer 'yes' or 'no' to questions put to them by the manager.

Advise Pinch, Nick and Swipe who have all entered complaints of unfair dismissal.

Answer plan

While this appears to be a fairly straightforward question, there is in fact a great deal in it. It is essentially about procedure and therefore students need to be aware of what constitutes an adequate investigation, the rules of a fair hearing, consistency of decisions and how far past work record is relevant.

Issues which need to be considered are:

- the test in *British Homes Stores v Burchell* (1978);
- the elements of a reasonable investigation;
- dismissal of a group of employees (*Parr v Whitbread plc (trading as Threshers Wine Merchants)* (1990));
- the constituents of a fair hearing;
- the confirmation of dismissal for a reason other than the original reason;
- the band of reasonable responses test in *Iceland Frozen Foods v Jones* (1983).

Answer

In any unfair dismissal complaint, the burden on the employer is to prove that he had a statutory fair reason to dismiss the employee within s 98(1) and (2) of the ERA 1996. Once this has been established:

> ... the determination of the question of whether the dismissal was fair or unfair, having regard to the reasons shown by the employer, shall depend on whether in the circumstances (including the size and administrative resources of the employer's undertaking) the employer acted reasonably or unreasonably In treating it as a sufficient reason for dismissing the employee; and that question shall be determined in accordance with equity and the substantial merits of the case [s 98(4)].

Thus, Triggerhappy must prove only that it had a fair reason to dismiss the three employees and then the tribunal, looking at all the circumstances, will decide whether dismissal was reasonable or unreasonable.

When only the three dismissed employees were working, a theft occurred. Under the test in *British Home Stores v Burchell* (1978), it was held that in an unfair dismissal case, the employer must have a genuine belief, based on reasonable grounds after a reasonable investigation, that the employee is 'guilty'. Thus, Triggerhappy must show that the three points in the *Burchell* test have been met. Without doubt, it appears that a theft has occurred, but, on the facts presented, it appears that the *Burchell* principles have not been complied with. First, Sneak has told the company that he has reservations about Swipe's honesty, but the company has never investigated the complaints. While it is accepted that Sneak's accusations may be unfounded, it would appear that the company has not reacted to this in the present case, as allegations of dishonesty could naturally lead the company to suspect Swipe rather than the other two employees.

However, cases of blanket dismissals – that is, dismissal of a group of employees, all of whom could have been guilty but, after an investigation, the employer cannot pin down which one is – can be fair despite the fact that the employer cannot have a genuine belief in the guilt of all the employees.

In the leading case of *Monie v Coral Racing Ltd* (1980), the employee was an area manager with responsibility for 19 shops. Only he and his assistant knew the combination of the safe at headquarters. While Monie was away, his assistant discovered that £1,750 was missing from the safe. As there was no sign of a break-in, the company concluded that one or both were involved in the theft and dismissed them. The Court of Appeal confined the Burchell principles to cases where only one employee is suspected. *Parr v Whitbread plc (trading as Threshers Wine Merchants)* (1990) has confirmed this in relation to the dismissal of four suspected employees, but stressed that the employer must do a thorough investigation to limit the group to only those who definitely could have committed the theft. Therefore, while Triggerhappy does not have to show that it genuinely believes all three are guilty, it must show that its investigation revealed that any one of the three employees must be guilty. Here, Triggerhappy already has suspicions that Swipe is dishonest and appears at the appeal to decide that Pinch is not. This suggests that the original investigation which preceded the dismissals was inadequate and therefore not reasonable. If this is the case, then it will be difficult for Triggerhappy to argue that it has a genuine belief that all of the employees could be guilty based on reasonable grounds. The grounds and the belief can only form a reasonable investigation which, on the facts, does not appear to have happened.

In looking at reasonableness in s 98(4), a tribunal will look to both the fairness of the decision to dismiss and procedural fairness. Since October 2004, all employers must comply with the statutory disciplinary procedures laid down in the Employment Act 2002 (Dispute Resolution) Regulations 2004. These provide, by way of a minimum requirement, that the employer set out in writing the conduct that has led to the contemplation of disciplinary action and invite the employee to a meeting. After the meeting, the employer should inform the employee of its decision, inform the employee of his right of appeal and organise an appeal meeting if the employee so wishes. After the appeal, the employer should inform the employee of the decision. In the case of dismissal for gross misconduct, the employer can use a modified procedure, which involves writing to the employee after his dismissal telling him the reason for the dismissal and of his right of appeal. Should the employee wish to appeal, the employer should set up an appeal hearing and afterwards inform the employee of the decision. Failure to comply with these procedures renders any dismissal unfair (s 98A) and compensation can be increased by between 10% to 50%.

It is unclear from the facts whether the employees were invited to a first disciplinary hearing. If they were not, the subsequent dismissals may be unfair and they may be entitled to increased compensation. The only way that the employer could not hold a first hearing under the statute is if the employees' conduct is deemed to be gross misconduct, a matter which would be up to the tribunal to decide. While it is clear that theft is gross misconduct and thus the tribunal may uphold the use of the modified procedure in the case of Nick and Swipe, it is not clear whether the tribunal would hold failing to report a fellow employee's theft as gross misconduct, which is the reason for Pinch's dismissal and therefore the standard procedure should have been applied to him. If all three have had a first hearing and they also have a contractual right of appeal, then the statutory procedures appear to have been observed, as long as the employees were informed in writing, prior to the first hearing, of their misconduct and were also, with their dismissal notices, informed of their right of appeal. While the rules of natural justice do not apply in unfair dismissal cases, the employer must give the employee a fair hearing. These rules are contained, in the main, in the ACAS *Code of Practice on Dismissal and Disciplinary Procedures* (2004). The rules of a fair hearing are first that the employee should know the case against him (*Hutchins v British Railways Board* (1974)). In the problem, it is not stated that the employees were told that their dismissals were for theft, but it appears that they were told that their dismissals were for failing to report theft by fellow employees. It is also unclear what was said in the appeal, but even if theft was mentioned at the appeal, the employees thought that they would be putting their case in relation to a failure to report theft, and to discover that they are accused of theft in the hearing has not given them adequate opportunity to prepare their case. The second rule of a fair hearing is that the employee must be given an opportunity to put his side of the case. On the facts in the problem, it seems highly debatable that this occurred. The employees were only allowed to answer yes or no to questions put to them by the manager conducting the appeal and it would appear that the employees' versions were not given, nor were any of them given the opportunity to put forward mitigating circumstances. This is very pertinent in Pinch's case, as he had been threatened by the other two employees if he revealed what had happened. It is relevant that this fact was not known by the company and further supports the argument that an inadequate investigation was conducted and that the employees were not given the opportunity to give their versions of the facts.

Another rule of a fair hearing is that the hearing should be unbiased, in that the person who chairs the hearing should not already have been involved in the case and formed an opinion (*Moyes v Hylton Castle WMC* (1986)). While the problem gives no details as to the manager who conducted the hearing, this may be another challenge available to the employees.

Two further comments should be made about the hearing. The problem states that the hearing merely reviewed the evidence. An appeal which is a complete rehearing of the case can rectify earlier deficiencies in procedure (*Whitbread and Co plc v Mills* (1988)). It is unknown how this will be affected by the statutory procedures but it is submitted that Mills will only be relevant where the employer has contractual procedures which are in excess of the statutory ones, for example, where an employee has two rights of appeal. However, in this case, as it appears that the employees have never put their side of the case and the hearing did not give them that opportunity, the defective investigation has not been rectified by the later appeal. In addition, it appears that originally the dismissals were for failing to report theft by a fellow employee. While an employer is entitled to lay down his own rules and state what he regards as gross misconduct, he cannot act autocratically. It appears from the facts that this rule of reporting has just been told to the employees in their dismissal letters. Therefore, the employees were originally accused of a breach of a rule of which they were unaware.

In addition, Swipe and Nick had their dismissals confirmed on the basis of theft. It would appear from the facts that they thought that they were dismissed for failure to report theft and then dismissed for a totally different reason, which they discovered after the appeal. Referring to the rules of a fair hearing above, this means that they went to the hearing not knowing the case against them and having been given no opportunity to answer any allegations. As such, this is yet further evidence of an unfair hearing as an appeal cannot confirm a dismissal for a different reason from that originally alleged without the whole process of investigation, hearing and appeal being conducted (*Monie v Coral Racing* (1980)). On the basis of the arguments presented, therefore, it would appear that all the dismissals are procedurally unfair.

Tribunals also look to the fairness of the decision to dismiss. In other words, was dismissal a fair sanction in the circumstances? Browne-Wilkinson J in *Iceland Frozen Foods v Jones* (1983) said that the task of a tribunal was:

> ... to determine whether in the particular circumstances of each case the decision to dismiss the employee fell within the band of reasonable responses which a reasonable employer might make.

This does not mean that the tribunal should find the dismissal unfair if it would not have dismissed, but it should ask itself if a reasonable employer would have dismissed. Substituting its own decision for that of the employer will lead to a finding that the tribunal decision is perverse. This means that the tribunal will look for a consistent approach by the employer, in that he must treat truly comparable cases the same and, particularly in conduct cases, will look to see if the employer took into account factors such as the employee's past work record and length of service. It is not inconsistent to treat two employees who have committed the same offence differently, if there is a considerable difference in their length of service and their work record.

In *Sherrier v Ford Motor Co* (1976), two employees were caught fighting. Despite an investigation by the employer, he could not discover who had instigated the fight. One of the employees had a 15-year unblemished record and the employer suspended him for five days without pay. Sherrier, on the other hand, had been employed for two years and had had six disciplinary sanctions imposed upon him, and so the employer dismissed him. It was held that the dismissal was fair.

In the problem, Pinch and Nick have 10 years' unblemished service and it could be argued that to dismiss one for suspicion of theft and the other for failing to report theft by fellow employees is too harsh, given their work record. In *Johnson Matthey Metals Ltd v Harding* (1978), an employee with a 15-year unblemished record was dismissed when the missing watch of a colleague was found in his possession. The EAT held that the dismissal was unfair in the light of the length of his previous good service. Given the facts in the problem, a tribunal may hold that, in the case of Pinch and Nick, a reasonable employer would not have dismissed them and that, therefore, dismissal was not within the band of reasonable responses. Given Swipe's shorter length of service, his previous disciplinary record and the allegations against his honesty, on the other hand, a tribunal may feel that the decision to dismiss Swipe was a reasonable one. It would appear, therefore, that in all the cases, the dismissals were procedurally unfair and additionally, the decision to dismiss may also be unfair in the case of Pinch and Nick, but probably reasonable in the case of Swipe. Thus, all three employees have good claims for unfair dismissal. It may be, however, particularly in the case of Swipe, that compensation is reduced due to the employee's conduct by s 122(2) of the ERA 1996, which allows a tribunal to reduce compensation to an amount which is just and equitable due to the employee's conduct before the dismissal. This does not mean conduct which contributed towards the dismissal but any conduct which the tribunal feels should be taken into account.

Much will depend on the procedures that the employer followed. In the case of Nick and Swipe, if the reason for their dismissals was theft, the employer is entitled to use the modified statutory procedure and merely allow a right of appeal after the decision to dismiss has been executed. This would mean that the dismissals are not unfair because of a breach of the statutory procedures but they are still likely to be procedurally unfair because of breaches of the rules of a fair hearing and the ACAS Code. In Pinch's case, much depends on whether the tribunal considers his conduct to be gross. If not, the standard procedure should have been used by the employer, and if he has not had a first disciplinary hearing, his dismissal will be automatically unfair. If he has, then the issues on procedural fairness discussed above will still render his dismissal an unfair one.

Notes

Question 39

Jack, Ken and Sally work for Rover Ltd. Jack and Sally have worked for the company for 10 months. Ken has worked for the company for 10 years.

Jack works in the factory. Recently, one of the machines got very hot and Jack felt there was a danger that it would cause a fire. He panicked and immediately pressed the fire alarm and, while other employees were leaving the premises, he threw what he thought to be a bucket of water over the machine. In fact, the bucket contained inflammable cleaning fluid and the machine caught fire, causing serious damage to the factory and halting production for a week. The bucket of cleaning fluid should not have been there, but had been left there accidentally by another employee. Jack has now been dismissed because of his actions.

Ken is one of 30 salesmen. The company wishes to reduce the salesforce by 20. The managing director, after discussions with the recognised trade union, decided that selection for redundancy would be on the basis of an employee's contribution to the company's future viability, based on criteria such as efficiency and management potential. Ken, who is the longest serving salesman, was today told that he has been selected for redundancy and given wages in lieu of notice.

Sally is pregnant. She suffers from severe arthritis but can work with painkillers. Since she has been pregnant, however, she cannot take the painkillers and therefore cannot work. She is three months' pregnant and has been off work for 10 weeks. Today, she received a letter of dismissal and a cheque to cover her notice period.

Advise Jack, Ken and Sally if they have any claim for unfair dismissal against Rover Ltd.

Answer plan

This is a problem which brings together procedure and potentially automatic unfair dismissal. It is the sort of question which can catch students out in that two of the parties do not appear to have the continuity for an unfair dismissal claim, but in both cases, if the reason is proved, no continuity is required. Given that there is a pregnancy dismissal and the question asks advice in relation to unfair dismissal, it is important not to get side-tracked into sex discrimination cases in relation to Sally.

Issues which need to be considered are:

- dismissal in health and safety cases under s 100 of the ERA 1996;
- redundancy as a fair reason to dismiss;
- procedure for a redundancy dismissal and the guidelines in *Williams v Compair Maxam Ltd* (1982);
- dismissal in cases of pregnancy under s 99 of the ERA 1996.

Answer

All the employees in the problem require advice in relation to unfair dismissal. At first sight, it would appear that Jack and Sally will have no claim because neither has the requisite one year's continuity which is required by s 108(1) of the ERA 1996. However, in some circumstances, an employee may pursue an unfair dismissal claim even if he or she has not been employed for one year and it is possible that Jack and Sally may fall within these provisions.

Jack saw a machine getting hot and, worried that it would catch fire, took certain precautions with somewhat disastrous consequences. As a result of his actions, he has now been dismissed. Protection in relation to dismissal on health and safety grounds is found in s 100(1) of the ERA 1996. This was introduced to comply with the Framework

Directive on the introduction of measures to encourage improvements in the health and safety of workers. Section 100(1)(e) provides that a dismissal is automatically unfair if the principal reason for the dismissal was that the employee:

> ... in circumstances of danger which he reasonably believed to be serious and imminent, took, or proposed to take, appropriate steps to protect himself or other persons from the danger.

By s 100(2), whether the steps taken are appropriate is judged by reference to all the circumstances, including the employee's knowledge and the facilities and advice available to him at the time. However, by s 100, the employer has a defence to a claim under s 100(1)(e), if he can show that it was so negligent for the employee to take the steps that he took that a reasonable employer might have dismissed him in the circumstances. There is no continuity period necessary to claim on this ground (s 108(3)(c)).

For Jack to be able to pursue a claim for unfair dismissal, therefore, he must show that he reasonably believed that danger was serious and imminent, that the steps he took were appropriate in the circumstances and that a reasonable employer would not have dismissed him.

The problem states that the machine was getting hot and that Jack thought that there was a danger of a fire. The problem then states that he panicked and pressed the fire alarm. The starting point for a tribunal would be to look at any training Jack has received, particularly what training he may have received in relation to machines getting hot. If he has received none, a tribunal may think that his belief that the machine would catch fire was reasonable in the circumstances. If, however, Jack has received training which he did not comply with, or his experience is such that he should have known to switch the machine off, the tribunal may reach the conclusion that, in all the circumstances, Jack's belief that danger was serious and imminent was not reasonable and the first part of s 100(1)(e) has not been made out. If Jack's belief is deemed to be reasonable, Jack then has to show that his conduct was appropriate in the circumstances and, again, his training and knowledge will be relevant. Jack doused the machine with what he believed to be water. If his training is such that this is inappropriate conduct, then the second part of the section is not made out. If, however, dousing the machine is the correct action or if he has received no training appropriate to the circumstances and it was reasonable to try and cool down the machine with water, it was not Jack's fault that the bucket contained inflammable fluid which had been accidentally left there. This would then raise the question of whether it was reasonable in the circumstances to expect Jack to check the contents of the bucket before he threw them. It is submitted that such checking would not be unreasonable if he expected the bucket to contain water and this expectation was reasonable.

Even if the action was not appropriate, this does not mean that the dismissal is fair. The employer must show that Jack's actions were so negligent that a reasonable employer *might* have dismissed. In other words, was the action so negligent that dismissal was within the band of reasonable responses from *Iceland Frozen Foods v Jones* (1983)? If it is proved that Jack was trained and experienced, that water should never be thrown over a hot machine in any circumstances and that Jack would know this and merely panicked, then it is submitted that the defence will have been made out. On the other hand, if Jack has no training and throwing water was a reasonable response, then the defence is not made out and it is likely that Jack's dismissal will be found to be unfair.

Ken has been employed for 10 years and his contract has been terminated by reason of redundancy. Redundancy is a fair reason for dismissal, but may be unfair in some circumstances. The first is where an employee is selected for a variety of reasons such as trade union membership or activities, health and safety reasons or maternity reasons. In these circumstances, if the reason for the selection is proved, the selection is automatically unfair and the dismissed employee does not require one year's continuity to claim. None of these reasons apply to Ken. It would appear, therefore, that Ken cannot argue that his redundancy is automatically unfair. While redundancy is a fair reason for dismissal, the employer must still act reasonably.

A tribunal will look at whether the employer has a fair unit of selection, whether the selection criteria are reasonable, whether the procedure the employer adopted was reasonable and whether the employer looked for alternative employment for his redundant employees. In Ken's situation, a fair unit of selection is the sales staff unless work is interchangeable, in which case the unit of selection should be broader and cover all of those involved in the work (*Gilford v GEC Machines* (1982)). If the union has agreed the unit, it is more likely that a tribunal will hold it to be fair. In Ken's case, it appears that all the sales staff have been considered and there is no evidence that work is shared with another group of employees. It would therefore seem that the unit of selection is fair.

The criteria used for selection should also be fair. This means that they should be objective and measurable and leave no room for subjective opinions. A criterion such as 'employees who in the opinion of management will keep the company viable' was frowned upon by the EAT in *Williams v Compair Maxam Ltd* (1982) as being too heavily reliant upon individual opinion. 'Last in first out' (LIFO) is always a good starting point and if the employer departs from LIFO, he should use objective criteria such as experience, skill and attendance.

In Ken's case, the employer wishes to retain those employees who will contribute to the future viability of the company. While this is similar to the words frowned upon in *Williams*, if such conclusions are drawn using objective criteria, then the selection procedure could still be fair. The criteria adopted by Rover is efficiency and management potential. While efficiency is objective and can be measured, management potential is subjective and is likely to be based on individual opinion. As such, the selection criteria can be challenged as non-objective and unfair.

The *Williams* case laid down guidelines for a fair procedure after selection where there is a recognised trade union. The guidelines are:

- the employer should give as much warning as possible to the union and employees concerned;
- the employer should seek the agreement of the union with regard to selection criteria and the means of achieving the necessary result;
- the employer should consider representations made by the union with regard to selection;
- the employer should consider alternative employment.

It would appear in Ken's case that Rover did consult with the recognised union. Failure to do so would not only make Ken's redundancy potentially unfair, but would also be a breach of s 188 of the TULR(C)A 1992. This section requires Rover to consult with appropriate employee representatives, which includes independent recognised union representatives, at least 30 days before the first dismissals occur as Rover is making 20 workers redundant, and further requires Rover to give certain information in writing to the union representatives. Failure to comply with s 188 entitles the union to apply for a protective award (s 189(1)(b)). To act fairly, however, consultation with the employee must take place, even if there has been consultation with the union (*Hough v Leyland Daf* (1991) and *Rolls Royce Motor Cars Ltd v Price* (1993)). The problem states that Ken was told of his selection for redundancy and given wages in lieu of notice. It would therefore appear that he was neither consulted nor warned of his selection as he was dismissed immediately. Nor would it appear that the employer considered whether there was alternative employment that Ken could do. As such, Rover has used unfair selection criteria and has not consulted or warned Ken, in breach of the guidelines in *Williams*, and his redundancy is therefore unfair. Rover cannot argue that even if it had consulted Ken, he would have been selected for redundancy and that the breach of a fair procedure has, therefore, had no effect on the final outcome, since the House of Lords decision in *Polkey v AE Dayton Services Ltd* (1987).

Sally is another employee who appears not to have the requisite one year's continuity. In 1994, however, new provisions were introduced to protect women who are dismissed on maternity grounds and render such dismissals automatically unfair (now s 99 of the ERA 1996). Maternity grounds include pregnancy or any reason connected with pregnancy and the amendments enacted in 1994 removed the need for one year's continuity when dismissal was under this head. Before the amendments, the employer could dismiss if he could show that pregnancy made the woman incapable of doing the job, for example, because she could no longer lift anything. Such exceptions have been removed, although if to continue working would be a breach of statute, the woman now has the right to be suspended on maternity grounds under ss 66 to 68. To satisfy the provisions, however, the dismissal must be causally connected with the pregnancy. It is insufficient that the woman be dismissed when she is pregnant. 'Any reason connected with her pregnancy' was given a broad interpretation pre-1994 in *Brown v Stockton on Tees Borough Council* (1988), when the House of Lords ruled that a supervisor, who was selected for redundancy because she was pregnant, was dismissed in breach of (the now) s 99. In other words, her pregnancy was the reason for her dismissal and not the redundancy. By analogy with *Brown*, it could be argued that Sally was dismissed for a reason connected with her pregnancy because her pregnancy meant that she could no longer take painkillers and therefore could not work. On such an interpretation, Sally's dismissal is automatically unfair.

In addition to the above, since October 2004, employers are required to comply with statutory disciplinary procedures in all cases of dismissal except collective redundancies. While it may be that the procedure does not have to be observed in respect of Ken as 20 employees are being made redundant and the union has been involved, the procedures must be observed in respect of Jack and Sally. In both cases, this would be the standard procedure of an invitation in writing to a first meeting with the employer stating the reason for the potential dismissal, a meeting being held, the employer informing the employee of the decision and of the right of appeal, the employer setting up an appeal meeting if the employee so requests and the employer informing the employee of the decision after the appeal (Employment Act 2002 (Dispute Resolution) Regulations 2004). It is unlikely that a tribunal would hold that Jack is guilty of gross misconduct and the modified procedure should apply to him. While the discussion above states that it is likely that the reasons will be proved, the non-compliance with the statutory procedures means that a tribunal can award an additional 10% to 50% compensation for such a failure.

In Ken's case, the issue is different. While the statutory procedures do not apply, if a tribunal decided that the selection criteria were objective and fair, the reason the dismissal would be unfair is the lack of consultation and warning.

Notes

10 Redundancy

Introduction

Questions on redundancy very often involve other areas discussed earlier in this book. In order to claim a redundancy payment, an employee must show that he or she has been dismissed for reasons of redundancy and therefore previous questions elucidating what constitutes a dismissal are relevant. In addition, there is an overlap between unfair dismissal and redundancy, in that although redundancy may be one of the fair reasons for dismissal, the procedure adopted by the employer may render the redundancy unfair. Some examination questions may deal with this aspect under a general unfair dismissal question, but it is also a likely adjunct to a redundancy question and, therefore, students should be knowledgeable on both areas before feeling sufficiently prepared for either.

General issues which the student needs to understand include:

- the definition of dismissal;
- the qualifying period;
- the definition of redundancy in s 139(1) of the Employment Rights Act (ERA) 1996;
- the effect of misconduct during the redundancy notice period;
- the concept of suitable alternative employment;
- lay-off and short-time working;
- consultation and redundancy.

It has already been stated that questions on this area may also involve a discussion of the procedure involved in redundancy and therefore introduce the added factor of unfair dismissal. Issues relating to unfair selection for redundancy and procedural matters have already been discussed in Question 39 in Chapter 9, above, and are raised again in Question 45, below. These questions show how the two areas can interlink.

For specific questions on redundancy, students should be familiar with:

- the continuity requirements;
- what constitutes an employer ceasing business;
- the effect of an employer moving his place of business and the relevance of the employee's contractual terms;
- what constitutes a diminution in the employer's requirements and the effect of any flexibility clause;
- the effect of a strike or other misconduct during redundancy notice;

- what constitutes an offer of suitable alternative employment and a reasonable refusal;
- the consultation requirements.

Finally, questions in this area may bring in the Transfer of Undertakings (Protection of Employment) (TUPE) Regulations 1981. These may impact on continuity issues or liability and their interrelationship with s 218 of the ERA 1996 needs to be understood.

Checklist

Students should be familiar with the following areas:

- what constitutes a redundancy;
- what constitutes a dismissal for redundancy;
- the qualification for the right to a redundancy payment;
- the impact of the TUPE Regulations 1981;
- special provisions in relation to lay-off and short-time working, misconduct and suitable alternative employment;
- consultation provisions.

Question 40

Two weeks ago, the following events occurred at Mouldy Productions Ltd, a company manufacturing various types of plastic mouldings.

Amy, a married woman with two children, was dismissed after refusing to change from night shift working to day shift working. The company was entitled to introduce the change under the terms of her contract. The change was made to maximise profitability, although the company continued to need the same number of workers.

Jack, a maintenance worker, who had always worked at the company's Whitehaven premises, refused to move to its premises at Preston, 100 miles away. The company was moving all the maintenace workers because of a lack of work at the Whitehaven site. He was sacked without notice, having been employed for 103 weeks.

During the latter part of last year, the company conducted a reorganisation during which the company regraded a number of workers. One such worker, Leonard, was regraded downwards and suffered a consequent loss of pay and status. The regrading was on different terms from his original contract and included a provision in relation to compulsory overtime. Leonard rejected the new package and resigned. At his resignation, Leonard had been employed for four years.

All the above parties are now claiming a redundancy payment. Advise Mouldy Productions Ltd as to its liability in respect of such payments.

Answer plan

The first thing to note about this question is what it is asking. Given that redundancy situations can bring in a variety of other issues, such as sex discrimination or unfair dismissal, it is important to read the question properly and only answer the question set. For example, it would be easy in this question to get involved in a discussion of sex discrimination issues in relation to Amy, but the question asks for advice in relation to claims for redundancy pay only. If it had asked the student to advise on possible actions, that would have been a different question and sex discrimination would then have been a discussion point. This particular question, however, is very specific in what it requires the student to discuss and, therefore, the answer must be equally as focused.

Particular points to be considered are:

- what constitutes a dismissal for reasons of redundancy;
- the definition of redundancy in s 139 of the ERA 1996;
- how far the statutory notice period in s 86 of the ERA 1996 can affect continuity;
- what constitutes suitable alternative employment;
- what constitutes a reasonable refusal of suitable alternative employment.

Answer

Mouldy Productions Ltd is asking for advice in relation to potential redundancy claims by the three parties. In order to claim a redundancy payment, all the parties must first show that they have been dismissed for reasons of redundancy. Section 163(2) of the ERA 1996 provides a statutory presumption that, if an employee is dismissed and claims a redundancy payment, the dismissal is for redundancy, and the burden falls to the employer to rebut the presumption and show that the dismissal was for another reason. In *Willcox v Hastings* (1987), a business was sold with the two employees. The new owner wished to retain only one of the employees because he wished to employ his son. He sacked both of the original employees, however, who both claimed a redundancy payment. The employer argued that only one of the employees was redundant but did not specify which one. The Court of Appeal held that both were redundant as the presumption in s 163(2) arose and this had not been rebutted by the employer. In respect of all three parties, therefore, Mouldy Productions needs to rebut the presumption.

Amy was dismissed when she refused to change from night shift working to day shift working. The definition of redundancy is to be found in s 139(1) of the Act. This states that a redundancy has occurred if the dismissal is attributable wholly or mainly to:

(a) the fact that his employer has ceased, or intends to cease, to carry on the business for the purposes for which the employee was employed by him, or has ceased or intends to cease, to carry on business in the place where the employee was so employed; or

(b) the fact that the requirements of that business for employees to carry out work of a particular kind, or for employees to carry out work of a particular kind in the place where he was so employed, have ceased or diminished or are expected to cease or diminish.

In Amy's case, the employer has not ceased to trade nor is there a moving of the place of work; thus, Amy must show that the employer's requirements for the particular work she was employed to do have ceased or diminished. She will therefore try to establish that the change from night work to day work means that Mouldy Productions now requires a different type of work and that the night work has diminished or no longer exists.

Early cases established that a change in hours, rather than a change in the job duties, did not constitute a redundancy for the purposes of s 139(1)(b) if the employer's overall requirements for the work was the same. In *Johnson v Nottinghamshire Combined Police Authority* (1974), two employees were working from 9.30 am to 5.30 pm. The authority altered its hours so that one covered 8 am to 3 pm and the other 1 am to 8 am. Both refused to accept the change and were dismissed. The Court of Appeal held that there was no redundancy. The employer still required two employees doing the same amount of work, albeit at different times. On the other hand, should the employer change the job duties and thus diminish the requirements for part of the job, this will constitute a redundancy. In *Murphy v Epsom College* (1985), the college heating system was replaced, needing new skills to maintain it. The college plumber refused to take on the new duties and was dismissed and replaced by a heating technician. The Court of Appeal held that the plumber was redundant as the employer's need for a plumber had diminished because of a change in the nature of the job.

The question to ask in Amy's case is what particular work is she employed to do? She is employed on night work, but the change to day work is permitted by her contractual terms and conditions. The contractual approach to work of a particular kind has been re-emphasised by *Cowen v Haden Ltd* (1982). In that case, the employee was a divisional contracts surveyor but his contract contained a flexibility clause. The Employment Appeal Tribunal (EAT) held that he had not been made redundant because the test was contractual and therefore there was still work available that he was contractually bound to do. The Court of Appeal reversed the decision on the facts, holding that the flexibility clause had to be interpreted by reference back to the main job duties and therefore the employee was redundant, but, importantly, upheld the tribunal on the contractual approach. The contractual approach was applied in the later case of *Pink v White* (1985). Thus, in *Lesney Products Ltd v Nolan* (1977), the change from a night shift and day shift to a double day shift was not a redundancy.

In Amy's situation, although the change in shifts is permitted by her contract, we are not told whether the job duties have changed or if any other facets of the job have altered. In *Archibald v Rossleigh Commercials Ltd* (1975), it was held that the work of an unsupervised night mechanic was different from that of an ordinary mechanic and, in *Macfisheries Ltd v Findlay* (1985), the EAT held that a change from night shift to day shift could amount to a redundancy if it involved a change in duties and responsibilities. Thus, if there is a change in Amy's job, it could be argued on the basis of *Murphy* and *Findlay* that there is a redundancy situation. It has to be said, however, that on the facts this looks unlikely. It appears that Mouldy Productions Ltd has merely changed when the job is done and Amy is required to work either day or night by her contract. Furthermore, on the facts, it appears that there is no reduction in the workforce and thus Amy is unlikely to be successful in her claim for redundancy. Mouldy Productions can argue that she was dismissed for refusing to obey a contractual order.

Jack has been employed for 103 weeks. In order to claim a redundancy payment, he must have 104 weeks' continuity and thus, on the face of it, appears to be unable to claim. It is possible, however, that the statutory minimum notice period may apply and so bring his continuity period up to 104 weeks. It is therefore necessary to see if Jack potentially has been dismissed for redundancy.

It has already been seen that s 139(1)(a) envisages a redundancy situation when the employer is moving his place of business. This means that Jack appears to have been made redundant. Given that the test is contractual, however (*Cowen v Haden Ltd*), it is necessary to discover whether Jack has a mobility clause in his contract. There does not, on the facts, appear to be an express clause. There also appears to be no evidence on which to imply a clause, given that Jack has always worked at Whitehaven. If, on the other hand, when Jack started the job he agreed to be mobile and the contract envisages this by, for example, providing travelling and lodging allowances, such a clause may be implied (*Stevenson v Teesside Bridge and Engineering Ltd* (1971)). The facts do not say what the content of the contract is and thus, on the basis of *O'Brien v Associated Fire Alarms Ltd* (1969), it could be argued that there is no mobility clause, given that Jack has always worked at Whitehaven and never been mobile. In *O'Brien*, the employees worked from the Liverpool office, which was closing down, and were told to transfer to the Barrow office some 120 miles away. While they travelled around in their jobs, they only did so within a reasonable distance from their homes and thus, while there was an implied mobility clause, the Court of Appeal held it was restricted to being mobile within such reasonable travelling distance; therefore, the employer had no right to require them to move 120 miles away and thus they were dismissed on the grounds of redundancy. While the contractual test was criticised, in *High Table Ltd v Horst* (1997) the Court of Appeal pointed out that in *O'Brien* the employer had dismissed the employees for breach of contract. Once it was decided that the employees were not in breach, the presumption of redundancy applied.

If there is a clause in the contract, however, Jack would be required to move and therefore would not be redundant. Given that such a clause does not appear to be present, can Jack be instantly dismissed for refusing to move? The courts will now only accept instant dismissal in cases of gross misconduct, gross neglect or refusal to obey a lawful reasonable order. In this case, Jack was told to move. Such a move is not part of his contractual terms and, therefore, it can be strongly argued that Jack is not refusing to obey an order which is lawful or reasonable. As such, the employer is not entitled to dismiss him instantly and Jack's dismissal is unlawful.

There is no mention of a contractual notice period. However, by s 86 of the ERA 1996, Jack will be entitled to a minimum notice period of one week. Although the normal rule is that an instant dismissal terminates the contract on the day the dismissal takes place, s 145(5) provides that, for the purpose of computing the qualifying period for a redundancy payment, if the instant dismissal is unlawful, the date of termination shall be the date on which the statutory notice expires and not the actual date of termination. As such, given that Jack's dismissal was unlawful, s 145(5) will operate to extend his employment by one week, so giving him the required 104 weeks' continuity to claim a redundancy payment. On the basis of *O'Brien* and *Horst* above, the employer's reason for dismissal is unfounded; therefore, the statutory presumption will apply and Jack is entitled to a redundancy payment.

Leonard has been downgraded as part of a reorganisation. He has suffered a loss in pay and status and the new post includes compulsory reasonable overtime. As a result, he has resigned. The first question to ask is: has Leonard been dismissed? While he has terminated his contract, this could be a constructive dismissal if the employer is in breach of contract (*Western Excavating (ECC) Ltd v Sharp* (1978)) by s 136(1). In this situation, it appears that Mouldy Productions has unilaterally altered the terms of Leonard's contract and, in particular, has downgraded him and lowered his pay. This is due to a reorganisation and therefore appears to be permanent. In *Millbrook Furnishing Industries Ltd v McIntosh* (1981), a unilateral alteration in job content was deemed to be a constructive dismissal even though it was temporary and there was a pressing business need. In Leonard's case, it seems that his pay and status have changed. This has been done without apparent contractual authority and without his agreement. As such, his resignation is due to a repudiatory breach on the part of the employer, entitling him to resign and claim constructive dismissal under s 136(1).

In order to be entitled to a redundancy payment, Leonard must show that his dismissal is for reasons of redundancy under s 139. It has already been noted that a redundancy occurs when either the employer ceases or moves his business, or his requirements for work of a particular kind that the employee is employed to do have ceased or diminished. If Leonard's job has changed and overall the requirements of the employer for that type of work have reduced, then there will be a redundancy even if the employer still employs the same number of people doing other work (*Murphy*). If, however, Leonard's job has remained the same and the reorganisation is for cost-cutting purposes, then the requirements of the employer for that particular work have not decreased and a redundancy has not happened. In *Shawkat v Nottingham City Hospital NHS Trust (No 2)* (2001), the Court of Appeal held that the mere fact of a reorganisation, as a result of which the employer requires the employees to do a different job, is not conclusive of redundancy. The tribunal must then decide whether there is a change in the requirements of the employer for employees to do work of a particular kind. If there is a redundancy, Mouldy Productions could try and argue that they have offered Leonard suitable alternative employment which he has unreasonably refused (s 141). The first question for the tribunal would be whether the offer was of suitable alternative employment. This involves the tribunal looking at the nature of the employment in relation to the employee's skills and capabilities. If the job is the same, the question for the tribunal will be whether the drop in salary and the drop in status makes this unsuitable employment, given the salary may be made up by the overtime worked. Should the tribunal conclude that the offer is of suitable employment, if they feel that the refusal by Leonard is unreasonable, then he will lose his right to a redundancy payment. It is submitted, however, that the drop in pay and status would make this an offer of unsuitable alternative employment and thus Leonard's refusal would be irrelevant.

Thus, if there has been a redundancy in Leonard's case, he will be entitled to a redundancy payment, but on the facts it seems unlikely that the requirements of the employer have diminished and therefore no redundancy has occurred. This does not, however, prevent Leonard from taking alternative action against Mouldy Productions and claiming unfair dismissal, arguing that he has not been treated fairly.

_____

_____

_____

_____

_____

_____

_____

_____

_____

_____

_____

_____

_____

—————— Question 41 ——————

Contractual issues now dominate all aspects of the decision as to whether an employee was dismissed by reason of redundancy for the purposes of a claim for a redundancy payment.

Discuss.

Answer plan ——————————————————————

This question is a fairly straightforward one but it is important to always bear in mind what it is asking. It talks about all aspects of the decision, therefore it brings in contractual issues in relation to dismissal as well as in relation to the definition of redundancy and the answer must constantly refer to the contractual aspects of a redundancy situation.

Particular points to be considered are:

- the definition of dismissal in s 136 of the ERA 1996;
- how far contractual issues are relevant in defining dismissal, particularly constructive dismissal and the test in *Western Excavating (ECC) Ltd v Sharp* (1978);

- the definition of redundancy in s 139 of the ERA 1996;
- the relevance of the terms of the employee's contract in relation to the definition, looking in particular at cases such as *Cowen v Haden Ltd* (1982); *Chapman Goonvean and Rostowrack China Clay Co Ltd* (1973); *Johnson v Nottinghamshire Combined Police Authority* (1974); *O'Brien v Associated Fire Alarms Ltd* (1969) *Stevenson v Teesside Bridge and Engineering Ltd* (1971);
- contractual issues in offers of suitable alternative employment.

Answer

In order to claim a redundancy payment, an employee must first establish that he has been dismissed and, secondly, that the dismissal is for reasons of redundancy. In *Sanders v Earnest A Neale Ltd* (1974), the employees conducted a work-to-rule and eventually the factory closed down. It was held that the dismissals were not for reasons of redundancy but due to the work-to-rule which had led to a loss of production which, in turn, had led to the closure. There is a statutory presumption in s 163(2) of the ERA 1996 that, if an employee is dismissed and claims a redundancy payment, his dismissal is for reasons of redundancy, and the employer must rebut the presumption to escape liability.

The starting point for the employee, therefore, is to establish that he has been dismissed. Dismissal is defined in s 136 of the ERA 1996 as termination by the employer, with or without notice; a fixed term contract expiring without being renewed or an employee resigning in circumstances in which he is entitled to do so by the employer's conduct. In addition, by s 136(5), if the employment is terminated by the death, dissolution or liquidation of the employer, or the appointment of a receiver, there is a dismissal for reasons of redundancy. The majority of these situations do not raise contractual issues but, in respect of an employee resigning, contractual issues are vitally important in establishing whether the resignation constitutes a constructive dismissal.

The key part of the definition of constructive dismissal is that the employee must have been entitled to leave. There are two possible interpretations of the word 'entitled'. On the one hand, it could mean that the employer acted so unreasonably that the employee could not be expected to stay. Or, conversely, that the employer's conduct amounted to a repudiatory breach which the employee accepted as ending the contract. After a period of uncertainty, the Court of Appeal, in *Western Excavating (ECC) Ltd v Sharp* (1978), decided that the contractual approach was the correct one, Lord Denning stating that conduct which entitled the employee to leave and claim dismissal had to be conduct on the part of the employer which was 'a significant breach going to the root of the contract of employment'. Whereas a breach of an important express term will be the basis of a claim, the test is wider and a breach of an implied term can lead to a constructive dismissal. Thus, it is important for a tribunal to establish all the terms of the contract to discover if a repudiatory breach has occurred. While the contractual test may appear to be narrow, the development of the implied duty of mutual trust and respect has, in fact, opened up the area so that unreasonable conduct on the part of the employer may in fact be a breach of the implied duty and thus a repudiatory breach (*Bliss v South East Thames Regional Health Authority* (1987)).

The contractual approach, however, can create problems. First, if the breach is a unilateral variation in terms, the employee must decide within a relatively short period of time to resign, otherwise he risks his conduct being seen as acceptance of the variation (*Jeffrey v Laurence Scott and Electromotors Ltd* (1977), although see *Alcan Extrusions v Yates* (1996)). Secondly, if the breach is anticipatory and the employer rectifies the breach before the employee resigns, there is no constructive dismissal as the employer is no longer in breach (*Norwest Holst Group Administration Ltd v Harrison* (1985)). Thirdly, there can be no repudiatory breach if the employer feels he is exercising his contractual rights, even if he is mistaken as to the precise terms of the contract (*Frank Wright and Co (Holdings) Ltd v Punch* (1980)). This indicates that where there is a genuine dispute as to the terms, the intention of the employer is relevant.

Should the employee establish that he has been dismissed, in order to claim a redundancy payment, he must further establish that the dismissal is for reasons of redundancy. Should the employer attempt to rebut the presumption in s 163(2), the employee must show his dismissal was for one of the reasons in s 139(1). In other words, he must show that his employer has ceased to trade, that he has moved his business or that his requirements for the particular kind of work the employee is required to do have ceased or diminished or are expected to do so.

While the employer ceasing to trade will normally not raise contractual issues, three points should be mentioned. First, the protection in s 136(5), which states that the death, dissolution or liquidation of the employer constitutes a dismissal for redundancy purposes. Secondly, if the employer is taken over in circumstances where s 218 of the ERA 1996 applies, if the business is taken over as a going concern, the employee cannot claim redundancy from the old employer, even though there has been a fundamental change in the contract. On the other hand, if merely the assets are transferred, then the employee must claim redundancy from his old employer, otherwise he will lose his employment protection rights as a new continuity period begins with the new employment (*Woodhouse v Peter Brotherhood Ltd* (1972)). Thirdly, if the employer is taken over in circumstances where the TUPE Regulations 1981 apply, then, despite the change in terms, there is no breach and no redundancy, although the employee has the right, by reg 5(4)(A), to object to the transfer and not move. Should he do this, however, he falls into legal limbo, because the change of employer is not a dismissal and, thus, he will not be able to claim a redundancy payment.

In relation to the second part of the definition (the employer moving place of business), the question for the tribunal is whether there is a mobility clause in the employee's contract. If there is not, his place of work contractually is where he physically works and, thus, if his employer moves, he will be redundant, unless the move is a short distance away and has no real effect on the employee (*Managers (Holborn) Ltd v Hohne* (1977)). If the employee has a mobility clause in his contract, however, his place of work will be within the content of the clause and thus there is no redundancy. Such a clause may be express or implied. If express, this will cause few problems for the tribunal. Whether such a term is implied, however, will be a question of fact looking at all the circumstances of the case.

In *O'Brien v Associated Fire Alarms* (1969), two electricians worked for a company in Liverpool and had always worked there, although the company operated throughout Britain. The work diminished in Liverpool and they were asked to work in Cumberland. They refused and were dismissed. Their claims for redundancy payments were upheld by the Court of Appeal on the basis that there was no express or implied term requiring them to work anywhere but the Liverpool office. Conversely, in *Stevenson v Teesside Bridge and Engineering Ltd* (1971), a steel erector was not entitled to a redundancy payment when work dried up at the site where he mainly worked, since travelling between sites was found to be an implied term in his contract, given he had accepted this when interviewed and the contract envisaged mobility since it contained provision for travelling and subsistence expenses. Although in *High Table Ltd v Horst* (1997), the Court of Appeal adopted a factual test rather than a contractual one in deciding that an employee, who had always worked at one place, was redundant when work there ceased, this was despite a mobility clause in her contract and was because she had only worked in one place for five years.

The third definition of redundancy is perhaps the one where contractual issues predominate. Given that the employee is arguing that the work of the particular kind he was employed to do has ceased or diminished, the tribunal must look to his contract to identify the particular work. This contractual approach was taken by the EAT in *Cowen v Haden Ltd* (1982) and was endorsed by the Court of Appeal, although the decision was overturned on the facts.

However, this does not mean that any change of contractual terms is a redundancy (*Chapman v Goonvean and Rostowrack China and Clay Co Ltd* (1973)) and the tribunal must see if, in relation to the contractual terms, the function for which the employee is employed has ceased or diminished. This means that if the work still remains and the amount of work the employer requires remains the same, the fact he requires the work at different hours does not mean a redundancy has occurred (*Johnson v Nottinghamshire Combined Police Authority* (1974)). On the other hand, if the requirements for the type of work have diminished, there is a redundancy, even if the employer takes on more employees due to an increase in a different type of work (*Murphy v Epsom College* (1985)). Thus, an employer replacing a barmaid with a younger version will not constitute a redundancy because the employer still requires the same function to be performed, albeit by a different type of employee (*Vaux and Associated Breweries v Ward* (1968)), although if he dismisses all his employees and replaces them with independent contractors, then there is a redundancy, because his needs for employees have ceased.

While the contractual test is important, Horst and the later case of *Church v West Lancashire NHS Trust* (1998) both talk of a mixture of the factual/function test and the contractual test. This more flexible approach has been endorsed by the House of Lords decision in *Murray v Foyle Meats Ltd* (1999). In that case, employees worked as meat plant operatives. They normally worked in the slaughter hall, but contractually could be asked to work elsewhere and had occasionally done so. As a result of a decline in business, the employer needed fewer employees in the slaughter hall and Murray was made redundant. He argued that the pool of selection (employees in the slaughter hall) was too narrow and, given that he had worked elsewhere, selection should have been across the whole of the business. The House of Lords held that the requirements of the employer for employees to work in the slaughter hall had diminished and therefore the pool for selection had been correct. However, Lord Irvine LC commented that:

> ... both the contract test and the function test miss the point. The key word in the statute is 'attributable' and there is no reason in law why the dismissal of an employee should not be attributable to a diminution in the employer's need for employees irrespective of the terms of his contract or the function he performed.

While the contract test is still important, it appears that future decisions will rest on a more flexible approach.

One further aspect of redundancy may give rise to contractual issues and that is where the employer argues that the employee is redundant but that he has been offered suitable alternative work which the employee has unreasonably refused (s 141). While the reasonableness of the employee's refusal will normally involve considerations outside his contract, the question of whether the offer is suitable will entail the tribunal in considering the redundant job and comparing it to the offer to see if the offer matches the employee's skills and capabilities. In *Carron Co v Robertson* (1967), the court held that all factors should be considered such as the nature of the work, hours and pay, the employee's strength and training, his experience and ability and his status. In *Standard Telephones and Cables v Yates* (1981), it was held that the offer of unskilled assembly work to a skilled card wirer was not an offer of suitable alternative employment. Thus, the terms of the employee's original contract will be the starting point for the tribunal and will be an important factor in deciding if the employee has refused suitable alternative work unreasonably and thus disentitled himself to a redundancy payment.

It can be seen from the above, therefore, that contractual issues permeate all aspects of a dismissal for reasons of redundancy in that they may be a consideration in relation to dismissal, the definition of redundancy and part of the consideration of whether the employer has offered suitable alternative employment to his redundant employee.

Notes

Question 42

Express Deliveries Ltd is a freightforwarding firm in the Midlands. At the beginning of the year, it ran into financial difficulties and carried out a reorganisation. Ron, whose contract stated that he was a credit controller but that he was obliged to 'carry out any other duties that might be assigned to him', was reassigned to a bookkeeping post which involved a regrading from Grade 3 to Grade 4, although he remained on the same salary. The change occurred because of a reduction in the need for credit controllers. Ron has resigned and claimed a redundancy payment.

Penny was taken on by the company as a trainee manager to take over from Mr Tibbs who was due to take early retirement. Mr Tibbs changed his mind and therefore the company sacked Penny. Penny is also claiming a redundancy payment.

Wendy is employed by the company as a cashier. Early last month, the company instructed the cashiers that, within six months, they would be required to use the newly installed computers to handle all cash transactions. Wendy has no experience of computers and objects to the change. Last week, she resigned and is now claiming a redundancy payment.

Advise Express Deliveries Ltd.

Answer plan

This is another question which raises issues in relation to the definition of dismissal for reasons of redundancy and, in particular, in relation to one party, the inherent flexibility within an employment contract.

Particular issues to be considered are:

- the qualification requirement to claim a redundancy payment;
- the definition of dismissal;
- the definition of redundancy in s 139(1) of the ERA 1996;
- the relationship between flexibility clauses and work of a particular kind, in particular a discussion of *Cowen v Haden Ltd* (1982);
- the necessity for a reduction in the employer's requirements for employees;
- the inherent flexibility within the contract and how far a change in working methods constitutes a repudiatory breach and can constitute a redundancy situation.

Answer

Express Deliveries Ltd has asked for advice in relation to three parties claiming a redundancy payment. All the claims have arisen as a result of a reorganisation caused by the company's financial difficulties last year. In order to claim a statutory redundancy payment, all three parties must have been employed for two years at the relevant date (s 155 of the ERA 1996) and must have been dismissed for reasons of redundancy. By s

163(2) of the 1996 Act, if a dismissed employee claims a redundancy payment, there is a statutory presumption that the dismissal was for reasons of redundancy and the burden shifts to the employer to show some other reason for the dismissal. As such, Express Deliveries Ltd can challenge the three parties by first arguing that there have not been any dismissals; and, secondly, if they have all been dismissed, that those dismissals were for reasons other than redundancy.

Ron was employed as a credit controller, but due to the reorganisation has now been downgraded to bookkeeper, although his salary has remained the same. He has resigned and is claiming constructive dismissal. Given the fact that he has a flexibility clause in his contract, the first question to ask is has he been dismissed?

By s 136(1) of the ERA 1996, an employee shall be treated as dismissed by his employer if he terminates his contract, with or without notice, in circumstances in which he is entitled to do so by his employer's conduct. While early cases argued that any unreasonable conduct on the part of the employer set up a constructive dismissal claim, Lord Denning MR in *Western Excavating (ECC) Ltd v Sharp* (1978) held that the contractual approach is the correct one. His Lordship talked of the employer being guilty of conduct which is a significant breach going to the root of the contract, or which shows that the employer no longer wishes to be bound by one of the essential terms of the contract. Thus, if Ron can argue that Express Deliveries is in breach of an essential term of the contract, he can argue that he has been constructively dismissed.

While it would appear that Ron's contract will lay down his specific job duties, it also contains a wide flexibility clause which requires Ron to carry out any other duties assigned to him. Given that Ron's salary has remained the same, the two changes which have occurred are in relation to his duties and his status. If the change in duties is covered by the flexibility clause, then the only potential breach by the employer is the downgrading, and Express Deliveries may further argue that this is impliedly covered by the clause allowing a change in duties. Much therefore hinges on the flexibility clause and how the tribunal will regard it.

In *Nelson v BBC* (1977), the employee was employed as a Grade 3 producer and editor, but had only worked in the BBC's Caribbean service. When that service was cut back, the BBC argued that Nelson had been made redundant, but this was rejected by the Court of Appeal which said that to come to such a decision would be implying a restriction into a widely drafted express term in his contract. Following this decision, the EAT, in *Cowen v Haden Ltd* (1982), decided that a contracts surveyor had not been dismissed for redundancy because of the wide flexibility clause in his contract. However, this point was reversed by the Court of Appeal, which held that the flexibility clause was an adjunct to his job as a contracts surveyor and not an extra form of employment which allowed his employer to transfer him to a totally different job.

On the basis of this authority, it is necessary to see if Ron's new duties are fundamentally different from his old duties as credit controller. If they are, then the bookkeeping work does not fall within the flexibility clause and Express Deliveries is in repudiatory breach of contract which entitles Ron to resign and claim constructive dismissal (*Western Excavating*). If, on the other hand, the new duties are similar to the old and fall within the flexibility clause, there is still the question of whether the drop in status constitutes a repudiatory breach. It is submitted that the drop would be a repudiatory breach and further that there is no implied contractual right to downgrade within the flexibility clause (*Hall v Lodge* (1977)). Express Deliveries may argue that the changes are only temporary and thus not repudiatory. Such an argument was put forward in *Millbrook Furnishing Industries Ltd v McIntosh* (1981) but was rejected on the facts. On the facts in the problem, there is no evidence that these changes are temporary and they appear to have been in operation for some time. As such, Ron can argue that he has been constructively dismissed.

To a large extent, the arguments used to demonstrate that Ron has been dismissed are also pertinent in relation to the question of whether his dismissal is for reasons of redundancy. By s 139(1)(b) of the 1996 Act, a redundancy exists if the employer's requirements for employees to carry out work of a particular kind have ceased or diminished. Cowen demonstrates that the test is the work that the employee was employed to do and for this the tribunal must look to the contractual job duties.

However, in *Shawkat v Nottingham City Hospital NHS Trust (No 2)* (2001), the Court of Appeal held that the mere fact of a reorganisation, as a result of which the employer requires employees to do a different job, is not conclusive of redundancy. The tribunal must then decide if there is a change in the requirements of the employer for employees to carry out work of a particular kind. Furthermore, the cases of *High Table Ltd v Horst* (1997) and *Church v West Lancashire NHS Trust* (1998) state that the test to determine what is work of a particular kind that the employee is employed to do is a mixture of both a contractual and a functional test – that is, the tribunal must look at the work specified in the employee's contract and at the work the employee was actually doing. This more flexible approach was endorsed by the House of Lords in *Murray v Foyle Meats Ltd* (1999), although Lord Irvine in that case stated that there was no reason in law why the dismissal of an employee should not be attributable to the employer's need to reduce his workforce irrespective of the job the employee was employed to do. If, in reality, Ron has only done credit controlling, then the contractual and functional test will produce the same result.

Given that it has already been argued that the work Ron is employed to do is credit controlling and not bookkeeping, if the employer's requirements for credit controllers have diminished, Ron's dismissal is for reasons of redundancy. This will be the case even if the amount of work for credit controllers has increased if, for example, because of new technology, the requirements for employees to do that work has diminished. Likewise, if the amount of credit controlling has diminished, it is irrelevant if the amount of bookkeeping has increased because that was not the work, it has been argued, that Ron was employed to do. The only possible argument for Express Deliveries is to say that Ron was offered suitable alternative work which he unreasonably refused and thus he is not entitled to a redundancy payment (s 141(2) and (3)). It is unlikely, however, that a tribunal will accept that an offer involving a loss of status will be an offer of suitable alternative work, given the factors a tribunal must consider, as laid down in *Carron Co v Robertson* (1967) and seen in cases such as *Taylor v Kent County Council* (1969) and *Cambridge and District Co-operative Society Ltd v Ruse* (1993).

Penny was taken on as a trainee manager to take over from another employee who was expected to take early retirement. When this did not materialise, Penny was dismissed. While Penny has clearly been dismissed, it should be stated that unless she has been employed for two years she will not be entitled to a statutory redundancy payment, although Express Deliveries may have their own scheme which gives their employees better rights and Penny may have enough continuity to claim under the private scheme. In order to claim, however, Penny must show that her dismissal was for reasons of redundancy. It has already been stated that one of the redundancy situations in s 139(1)(b) is that the employer's requirements for employees to do work of a particular kind have ceased or diminished. While *North Yorkshire County Council v Fay* (1985) appears to go against this decision, this is in doubt since Horst, Church and Murray. Furthermore, in *Fay*, the employee was dismissed to make place for an employee who was redundant. This is not the situation here. In Penny's case, she was taken on to replace another worker who eventually remained. She was also taken on as a trainee not because of any increase in work. In *O'Hare v Rotaprint* (1980), a company expanded its workforce and anticipated increased production which never materialised. The EAT held that the dismissal of the extra employees was not a dismissal for redundancy because it could hardly have been said that work had diminished if, in fact, it never materialised in the first place. In Penny's case, the amount of work that the employer requires and the number of employees he requires to do that work have remained static. Thus Penny has not been dismissed for reasons of redundancy and is not entitled to a redundancy payment.

Wendy has resigned because her method of work has changed from manual to computerised. Again, it is necessary to establish whether Express Deliveries is in repudiatory breach of contract before turning to the issue of redundancy. While there is no flexibility clause in Wendy's contract, there is an implied term in any contract of employment that the employee must adapt to changes in working methods. In *Cresswell v Board of Inland Revenue* (1984), revenue officers refused to operate a new computerised system of PAYE administration. Walton J refused the employees a declaration that such changes were outside their contractual duties. It was stated, however, that such a change should be accompanied by relevant training and a failure to do so and the dismissal of an employee for incapability could be an unfair dismissal. Wendy has only just been told of the change and it will not be brought in for six months. Provided that Express Deliveries institutes the proper training, it is within its contractual rights to alter working methods and, as such, there has been no breach on its part. Wendy has thus resigned and not been dismissed and is not entitled to a redundancy payment. Even if there had been a dismissal, a change in working methods is not a diminution in the employer's requirements for work of a particular kind (*North Riding Garages v Butterwick* (1967) and *Vaux and Associated Breweries Ltd v Ward* (1968)) and thus there is no redundancy.

Notes

_____

_____

_____

_____

_____

_____

_____

_____

_____

_____

_____

_____

Question 43

Fragrancies is a company marketing and selling cosmetics and other beauty products. Due to financial difficulties, Fragrancies went into negotiations with Smashing Smells, a company manufacturing perfume, with the aim of selling off the beauty products side of the business. The cosmetic side of the business was to be wound up. Todd was employed as a technician developing cosmetics. He was given three months' notice of redundancy but, two months before his notice expired, Fragrancies discovered that he had been selling technical details to a rival firm. It sent Todd a letter telling him of its discovery, but stating that due to the liquidation he could work his notice.

Ron worked for the cosmetics side as a salesman. When he was given three months' notice of redundancy, because of the liquidation of that part of the company, he went on strike until the company was wound up.

Smashing Smells operates tight security and employs security men. It decided to put out the security operation to tender and Group 8 won the contract. Last week, Group 8 took over the security. Len worked as a security guard. He was dismissed by Smashing Smells two hours before the transfer took place because he is 62 and Group 8 refused to take employees over the age of 60.

Advise Ron and Todd of their entitlement to a redundancy payment and Len of any legal rights he may have.

Answer plan

This is a complex case involving three employers and it is necessary to establish the claims which lie in relation to each of the employers. Thus, Ron and Todd will be claiming against Fragrancies. Len may have a claim against Smashing Smells or Group 8. Ron and Todd will be claiming under the ERA 1996 and Len may have a claim under that Act or may have a claim under the TUPE Regulations. In a question like this, it is important to identify the strands at the beginning otherwise the answer will not be coherent and logical.

Particular issues to be considered are:

- the situation of employees where the employer is wound up under s 136(5) of the ERA 1996;
- the position of the employee whose misconduct is discovered during notice of redundancy under s 140(1);
- the exception to the above in s 140(2);
- the definition of a transfer of an undertaking in the TUPE Regulations 1981;
- the impact of *Watson Rask and Christiansen v ISS Kantineservice A/S* (1993); *Dr Sophie Redmond Stichting v Bartol* (1992); *Dines v Initial Health Care Services* (1994); *Suzen v Zehnacker Gebaudereinigung GmbH Krankenhausservice and Leforth GmbH* (1997); *Betts v Brintel Helicopters* (1997);
- the meaning of employed 'immediately before the transfer' in *Litster v Forth Dry Dock and Engineering Co Ltd* (1989);
- the interpretation of reg 8 of the TUPE Regulations 1981.

Answer

The problem involves a discussion of two different pieces of legislation. In relation to Ron and Todd, the issues to be discussed is whether they can claim a redundancy payment from Fragrancies as there is no transfer of the cosmetics side of the business, it is being wound up. In relation to Len, the question is whether he has been transferred as part of a transfer of an undertaking or not and thus where liability may lie in relation to the dismissal.

Ron and Todd wish to claim a redundancy payment from Fragrancies. An employee is entitled to a redundancy payment if he is dismissed by reason of redundancy. By s 136(5) of the ERA 1996, the liquidation of the employer shall be treated as a dismissal for reasons of redundancy unless the exception in s 140(1) applies. Section 140(1) provides that where the employee is under notice of redundancy, an employee shall not be entitled to a redundancy payment where his employer is entitled to terminate the contract by reason of the employee's conduct and:

- terminates without notice;
- terminates with shorter notice than the redundancy notice; or

- terminates with the same notice as the redundancy notice but accompanies the notice with a written statement that he would be entitled to terminate without notice by reason of the employee's conduct.

Thus, if s 140(1) applies, the reason for the employee's dismissal is his conduct and not redundancy; he is not entitled to a redundancy payment.

Todd was under notice of redundancy when the company discovered that he had been selling technical details to a rival firm. The employee owes a duty of fidelity to his employer and breach of this duty will constitute gross misconduct. Part of this duty is the requirement not to divulge confidential information (*Cranleigh Precision Engineering Ltd v Bryant* (1964)); thus, Todd has broken this duty and committed gross misconduct which would entitle Fragrancies to dismiss him without notice. The employer must have evidence, however, that the employee is guilty. If the employer merely has a reasonable belief in the employee's guilt, s 140(1) will not operate (*Bonner v Gilbert (H) Ltd* (1989)).

Todd has been guilty of gross misconduct, but to be disentitled to a redundancy payment, s 140(1)(c) must apply. There has been much debate on the meaning of the section. One argument is that the section means that the employee has been dismissed for redundancy, but in circumstances where the employer could have dismissed for cause, either by giving no or shorter notice or the same notice but expressly stating the dismissal is for cause. The second interpretation is that the cause rebuts the presumption that the dismissal is for reasons of redundancy but the employer must comply with the procedural requirements for the rebuttal to be effective. *Sanders v Earnest A Neale Ltd* (1974) leans towards the first interpretation while stressing the importance of the procedural requirements. In *Simmons v Hoover Ltd* (1977), the EAT held that if an employee is dismissed but the dismissal is not wholly or mainly attributable to redundancy but to misconduct, then the procedural aspects of s 140 put the employee on notice to that effect and should the employer fail to comply with the procedural requirements, he cannot rely on the section. In Todd's case, although the employer knew about the misconduct, he did not terminate the contract immediately or give shorter notice than the redundancy notice. Fragrancies made Todd aware that the misconduct had been discovered, but said that given the liquidation was happening he could work out his notice. It does not appear that Todd was told that the employer could terminate without notice because of his conduct, and thus could hardly be said to make Todd aware that he was being dismissed for his misconduct. As such, it is submitted that Fragrancies has not satisfied the procedural requirements in s 140(1)(c) and, thus, Todd is entitled to a redundancy payment.

Ron also appears to fall within the provisions of s 140(1) as he went on strike, which is a breach of contract. There is an exception to s 140(1), however, in s 140(2). This provides that if, after being given notice of redundancy an employee goes on strike, s 140(1) shall not operate to deprive him of a redundancy payment. This section protects the employee who strikes in protest of redundancy but does not protect an employee who is on strike and then is selected for redundancy (*Simmons v Hoover*). Therefore, as Ron has taken strike action in protest at the redundancy, he falls within the provisions of s 140(2) and is entitled to a redundancy payment.

Len was employed by Smashing Smells as a security guard. The security operation has been taken over by Group 8. The first point to establish is whether this is a transfer of an undertaking to which the TUPE Regulations 1981 will apply. These Regulations were introduced to bring into operation the Acquired Rights Directive (77/187/EEC) and, as such, their interpretation is subject to the Directive. Before amendments made by the Trade Union Reform and Employment Rights Act (TURERA) 1993, the TUPE Regulations did not apply to transfers which were not commercial ventures. After the decision of *Dr Sophie Redmond Stichting v Bartol* (1992) in the European Court of Justice (ECJ), the Regulations were amended to include non-commercial ventures which were transferred. From *Stirling v Dietsmann Management Systems Ltd* (1991), it appeared, however, that the Regulations would not apply where the transfer did not involve a transfer in the ownership of assets and where a peripheral part of the employer's business was transferred but not the main part.

This interpretation is now incorrect since the ECJ decision of *Watson Rask and Christiansen v ISS Kantineservice A/S* (1993). In this case, the catering service of a company was put out to tender. The company who won the contract took over control of the employees and the existing catering equipment. The ECJ held that the Directive applied where there is a change in the person who is responsible for the business, regardless of whether there was any change in the ownership of the undertaking. This has been followed in *Wren v Eastbourne Borough Council* (1993) and *Dines v Initial Health Care Services* (1994). It is unlikely that Smashing Smells is only employing one employee in security and equally unlikely that, if it employs more than one, only Len is being transferred; therefore, cases like *Suzen v Zehnacker Gebaudereinigung GmbH Krankenhausservice and Leforth GmbH* (1997) and *Betts v Brintel Helicopters* (1997) are not relevant. It should also be noted that changes to the Regulations, expected to come into effect in October 2005, make it clear that a transfer applies when a service provider changes and that there will be a TUPE transfer if the transferor ceases activities that are taken up by the new contractor, as long as there is an organised grouping of employees whose main purpose is to carry out that activity (draft regulation 3). Given existing case law, the transfer of the security service will be the transfer of an undertaking under the Regulations, but the situation will be much clearer when the amended regulations come into effect.

As the transfer does fall within the Regulations, reg 5(2) provides that the transfer operates to transfer all the transferor's rights, powers, duties and responsibilities over to the transferee. This means that in relation to employees transferred over to Group 8, their contractual terms should remain the same. Regulation 5(2) therefore transfers liability from the transferor to the transferee. Such liability, however, only transfers in relation to employees employed immediately before the transfer (reg 5(3)). Len was dismissed two hours before the transfer took place. Under the old authority of *Secretary of State for Employment v Spence* (1987), 179 employees were dismissed three hours before the transfer took place; they were held not to be employed immediately before the transfer, but this is now subject to the House of Lords decision in *Litster v Forth Dry Dock and Engineering Co Ltd* (1989). This judgment inserted the words into reg 5(3) 'or would have been so employed had he not been unfairly dismissed by reg 8'. In addition, in *ECM (Vehicle Delivery Service) Ltd v Cox* (1999), the EAT held that a transferee cannot avoid the TUPE Regulations by refusing to take on the transferor's workforce. Whereas it does not appear that Group 8 are refusing to take on all the workforce, this decision may help Len.

Thus, Len may have been transferred to Group 8 if his dismissal is unfair by reg 8. That regulation provides that a dismissal of an employee as a result of the transfer will be automatically unfair unless it is for an economic, technical or organisational reason which entailed a change in the workforce (reg 8(2)), in which case, there is a fair dismissal under some other substantial reason, although the employer still has to satisfy the requirements of reasonableness. In *Wheeler v Patel* (1987), it was held that the dismissal of employees as a condition of the transfer taking place did not fall within reg 8(2). In *Meikle v McPhail* (1983), it was held that a redundancy situation caused by the transfer did fall within reg 8(2).

In Len's case, it appears that the reason for his dismissal was not an economic, technical or organisational reason involving a change in the workforce. Even if such a reason was proved, there has been no warning or consultation and as such the employer has failed to comply with the requirements of reasonableness in s 98(4) of the ERA 1996. As such, Len has been unfairly dismissed and, on the basis of *Litster*, liability for that dismissal has transferred to Group 8 and it is that employer he should sue.

Notes

_____

_____

_____

_____

_____

_____

_____

_____

_____

_____

_____

_____

Question 44

The statutory protection in s 218 of the ERA 1996 was grossly inadequate in protecting employees involved in a transfer of a business. The implementation of the Acquired Rights Directive in the form of the TUPE Regulations was meant to alleviate the deficiencies in the statutory protection; however, the original misimplementation of the

Directive reduced the protection afforded to employees and, despite amendments and reinterpretation, it is still questionable whether the Directive has been fully implemented.

Discuss.

Answer plan

This question is really three questions in one and requires a fairly detailed knowledge of both the TUPE Regulations and s 218 of the ERA 1996. It is asking the student to show the limitations of s 218, to show how the original Regulations did not comply with the Directive and to demonstrate whether the amended Regulations are still misimplementing the Directive. To answer this question, a student must be aware of the provisions in s 218, the amendments to the Regulations made in 1993, the changes in the interpretation of the Regulations imposed by ECJ decisions and be able to analyse whether the Regulations now properly implement the Acquired Rights Directive. Students should also be aware of changes which come into effect in October 2005.

Particular issues to be considered are:

- the definition of an undertaking pre-1993;
- the changes made by the TURERA 1993;
- the interpretation of a transfer within the Regulations and the changes required by ECJ decisions;
- the protection afforded by reg 5(2) compared with that of s 218;
- the difference in transfer of liability under s 218 and reg 5(2);
- the impact of *Litster v Forth Dry Dock and Engineering Co Ltd* (1989);
- the protection in reg 8 compared with s 218;
- how far the present Regulations comply with the Directive;
- the amendments expected to take effect in October 2005.

———————————— Answer ————————————

The TUPE Regulations 1981 were brought into force to implement the Acquired Rights Directive. At the time the Regulations came into force, there was already some protection for employees where a business was transferred in the form of Sched 13, para 17(2) to the Employment Protection (Consolidation) Act (EP(C)A) 1978 (now s 218 of the ERA 1996). This provides that when a trade, business or undertaking is transferred, continuity of employment will be preserved. The provision itself is, however, limited in that for continuity to be preserved, the business must be transferred as a going concern. Transfer of the assets alone will not preserve continuity (*Woodhouse v Peter Brotherhood Ltd* (1972)), but both the assets and the business must be transferred for the provision to apply, so that, if only the business itself goes and not the assets, again, that does not fall within the section (*Blumstead v John Cars Ltd* (1967)). Furthermore, whether the business is transferred as a going concern is a question of fact for the tribunal. In *Crompton v Truly Fair (International) Ltd* (1975), it was held that there was no transfer of a business when the old employer made children's clothes and the new employer made men's trousers. Such decisions left employees in a vulnerable position because if there was no transfer of the business, they had to claim a redundancy payment from their old employer and a new continuity period would begin with the new employer. If the employees mistakenly thought there was a transfer of a business and failed to claim redundancy from the old employer, this would often lead to no redundancy or unfair dismissal protection from the new employer if he sacked them less than one or two years after the transfer, or reduced awards, given that awards are based on years of service. Furthermore, s 218 only preserves continuity and no other rights.

The Acquired Rights Directive was implemented by the TUPE Regulations and gave much greater protection to employees. The purpose of the Directive and the Regulations is to preserve the whole of an employee's contractual rights through the transfer and not just his continuity rights. Thus, should a transfer occur within the meaning of the Regulations, the employee will keep all his contractual benefits, apart from future pension rights which can be excluded (*Walden Engineering v Warrener* (1993)), and liability for dismissal transfers to the transferee. The original Regulations, however, did not fully implement the Directive and thus only gave protection in relation to certain transfers. Furthermore, it is still questionable whether the amended Regulations fully implement the Directive and give full protection.

The original Regulations defined an undertaking in reg 2. This original definition excluded transfers of undertakings which were non-commercial ventures (arguably because of the government's commitment to Compulsory Competitive Tendering (CCT)). Thus, in *Woodcock v Committee of Friends School* (1987), it was held that the Regulations did not apply to an undertaking which had charitable status. Attempts to equate the definition of an undertaking under the Regulations to the definition in s 218 were prevented by the EAT in *Stirling v Dietsman Management Systems Ltd* (1991), the tribunal saying that the definition under s 218 could not be used to widen the definition of a commercial venture in the Regulations.

It was clear, however, that the Directive was not limited to commercial ventures following the ECJ decision of *Dr Sophie Redmond Stichting v Bartol* (1992), when the Court held that the Directive applied to the transfer of employees from a foundation, funded by a local authority to help drug addicts, to another with the same function. As such, the TURERA 1993 amended reg 2 to include transfers of non-commercial ventures.

While this was more in line with the Directive, interpretation by national courts still limited the protection given to employees by the definition of transfer. The EAT in Stirling said that to have a transfer within the meaning of the Regulations, there had to be some transfer of ownership of assets and the part transferred had to be a major and not peripheral part of the employer's business. On this interpretation, if an employer put out a service to tender, such as catering or security, given that no ownership of assets was transferred, merely employees, this was not a transfer within the Regulations and thus the employees were protected only in relation to their continuity rights by s 218.

In *Watson Rask and Christiansen v ISS Kantineservice A/S* (1993), the ECJ again interpreted the Directive. In that case, a company tendered its catering provision which it had previously run itself, employing the catering staff. The company that won the tender merely took over control of the existing employees and equipment. It changed the terms of the employees' contracts and then the employees resigned and claimed constructive dismissal. The transferee claimed that there had not been a transfer within the provisions of the Directive as there was no transfer of assets and the transferee was only providing a service for the transferor. The ECJ held that a relevant transfer had occurred. This happened when there is a change in the legal or natural person who is responsible for carrying out the business and who incurs the obligations of employer vis-à-vis the employees. As such, *Stirling* is now not good law and *Watson Rask* has since been applied in our national courts (*Wren v Eastbourne Borough Council* (1993) and *Dines v Initial Health Care Services Ltd* (1994)). However, where an employer loses, for example, one contract which affects only a number of its employees, it is then a matter of fact for the tribunal whether an undertaking has been transferred (that is, an economic entity as opposed to an identifiable activity). This is the result of *Suzen v Zehnacker Gebaudereinigung GmbH Krankenhausservice and Leforth GmbH* (1997) and followed in *Betts v Brintel Helicopters* (1997). According to Lindsay J, in *Cheesman v R Brewer Contracts Ltd* (2001), this implies a degree of structure and autonomy, which can be concluded by looking at factors such as the identity of the workforce, the management structure, the way work is organised, the operating methods and the resources.

The effect of a transfer on an employee's contract is in reg 5. This provides that the transferee shall acquire 'all the rights, powers, duties and liabilities' under or in connection with the contract. Regulation 7, however, excludes the transfer of pension rights and, while an employment tribunal argued in *Perry v Intec Colleges Ltd* (1993) that this was contrary to Art 3(3) of the Directive, the EAT, in *Walden Engineering v Warrener* (1993), has decided that the Regulations do not conflict with the Directive as Art 3(3) protects acquired rights not future rights.

While reg 5(2) appears to give wide protection, it is in fact limited, as the Regulation only applies to those employees employed immediately before the transfer. In *Secretary of State for Employment v Spence* (1987), the Court of Appeal held that the Regulation did not protect employees who were sacked three hours before the transfer took place. In the later case of *Litster v Forth Dry Dock and Engineering Co Ltd* (1989), the House of Lords held that such an interpretation would go against the purpose of the Directive and inserted the phrase in the Regulation 'or would have been so employed had he not been unfairly dismissed by reg 8', thus protecting those employees dismissed as a result of the transferee's insistence. It should be noted, however, that the dismissals are not void, the decision merely establishes that liability for the dismissals rests with the transferee and not the (normally) bankrupt transferor. This appears to go against the ECJ decision of *Bork (P) International A/S v Foreningen af Arbejdsledere i Danmark* (1989), which made it clear that the Directive was intended to prevent dismissals before the transfer. The problem of dismissal is probably the most pertinent for a transferred employee. Under the Regulations, the employee is protected in two ways. First, reg 8 provides that a dismissal as a result of a transfer is automatically unfair unless the employer can show that the dismissal is for an economic, technical or organisational reason entailing a change in the workforce (reg 8(2)). Should the dismissal fall within reg 8(2), then it is a fair reason under some other substantial reason, although the employer will have to satisfy the requirements of reasonableness in s 98(4) of the ERA 1996. It has been held that a dismissal as a condition of the sale does not fall within reg 8(2) (*Wheeler v Patel* (1987)), nor does a reduction in salary after the transfer (*Berriman v Delabole Slate Ltd* (1985)), but that a redundancy caused by the transfer does (*Meikle v McPhail* (1983)). However, the Advocate General, in *D'Urso v Ecole Marelli Elettro-meccanica Generale SpA* (1992), expressed the opinion that a constructive dismissal caused by a change in terms would only be fair if such a change would have occurred despite the transfer. This raises doubts as to whether reg 8(2) complies with the Directive.

The second protection for the employee in relation to dismissal is found in reg 5(5). This provides that an employee can claim constructive dismissal if the transfer results in a substantial change in his working conditions to his detriment. This would appear, however, to go against the ECJ decision in *Watson Rask* where the change was minor (a change in the pay day) and yet the ECJ held that the employee was protected by the Directive. Furthermore, the protection in regs 5 and 8 is somewhat restricted by the new reg 5(4)(B). This gives the employee the right to object to his being transferred, but then provides that such an objection terminates his contract on the transfer and there will be no dismissal. While this appears in line with the ECJ decision in *Katsikas v Konstantinidis* (1993), which upheld the German equivalent of the TUPE Regulations giving the employee a right of objection, reg 5(4)(B) leaves an employee in a vulnerable position. He cannot claim redundancy from his old employer because he has not been dismissed and he does not wish to work for the new employer. It is again debatable whether the effect of reg 5(4)(B) is a proper implementation of the Directive.

Thus, while changes made by both legislation and ECJ decisions have brought the Regulations more in line with the Directive, it is still questionable whether the Regulations fully implement the Directive at present and give employees who are transferred with an undertaking the full protection to which they are entitled under European law.

Amendments made to the Directive in 1998 (98/50/EC) to a large extent, while clarifying the situation, merely codify ECJ jurisprudence. Article 1 states that a transfer means:

> the transfer of an economic entity which retains its identity, meaning an organised grouping of resources which has the objective of pursuing an economic activity, whether or not that activity is central or ancillary.

This definition is contained in the draft TUPE Regulations 2005, reg 3 of which provides that there is a TUPE transfer if the transferor ceases activities that are taken up by the transferee, provided there is an organised grouping of employees whose main purpose was to carry out those activities before the transfer. Thus the common situation of transferring a service will now fall within the Regulations. In addition, proposed changes to the Pensions Act 2004 will require the transferee to provide equivalent future pension protection. As such, the changes will reflect the amendments to the Directive; it is still questionable whether there is still a full implementation of the protection orginally envisaged by the Acquired Rights Directive 1977.